The Ideal in Law

The Ideal in Law

Eugene V. Rostow

The University of Chicago Press
Chicago and London

The University of Chicago Press, Chicago 60637
The University of Chicago Press, Ltd., London

© 1978 by The University of Chicago
All rights reserved. Published 1978
Printed in the United States of America
83 82 81 80 79 78   5 4 3 2 1

Library of Congress Cataloging in Publication Data

Rostow, Eugene Victor, 1913–
   The ideal in law.

   Includes index.
   1. Law—United States—Addresses, essays, lectures.
   2. Law and ethics—Addresses, essays, lectures.
   I. Title.
KF379.R69   340′.0973   77–81733
ISBN 0–226–72818–8

Eugene V. Rostow is Sterling Professor of Law and Public Affairs, Yale University. His books include *A National Policy for the Oil Industry* (1948), *Planning for Freedom* (1959), *The Sovereign Prerogative* (1962), *Law, Power, and the Pursuit of Peace* (1968), and *Peace in the Balance* (1972).

For E.G.R.
Once more, with love

Contents

Preface

The papers included in this volume, diverse as they are in nominal subject matter, address a single theme: the role of ethics in law, and of law in ethics. That cobweb of relationships has been the theme of all my work. Looking back on more than thirty years in academia, I realize that while I have taught and written in several fields, the moral element in law, and the weight of law in the process of social and moral development, have been my unvarying preoccupation.

The present book originated in an invitation to participate in a series which came to an end as this manuscript was being finished. The editor's proposal was that I do a short book on the notion of justice in law—a reflective book as much for the general as for the professional reader. We agreed on the enterprise in 1961. All I can plead by way of excuse for the delay is that it was caused by detours I felt obliged to make.

As I began to contemplate the project, I decided to proceed in the classic manner of the law schools, by the case method. The case I chose to test my views on jurisprudence is the most important in our moral experience: the treatment of Blacks in American law. I could imagine no part of our lives more fundamental in itself, nor one of comparable value in illuminating the interplay of custom and morality in the evolution of law, and the influence of law on history.

During the next five years, the manuscript grew slowly. Other tasks pressed their claims. But this venture was a constant companion. I read widely in the literature, and lectured on various phases of the topic at the law schools of Northwestern and Western Reserve universities, and of the University of Utah. Fleece from those lectures appear in chapters 1, 2, and 3.

The challenge of the book remained in the forefront of my mind throughout my sojourn in Washington between September 1966, and January 1969. In 1968, I had the privilege of delivering the annual Fourth of July Oration from the steps of Monticello, under the auspices of the Thomas Jefferson Memorial Foundation—a mise-en-scène to brighten any American eye. My subject on that occasion was "The Consent of the Governed," and much of the speech, as it has developed since that sunny moment, appears in chapters 1 and 4.

When I returned to Yale in 1969, I was anxious to finish the book as I had planned it. But obstacles multiplied. I was diverted by continuing interests in the field of foreign policy. At the same time, the Civil Rights Revolution of the sixties, and its aftermath, had stimulated a lively and useful scholarly interest in the position of Negroes in American life. What would have been, among other things, a brief review of the treatment of the Black in American law, if the original plan had been carried through, was no longer so urgently needed.

It was therefore decided to publish the book in its present form. It is still a book with a single theme, whose argument is developed and given body by the critical analysis of experience as well as by expository writing of the more conventional kind. But the realms of experience—the "cases" drawn upon to bring out my views about the nature and functions of law—are no longer confined to one area, that of the Black as a participant in the evolution of American society.

I also decided not to revise the texts of these papers significantly, save to minimize duplication. I still stand by their basic contentions. To have brought their scholarly apparatus up to date would have been a time-consuming task, and, from the point of view of this book, not a notably useful one.

It is a pleasure to thank many whose kindness and hospitality helped stir me to write some of these chapters: Dean Samuel Thurman, of the University of Utah Law School, who extended the invitation to deliver the William H. Leary Lecture there in 1965; Dean John Ritchie, and Professors Willard Pedrick and Nathaniel Nathanson of the Northwestern University Law School, who asked me to participate in the 1965 Julius Rosenthal Memorial Lectures, published as *Perspectives on the Court* by the Northwestern University Press in 1967; Acting Dean Oliver C. Schroeder, Jr., who encouraged me to go over the whole ground in detail, before a critical and sympathetic audience at the Western Reserve Law School in 1965; the Honorable Henry J. Taylor and his colleagues of the Thomas Jefferson Memorial Foundation, who tapped my shoulder with their memorable invitation to deliver the Fourth of July Oration for 1968 at Monticello; the Honorable Francis T. P. Plimpton, then President of the Association of the Bar of the City of New York, and Merrell

E. Clark, Jr., Chairman of its Centennial
Committee, for persuading me to organize the
Centennial Convocation of the Association in
1970, under the title "Is Law Dead?" which is
also the title of the volume of the proceedings
published by Simon & Schuster in 1971; Professor Edward S. Mason, editor of "The Corporation in Modern Society" (1960), who
induced me to write "To Whom and for What
Ends is Corporate Management Responsible?"; the officers of the California State Bar
Association, and especially that delightful and
remarkable old warrior, the late Herbert W.
Clark of San Francisco, who asked me to give
the Alexander F. Morrison Foundation Lecture for 1961, "The Lawyer and His Client";
friends in several British universities during
my tenure of the Pitt Professorship of American History and Institutions at King's College,
Cambridge, during the academic year 1959–
60, whose kindness encouraged the writing of
chapter 6; Dean Ewald T. Grether, and the
trustees of the Barbara Weinstock Foundation, for the honor of their invitation to deliver
the Barbara Weinstock Lecture on the Morals
of Trade at the University of California in
1962, "The Ethics of Competition Revisited";
and, finally, my old friend and colleague Professor Henri Peyre of Yale, who persuaded me
to lecture on Montesquieu as a legal philosopher at a celebration of the two-hundredth
anniversary of that great man's death.

Preparing a lecture for Professor Peyre's
ceremony turned out to be one of the most
important events of my intellectual life. At
that stage of my studies, Montesquieu precipitated my own ideas about law as a social institution into a pattern of new coherence, which
has become the framework for my work thereafter. I began to understand the singular

contribution Montesquieu has made to all subsequent thought about the nature of society,
and the power of his influence in the long line
which extends from Plato and Aristotle into
modern sociology, legal philosophy, political
theory, and philosophy proper. The first of the
modern social theorists, he is a true progenitor
not only of the American constitution but of
the outlook I find most congenial, and most
fruitful, in the study of society as the environment of man. Scrupulous in his deference to
the uniqueness of each culture, he insists with
equal emphasis that social studies can never
be morally neutral. To Montesquieu, the goal
of social studies must be the improvement of
society, and the achievement of social conditions which liberate man as a mature and responsible citizen and encourage his propensity
for moral improvement and for civilization
more broadly conceived.

E.V.R.

New Haven, Connecticut
Washington, D.C.
King's College, Cambridge
Balliol College, Oxford
Peru, Vermont

One

What Is Law?

I

The Roman jurists thought law could not be defined at all—that it pervaded society so deeply, and in so many ways, that the idea of law could never be captured in a single perspective. The Roman view is certainly wise, and probably correct. But first chapters should define a beginning. For the purposes of this book at least, as an effort to consider the notion of justice in law, we can begin, rather gingerly, with the proposition that law is the pattern of behavior deemed right by a society and the accepted methods of that society for determining its pattern of right behavior. In this sense, law is something more than what men do in fact, and something less than what they piously wish they did. It is what they think they ought to do, and what they usually do: their mores, and not their customs alone. In short, law should be perceived as the way in which each culture seeks to fulfill its ideal of justice—through procedures it deems fair, to reach results as close to being "just," in its view, as the circumstances of the moment permit. It is a way of making social policy, and a way of thinking about it as well.

Law is also an institution of immense ceremonial and operational importance. It orchestrates the social process by conducting the process of law, making the decisions it requires, and seeking to justify them in words of great moment and influence. Law thus demands a continuing popular debate about the most difficult moral problems of the society, and constitutes one of the key voices in that debate. The voice of the law should and often does insistently appeal to the principles each society deems essential to its rectitude. All cultures respect the idea of law. Some revere it. And even in societies where the rule of law has been lost for a time, it provides a yearning aspiration whose power is a weapon in the struggle for liberty.

It follows from this definition that each society has its own legal system, for in each society the configuration of custom, history, values, and ideas is necessarily unique. This is true even for societies closely linked in background and experience, like Denmark and Sweden, for example, or England and Scotland, or Louisiana and Minnesota. Each legal system has certain common features, and all share several common norms. But in each the shadings, the tone, and the emphasis are different.

A human society is a living organism animated by ideas—by beliefs, habits, customs, values, and perceptions of the external world. Perhaps "beliefs" is the most comprehensive word to describe ideas of this order, which run along the nerves of society like signals. Human societies are not congeries of people, buildings, and statistics, but communities drawn together by shared loyalties and shared ideals: symbols, myths, if you will, but symbols and myths which evoke what is most precious in the life of men. The appeal of a flag, or an ark, or a cross, or a book is not diminished because it is old or because all the believers do not understand all that their standard implies. Thus Magna Carta and the Declaration of Independence, the Constitution and the Supreme Court, embody an ideal to which men rally, and for which they are willing to die: the ideal, that is, that authority should be subject to law, which the community itself defines and enforces.

In the end, the beliefs that a culture shares as a collectivity determine its response to events, pressures, and threats, and govern its choices among possible policies. For each culture, as for each individual, the past is inescapable. Its response to each new stress is influenced in considerable part by favorable and unfavorable elements in its collective memory of earlier behavior: by the example of its heroes and its martyrs, its prophets and its fallen angels. Thus each community follows its own particular path. That path is not a rigid linear projection of the past. Each culture is capable of gradual change, even of mutation, at its own pace. But the path defining the range and purpose of possible change is greatly affected by the past.

The path of change in law is greatly affected as well by another element in every culture and its legal system—what Montesquieu called "the spirit" of its laws—the aspirations for its law which characterize each society. The inner code—the element of the ideal in law, guiding it toward its future—is the ultimate social force shaping each legal system and the way in which it responds to deviations from its norms.

For example, several recent presidential elections represent deviations from the pattern of the past in American constitutional law. Franklin D. Roosevelt was elected four times, breaking the two-term tradition that went back to Washington. And in 1960 the American people chose a Catholic as President for the first time. In the first case, the deviation was repudiated and the tradition reaffirmed. An amendment to the Constitution now forbids a President to be elected more than twice. It embodies the strongest principle of the American polity —the distrust of power. But Kennedy's election vindicated principles of equality and religious tolerance which are among the animating notions of the American constitutional order. After Kennedy's election, there was no impulse to return to the earlier practice, always understood to be a shameful breach of the principle of equality. On the contrary, there was nearly universal relief at the triumph of an ideal that nearly everyone accepts as right.

In this perspective, President Carter's election in 1976 represents the same principle. Electing a Southerner as President opened a door which had in fact been shut since the Civil War.

The role of Montesquieu's famous essence in the formation of law is illustrated even more vividly in the process which led to the doom of President Nixon in 1974. It became apparent in 1973 that abuses of power had occurred in the White House—abuses intolerable to the spirit of American politics. The revelations stirred the constitutional instincts of the nation, always the strongest force in its public life. No man, and no group of men, could stop the enquiry. At the same time, the nation was determined not to repeat what were generally—and rightly—recalled as the constitutional errors committed during the impeachment proceedings against Andrew Johnson in 1868. No one wanted the American Constitution transformed into a Parliamentary system, with the President as its Prime Minister, and Congress as its sovereign. A bill of impeachment must not become a vote of no confidence. The nation and its institutions groped their way forward slowly, avoiding one wrong turning after another, in order to satisfy both imperatives—that all responsible for the abuses be punished, and that the constitutional norms be fully respected in the process.

This view of the moral element in law rests on a distinction of the utmost importance, often blurred in the literature: the distinction, that is, between the ethical norms and aspirations of a particular society at a particular time, and those of the commentator, critic, or scholar himself. The individual may and should have his own moral vantage point, as Montesquieu did; he is, indeed, under an obligation to criticize the moral code of any particular society. But the institutions of a society must function in accordance with the moral code of that society. For them, no other course is possible, or proper.

II

Among the cultures of the world, the American is one of those most deeply committed to the idea of law—and to the idea of a particular law, the law whose libertarian ideals are expressed in the Declaration of Independence and the Constitution. In part, the passion of this commitment reflects the Old Testament Protestantism of the sects whose creeds constitute the dominant model for the American personality. For the Old Testament, it should not be forgotten, is concerned not with theology but with the authority of The Law. In part, the special American attitude toward law is the consequence of the role of the written Constitution, and of the Supreme Court as its expositor and guardian: the great unifying force, and spiritual center, of the nation's life. In part, of course, it represents the flowering of the British tradition—but its flowering in a different soil, under different circumstances, and with rather different results.

Whatever its sources may be—and they are many—the American principle of legality is among most powerful of the dreams and hopes which make our people one.

For example, it is the heart of the American mystery that the Revolution of 1776 be deemed a rightful act, a lawful act, and not simply a coup d'etat, to be followed by another, and later on by more. The Declaration of Independence was not a clever piece of political propaganda, putting a plausible face on a naked seizure of power, but the statement of a principle basic to our nature, and to the nature of our society.

We are people of the Book, who must live by the Law. If as a people we break the positive law, we must know first that our act is justified in the nature of law, and as a matter of law—justified because the law we broke was void, or had been repudiated, or was contrary to Higher Law.

The authority of the Constitution and the legitimacy of the social order based upon it derive in the end from this conviction about the character of the Revolution.

The principles of liberty and equality set out in the Declaration of

Independence and codified in the Constitution are the most powerful influence in our history. Year after year, they burst the bonds of hatred and of habit, reshaping our minds and then our institutions. Their moral power gives coherence and direction to our public life.

The moral power of the Declaration of Independence and the Constitution is not rooted in appetite, or in success. The ideas of the Declaration are part of our bone not because the revolutionaries were romantic adventurers, not because they won, but because we believe in what they did and said. The Declaration has been and remains one of the chief themes in the symphony of our history because to us, as communicants in the creed of American society, its ideas have the sanction of being right—right as a justification for the Revolution, and right also as a statement of our most cherished ambitions for American society.

I do not intend by this contention to minimize the significance of violence and lawlessness in our history. From our treatment of the Indians to the days of the Ku Klux Klan and the Molly Maguires, we have known crime in our labor and race relations, in our politics, and in business. What I do mean is that thus far, at any rate, our instinct after an outburst of violence has always been to seek a generous solution through law for the conflict which gave rise to violence. Thus the Clayton Act and the Wagner Act followed the bloody strikes and bloody labor struggles of the generation before 1912, and then later of the twenties and early thirties. And now civil rights and poverty legislation have been passed in the wake of recent efforts— and sometimes violent and disturbing efforts—to see to it that the promise of the Fourteenth Amendment is in fact at last fulfilled.

The idea of legality is fundamental to the theory of the Declaration both as a revolutionary and as a constitutional act.

The case for revolution which Jefferson wrote does not depend upon his eighteenth-century language of universal natural rights. It is based on a more general theory about the nature of a free political community, a free people, and a free nation.

I do not apologize for Jefferson's theory of natural rights, or suggest that it is no longer sensible to speak of mankind in general, in the tolerant and civilized eighteenth-century way, rather than about the Russians, the Americans, and the Chinese who live in different societies and are shaped by different cultures. Of course men are products of particular cultures. But they are also men, more and more obviously caught up in a shared and universal dilemma. The state of our tortured planet requires us somehow to invoke our common humanity in order to control and restrain our all too common inhumanity.

The Declaration put the essential legal justification for the Revolution of 1776 in these terms:

> We hold these truths to be self-evident, that all men are created equal, that they are endowed by their Creator with certain unalienable Rights, that among these are Life, Liberty and the Pursuit of Happiness.—That to secure these rights, Governments are instituted among Men, deriving their just powers from the consent of the governed.—That whenever any Form of Government becomes destructive to these ends, it is the Right of the People to alter or to abolish it, and to institute new Government, laying its foundation on such principles and organizing its power in such form, as to them shall seem most likely to effect their Safety and Happiness.

These propositions rest on two doctrines which are the implicit predicate of the Declaration.

The first is the theory of the state as a social compact, formulated for the modern world by Locke and Rousseau, but with roots that extend back through the Middle Ages to classical Greece. While the idea of a social compact is of course something of a metaphor, it remains the essential principle of all modern democracies and, indeed, of any community where authority rests on living custom rather than on force or divinity. For all who believe in popular and representative government, the powers of government must be deemed to derive from the consent of the people as the ultimate source of sovereignty, and not from the barrel of a gun. In formal terms, the American Constitution *is* a social compact, adopted by "we, the people," and binding all who share the culture of American society, in which the citizen participates freely in the making of law and in its public life.

The second doctrine basic to our Revolution is a particular theory of the British Empire, first formulated by Franklin and generally accepted in the colonies by 1776. According to that theory, the colonies were societies of free men, established in the wilderness under their own legislatures, and linked by Britain only through allegiance to the Crown. The Parliament of Westminster had no authority over the colonies, Franklin argued, any more than the colonial legislatures had authority in England. In the years immediately before 1776, the attempts of Parliament and of the King to govern the colonies breached older habits and the constitutional rules on which the association with Britain had been based. These were acts of usurpation, Jefferson and his colleagues charged. Repeated efforts at conciliation having failed, the colonies were therefore justified in "snipping the thin gold thread of voluntary allegiance to a personal sovereign," as Professor Becker put it.[1]

Thus the American revolutionaries could claim that the King had violated the law of their relationship, and that their Revolution was no more than a recognition of the fact that the ties of allegiance had ceased to exist.

There is therefore no paradox—at least for an American mind—in the position of the Founding Fathers, who fought a revolutionary war in rebellion against constituted authority, and then organized American society under a new system of laws, made by the revolutionaries, and intended by them to be eternal. The harshest war of the nineteenth century confirmed their thesis that the Union of 1788 was an indissoluble compact, made directly by the people, and not to be broken by the states.

III

Thus far, I have talked about law almost as an anthropological phenomenon, without mentioning the authority of the sovereign. Many theories of law insist that law is no more than a sovereign's command, obeyed largely out of fear of punishment. Writers of this persuasion often claim, for example, that international law is not really "law," and that international politics are not governed by its rules, because the society of nations has no sovereign.

This familiar opinion reflects the power in our minds of ancient symbols of royal, and indeed of divine authority. For the most part, international law is enforced about as effectively as national law, both as the embodiment of mores and as an influence upon behavior. And for the international society of states, it is "law" in every sense of the term. Effective lawmaking occurs in many societies, such as that of the United States, where the wafer of sovereignty is broken into hundreds if not thousands of fragments. In such societies, soci-

---

1. CARL BECKER, THE DECLARATION OF INDEPENDENCE 132 (1922, 1956).

eties of pluralism, the authority to declare and interpret laws is dispersed among a multitude of institutions, public and private. In the United States, for example, the sovereign prerogative is shared by the President, Congress, and the Supreme Court, on the one hand, and by officials of states, counties, cities, universities, churches, corporations, trade unions, and dozens of other private and semi-private institutions, on the other.

No legal system can function without at least a marginal invocation of the police power. But the respective roles of habit and command in the effectiveness of law cannot be so simply explained. The most sovereign of sovereigns cannot promulgate any laws that happen to catch his fancy. No matter how completely a ruler's power is concentrated and respected, he cannot obtain obedience to rules that depart too far from the pattern of custom, or require people to behave in ways they consider wrong, save at the cost of totalitarian coercion. He could hardly legitimize polygamy, for example, in a religious society of monogamy, or stamp out polygamy if his people were attached to it as a matter of faith. Obedience to law, like law itself, springs in the main from custom, oriented to and by "the spirit of the laws," in Montesquieu's sense. Lincoln called this element of law the "mystic chords of memory" which stretch "from every battlefield and patriot grave to every living heart and hearthstone" of the land. In the end, Lincoln's "chords of memory" determine how societies behave. In pluralist societies, laws that correspond to its customs, or represent aspirations for the law that society is willing to see translated into patterns of actual behavior, can become effective without much use of the police power.

In a society governed by law—what the German jurists call a *Rechtsstaat*—custom, aspiration, and command are in harmony most of the time. For the idea of peace is an indispensable element of the notion of law. Arbitrary power may maintain order in society for a time without the regularities of law, but peace is beyond its reach. In its simplest sense, the law of each society is the system of peace appropriate to its code of values: a peaceful way to resolve conflicts and make social policy through known procedures and in accordance with known and accepted principles—an alternative both to tyranny and to anarchy.

A society does not invariably live in accordance with its own rules of right behavior, nor always follow its established procedures for resolving conflicts about what right behavior is. It is clear, for example—or at least it was clear until recently—that American society accepted the model of monogamous marriage as a norm. Monogamous marriage was the pattern of behavior deemed right, even though adultery and other deviations from the norm were hardly unknown. Similarly, it has been and is the norm of the legal system that decisions of social policy be made through elections, the votes of Congress and the state legislatures, and the judgments of courts, although, like others, American society has endured the stress of periods of turbulence, and one of civil war.

While a model for behavior can remain an effective norm of law if it is not universally respected, it ceases to be a norm, and becomes a myth, when it no longer corresponds to the generality of practice, and society abandons any effort to vindicate or protect it.

The perspective outlined here, then, views the institutions of law, ranging from legislatures and courts to the officers, directors, and trustees of corporations, universities, and trade unions, as participants in a process through which society secretes law, and laws helps to shape society. That process *is* the law—a process of peace, conducted in highly structured ways, and dominated by the society's commitment to fulfill its ideal of justice through law.

The outlook toward law which I shall try to develop in this book—it has been called "legal idealism," which I find not an inappropriate label—combines the outlooks of history and philosophy. To my mind, there is no real distinction between the two ideas. History without philosophy is no more than antiquarianism. And philosophy without life is the play without the Prince. Philosophy is a serious subject, seriously concerned with the human condition, not another word for mathematics or grammar.

It is indispensable, in my view, to examine the process of law through extended periods of time. That process, I have contended, involves interactions among the law of the past, the moral ideas of society, and the realities of social experience. Those interactions are mediated by the procedures of the law, which involve disciplined and highly particularized methods of systematic thought. To understand law as a factor in the social process, and the social process as a factor in law, however, one must not be mesmerized by the elegance and intellectual charm of the rationality of law, important as it is. A static and purely analytical view of judicial technique necessarily misses the point. Law is an indispensable part of the long tides of social change. Holmes posed the challenge in his famous definition of law as a prediction of what in fact the judges will do. We can never assume that the judges will do tomorrow what they did yesterday. That is not to reproach them as usurpers. They would betray the most vital rule of their craft if adherence to precedent were the whole of their work. Yet on what basis can we anticipate the law that is always in gestation? Only, I submit, by understanding all the forces which press upon it and demand its arbitraments. What I am saying, then, is that law must be viewed in a matrix, and that any attempt to confine it more narrowly is bound to be misleading. A "value-free" science of law, and a philosophy of law cut off from the study of society at large, are contradictions in terms.

I have on occasion said that law is the universal social science, necessarily embracing all other ways of viewing man in society. Yet law is more than a synthesis or anthology of what we can learn from economics, sociology, political theory, anthropology, psychology, cybernetics, semantics, and the rest. It is an autonomous force in human affairs. It draws strength from a long tradition and a prestige in the minds of men based on centuries of trust. Men grumble about lawyers and suspect them of cynicism or worse, because, in the famous phrase, they can be hired "to prove black is white, or white black." But at another level, men understand the social value of the protection the law affords them. When they are in trouble, they ask lawyers to stand between them and the wrath of the state, and they abide by the decision of upright judges.

There are relations of reciprocity between law and the flow of history. Law responds to other social forces, but it also has an influence upon them. Men do not lightly ignore what their lawgivers tell them is just. The law is not a passive register of history, although it must often defer to powers which for the moment have the larger battalions.

Some wish to restrict or confine the moral element in law, or even to deny its existence altogether. Such men yearn for a "pure" system of law, predictable, determinate, ordered—altogether free of the ambiguity of human choice and human passion. They would separate law and morals, and admit as the permissible moral qualities of law only its formal or structural attributes, for example, that laws be general and publicly known, that trials be fair, that like cases be treated alike, and that there be no retrospective punishment. Professor Fuller calls such aspects of law its "internal morality."[2] They are indeed fundamental. They characterize all legal systems and are

---

2. LON C. FULLER, THE MORALITY OF LAW 33–94 (1964). See also JOSEPH RAZ, THE CONCEPT OF A LEGAL SYSTEM (1970).

necessary features of the legal mode in thought. But they do not begin to identify the moral content of the law.

The crusaders for a positivist view of law mistake the tentative relationship between fact and theory in the natural sciences. They call for a "science" of law which would end uncertainty, and allow us to escape the torment of the endless challenge to law in the name of justice. But they pursue a chimera. No such "science" of law can exist.

Views of this order rest on an equal misapprehension of natural science and of law. The problem of knowledge is no different in the natural sciences than in the study of man and society. There are not two cultures and two modes of thinking, but only one. The articulation of evidence and hypothesis is the same demanding task in history and in histology, in law and in physics. And the theories of science are no less controversial and no more durable than those of law or economics. Law, on the other hand, has no meaning save as a way of doing justice. Indeed, the quest for justice in one sense lies behind the endless ratiocination of legal literature. The doctrine of precedent, and the care of lawyers to respect or distinguish precedents, reflect only the principle that like cases ought to be decided alike—that is, that people are equal before the law and have equal rights. Attempts to separate law from the idea of justice invariably flounder. Even if law could be made "scientific" in terms of the most positivist legal philosophies, the achievement would leave it dead.

The position of the Negro in our law and society is a case in point. Slavery and, after slavery, racial discrimination were accepted by custom and sanctioned by law. But the conscience of the community and the conscience of the law recognized them as evil. That fact has been and is a propelling force in the evolution of law. Custom, even ancient custom, has a legitimate place in the development of law. But it yielded in the end to the convictions summed up in the gospel of liberty, equality, and fraternity. As Myrdal predicted in his great book, *An American Dilemma,* moral forces, and above all the moral principle that all men are created equal, dominate American life and would ultimately prevail. Other factors were at work in the social process and in the process of law—factors of political and economic interest, the mysterious social impact of war, and the gradual integration of the nation under the pressure of technological change. When examined, however, all these factors are seen to have affected the position of the Black in our society and law only because they reinforced the underlying conviction that slavery and racial discrimination were evil. And, in turn, efforts to eradicate the injustice of our treatment of the Negro inevitably encouraged more general processes of libertarian advance.

It is often asked whether the substantive moral element in law—its substantive content, that is, as distinguished from the formal moral attributes of legality—is anything more than the will of the majority, expressed through the legislature and, ultimately, through the votes of twelve men in a jury box. As Lord Devlin has brilliantly shown,[3] a modern secular democracy has no alternative. Having abandoned the bishops of an official religion, its moral code at any moment draws its sanction, just as its political authority does, from the will of the people at large. "A free society is as much offended by the dictates of an intellectual oligarchy as by those of an autocrat."[4]

So far as the law at any moment is concerned—the law in action and on the streets—the men in the jury box do have the last word. They hear instructions from the judge. They function in the shadow of their loyalty to the legal process, with all its majesty and all its taboos. But their will, expressed in a verdict, *is* the law, for the time being at least, whatever may be written in the books. It was not uncommon, even ten years ago, for Southern white juries to refuse to convict white men who had almost surely killed or injured Blacks or white civil rights "agitators"; and it is not uncommon today for Black juries to refuse to convict Blacks who have almost surely killed or injured white policemen. Events like these leave us with the hollow proposition that under the actual living law represented by such decisions—the law at the end of a policeman's nightstick, the law twelve men or women in a jury box will enforce—such conduct is not criminal. We know that if this rule be in fact the law, it is bad law. What criteria justify us in making that assertion? What forces in the nature of our culture, and in the nature of our law, can lead such jurors to change their minds?

Those are the ultimate questions.

3. PATRICK DEVLIN, THE ENFORCEMENT OF MORALS 86–101 (1965).
4. *Id.* at 93.

Part One

Custom versus the Ideal

A Case Study in the Evolution of Law and Mores

The two papers which follow recall in broad outline the great moral struggle in which American society has been engaged since the seventeenth century: the challenge of doing justice to the Blacks, in accordance with the code of justice we profess. The principle of human equality is the first axiom of the American code—the only possible rule for a nation of immigrants, reshaped in Jefferson's image. Tocqueville perceived equality as the basic idea of American society and the dominant influence on its laws, its customs, its outlook, and its atmosphere. On the other hand, the British, European, and American cultures, and the assumptions with which they approached the problem of race until the day before yesterday, gave rise to a pattern of custom far less catholic and universal than the Jeffersonian ideal. On this subject, Jefferson himself, after all, was never able to resolve the conflict within himself.

The contest between these two immense forces in our national personality and character, and the ways in which that contest has been reflected in the law and influenced by law, is to me the First Book of our national life, and the most vivid—and most important —of possible occasions for examining the formative influences in American law.

Two

The Negro In Our Law—I

I

One could start the story at any one of a number of points. I shall
state my theme in its most general form by recalling *Somerset*'s case.[1]

In 1769, a Virginian named Stewart or Steuart took one of his
slaves with him on a business trip to England. The slave's name is
given as James Somerset or Sommersett. He left his master in 1771.
Stewart then had Somerset seized and placed in irons on a ship in the
Thames, planning to send him to Jamaica, and there to sell him for
plantation work. Somerset's friends applied for a writ of habeas
corpus, which came before Lord Mansfield, who referred it to the
whole Court of King's Bench. The case was argued at length, and
with fervor, exciting considerable general interest.[2] There are several
versions of Mansfield's opinion freeing Somerset.[3]

The first version of this chapter was delivered as the William H. Leary Lecture
at the University of Utah Law School on May 11, 1965. It was published in
a slightly different form in 9 UTAH LAW REVIEW 841 (1965). © 1965 by the
University of Utah, Salt Lake City, Utah.

1. Somerset v. Stewart, Lofft 1, 98 Eng. Rep. 499 (K.B. 1772).

2. See 2 BOSWELL, THE LIFE OF SAMUEL JOHNSON 476–77 (Hill ed., Powell
rev. 1934); 3 *id* at 87, 212. Lord Mansfield refers with approval to the arguments of counsel and adds, "I cannot omit to express particular happiness in
seeing young men, just called to the Bar, have been able so much to profit by
their reading." Somerset v. Stewart, Lofft 1, 18, 98 Eng. Rep. 499, 509 (K.B.
1772). Mansfield assumed that the decision would free 14,000 or 15,000
slaves then living in England. *Id.* at 17, 98 Eng. Rep. 509.

   The case is discussed in Edward Fiddes, *Lord Mansfield and the Somerset
Case*, 50 L. Q. REV. 499 (1934); W. M. Wiecek, *Somerset: Lord Mansfield and
the Legitimacy of Slavery in the Anglo-American World*, 42 U. CHI. L. REV. 86
(1974); LESTER and BINDMAN, RACE AND LAW 28–34 (1972); C. H. S.
FIFOOT, LORD MANSFIELD 41–42 (1936).

3. *Supra* note 1; 20 How. St. Tr. 1, 1369 (K.B. 1772).

Lord Mansfield refused to give effect in England to the master's authority over the slave derived from the law of Virginia, even though Virginia was then a colony in which slavery was allowed by act of the British Parliament. It was plausibly argued that slavery, like marriage, for example, the legitimacy of children, divorce, and other relations of status, should be considered in the light of the law of the state where the relationship was formed and where master and slave were domiciled—in this instance, Virginia. Following this line of thought, counsel for Stewart, in the name of comity, asked the court to treat the legal relationship between master and slave as valid in England because it was valid in Virginia. The argument would surely have prevailed if the English court had deemed slavery to present a normal problem of civil status. This Lord Mansfield would not do. The court asked to decide a case always has the ultimate power to refuse to enforce relationships created elsewhere by the law of another state, when those relations deeply offend the conscience of the court, and violate the public policy of the state which must recognize and enforce the relationship. The question has arisen over the years in connection with the recognition of foreign laws regarding polygamy, divorce, confiscation, and the like.

Of slavery Mansfield wrote, "So high an act of dominion must be recognized by the law of the country where it is used. . . . The state of slavery is of such a nature, that it is incapable of being introduced on any reasons, moral or political; but only by positive law, which preserves its force long after the reasons, occasion, and time itself from whence it was created, is erased from memory: It's so odious, that nothing can be suffered to support it, but positive law."[4] There being no positive law, a phrase which for him meant legislation or binding precedent authorizing such slavery in England, Lord Mansfield concluded, "I cannot say this case is allowed or approved by the law of England; and therefore the black must be discharged."[5]

---

4. Somerset v. Stewart, Lofft 1, 19, 98 Eng. Rep. 499, 510 (K.B. 1772).

5. *Id*. The judge conceded that contracts for the sale of slaves were enforceable at law in English courts. *Id*. at 17, 98 Eng. Rep. at 509.

Somerset and its many-sided influence in American law, American politics, and the evolution of the American conscience are considered at length in Professor Wiecek's article, *supra* note 2; in DAVID BRION DAVIS, THE PROBLEM OF SLAVERY IN THE AGE OF REVOLUTION 1770–1823 at 471–522 (1975); and in Professor Robert M. Cover's excellent study, JUSTICE ACCUSED (1975), which meticulously examines the treatment of slavery by American judges,

Mansfield's position has powerful echoes of the Roman law, where slavery was regarded as contrary to the law of nature. It was generally said by the Roman lawyers that slavery could be upheld only on the basis of customary law, *ius gentium*.[6] Mansfield's opinion echoes Blackstone as well—and Montesquieu, upon whom Blackstone depended heavily in this instance.

Cardozo, bracketing Mansfield with Marshall to illustrate the magisterial style in writing opinions, was once misled into quoting from a more eloquent passage with which Campbell had embellished Mansfield's prose: "I care not for the supposed dicta of judges, however eminent, if they be contrary to all principle. . . . Villainage, when it did exist in this country, differed in many particulars from West India slavery. . . . At any rate villainage has ceased in England, and it

---

writers about law, and legislatures before the Civil War, in the shadow of Lord Mansfield's famous judgment, and the constitutional compromises about slavery which it helped to make explicit.

Professor Cover's special concern is the dilemma of those American judges of the period who believed slavery to be morally wrong. For them, cases involving slavery presented, in exceptionally acute form, the familiar conflict between the law the judge is bound by his duty to enforce and his conscience, that is, his own opinion of its morality. The citizen's obligation in a democratic society to law he believes to be immoral is discussed in chapter 4 *infra*. For all its usefulness, Professor Cover's book is weakened by an unresolved conflict in its analytical framework. Cover builds his book around a contrast I find unsatisfactory, between what he calls "positivism" and "natural law" or "morality." Positive law at every point in its evolution has a moral idea, which animated its formulation originally, and has influenced its development. The problem, as I see it, is not the difference between "positive law" and "morality," but the interplay among the morality of the existing positive law; the emerging moral code of the community; and the personal moral code of the individual judge or writer about law. The judge's duty, surely, is to interpret and apply the emerging moral code of the community, as Mansfield did in *Somerset,* and apply it to the construction of the existing law, and not to impose his private morality on the law of the society he has taken his oath to serve.

At times, Professor Cover accepts this distinction, and discusses the judge's duty in these terms. Through most of his book, however, he seems to assume that there is a body of precepts which exist somewhere "out there," as he says, "a brooding omnipresence in the sky," which can be identified by the individual as "morality" or "natural law," presumably by intuition or revelation. Although he never quite says so, he seems to be arguing that the upright judge should subordinate existing law to *his* vision of morality.

See DAVID G. RITCHIE, NATURAL RIGHTS (5th ed. 1952).

6. JOLOWICZ, HISTORICAL INTRODUCTION TO ROMAN LAW 105, 135–38, 269–71 (2d ed. 1952).

cannot be revived. The air of England has long been too pure for a slave, and every man is free who breathes it."[7]

However authentic the rhetoric attributed to Mansfield's opinion may be, the court's decision in *Somerset* was clear: let the Black go free.

This was the law of England in the 1770s.[8] It was not then the law of the American colonies, and for many long years it was not the law of the United States. One must add that it is not even now the law in fact in every part of the United States.

Yet in the 1770s, and throughout our history as a nation, every judge, and every thoughtful man, knew that the principle of Somerset's case should have been our law too. That conviction, like the knowledge of evil, has been the source of much in our law, and in our lives: a restless, uneasy pressure for change; a sense of guilt; a zeal for liberty.

This is the question I shall try to address in this paper—the place of the Negro in our law, why it was what it was, and how it became what it is today.

I should begin by making it clear that my work is not drawn from fresh research in the vast archives of the subject. It is, rather, an attempt at reflection and observation intended to help us govern ourselves by examining the future in the perspective of the past.

For I am of the school that views policymaking as the goal of historical studies, as it is the proper goal of every other approach to the study of society. We renew contact with what came before not in

7. CARDOZO, LAW AND LITERATURE 13–14 (1931); see 4 CAMPBELL, LIVES OF THE CHIEF JUSTICES OF ENGLAND 133–35 (1889). The final flourish echoes a remark in *Cartwright's* case as reported in 2 RUSHWORTH, HISTORICAL COLLECTION 468 (1721), where the court did indeed say that "England was too pure an Air for Slaves to breath in."

8. *Somerset* leaves many legal questions unanswered: Did the writ, for example, dissolve the relation of slavery like a bill of divorcement, or only deny the master the power to exercise any control over the slave in England? What would happen to the relationship if the master and slave returned to Virginia after a sojourn in England—the exact factual analogue to the *Dred Scott* case less than a hundred years later. In 1827, Lord Stowell answered that question as the Supreme Court did in *Dred Scott,* in the case of The King v. Allen, 2 Hagg. 94, 166 Eng. Rep. 179 (Adm. 1827) (popularly known as *The Slave Grace* case); *cf.* The Antelope, 23 U.S. (10 Wheat.) 66 (1825). See also 1 W. W. STORY, LIFE AND LETTERS OF JOSEPH STORY 559 (1851). According to Stowell and Story, *Somerset* simply suspended the status of slavery while Somerset remained in England, but if he returned with his master to their original domicile, the status of slavery was resumed or revived.

the spirit of nostalgia or antiquarianism, but because we know that the memories of our experience as a people, conscious and unconscious, play a large part in determining what we are and how we perceive the world around us. The forces that shape our national personality and character correspondingly restrict our freedom of choice. They define the range within which planned change is possible at any moment of time. And they prescribe the hierarchy of values we seek to fulfill in making such choices as are in fact open to us.

I have two general themes in mind.

The first is the inherent importance of the problem. From whatever vantage point we view our history, and the prospects for its future, the status of the Negro is a central and a tormenting issue. Fundamental conflict over the legal position of the Negro was a basic element in the constitutional system launched in 1787, and variant forms of that conflict have been key factors in almost every stage of its development since. The clash between our professed principles and the Negro's place in society has been the essence of the compromises, in war and in peace, through which we have sought one equilibrium after another in adding states to the Union, and in defining and re-defining the relative authority of the states and of the nation. The question of rights, privileges, and immunities for the Negro has been a crucial factor in determining the underlying alliances of the political order throughout our experience as a republic. And the Negro's plea for recognition as a human being, "created equal" and, therefore, entitled to equal treatment by the law, has been and is the haunting cry which never quite stops echoing in our inner ear, however strong the opposing forces of custom and racial feeling. In recent years, it has been a moving force requiring growth in almost every distinguishable branch of constitutional law, and in many other areas of law as well, from libel and reapportionment to wills, contempt of court, and the law of covenants which do and do not run with the land. Once the country came to agree with the Supreme Court that the Emperor was indeed naked—that our treatment of the Negro has been completely contrary to the most sacred principles of our polity—the idea of the New Model in our law and social arrangements spread with startling rapidity.

My second broad interest here is the richness of the topic as a case study in jurisprudence. The place of the Black in our legal system offers a unique opportunity to examine the role of law in the social process, and of the social process in the formation of law. After all, our spectrum extends from chattel slavery—and our law of slavery was the worst in the history of law—past *Dred Scott*,[9] the Civil War, and the *Civil Rights Cases*[10] of 1883 to the extraordinary if sometimes slow and uneven progress in the direction of equal rights for the Negro made in recent years by the Supreme Court, the Congress, and the people themselves. Such an examination requires us to test all the dazzling hypotheses of legal philosophy about the nature and purposes of law, and about its relationships to custom, reason, authority, morals, and the idea of justice. It permits us to distinguish theories which are consistent with experience from those which are not. In the nature of knowledge, this is an indispensable task. For theories—that is, sets or systems of propositions about reality—can never be proved true. They can, however, be shown to be untrue by demonstrating that our best measures of the external world, approximate as they necessarily are, are incompatible with propositions logically deduced from a particular theory about it. In this way we can at least narrow our search for explanations, and direct our attention to the factors most likely to prove fruitful in revealing the nature of the social process.

What I have particularly in mind is the part which moral elements —that is, both mores and aspiration—play in the process of making law. These are much controverted issues, and my views are not stylish. But I should contend that the student of law evades his principal responsibility, and his most difficult one, if he takes an exclusively analytical, linguistic, and positivist approach to law.

The status of the Negro in American law is not a pretty story, nor one for squeamish stomachs. It does not permit us to evade the share which inhumanity has played, and plays still, in human affairs, when the strong have a chance to hurt the weak. It does not allow us to forget how close to the surface primitive savagery is, and how powerful the beast within. Here, in sharp and often painful focus, we see the full array of passions and interests which enter into destiny: the force of habit, of greed, and of fear; the power and the weakness of conscience and religion; the thrust of dark passions and aggressive instincts that civilization must always seek to tame, or at least to

9. Dred Scott v. Sanford, 60 U.S. (19 How.) 393 (1857).
10. 109 U.S. 3 (1883).

confine; the mysterious impact of war on men and on societies; the contribution great men and women can sometimes make, if they are in the right places at the right times; and the ways in which social change occurs, often, usually, in what seem to be sudden sharp bursts after long periods of latency.

The chronicle is one of horror, but not only of horror. Our treatment of the Negro has created a constant tension between the actual state of things and the acknowledged ideal in our lives. Many chapters of the story are degrading and disgraceful. But the presence of the Negro has been a perpetual challenge to the Puritan spirit at the heart of our psyche. It has required moral exertion of us and given martyrs and heroes their occasions of glory. Thus, the moral element in our affairs has been strengthened and deepened to become their ruling power.

II

The slavery of the American colonies was not an isolated phenomenon. In part, it represented a survival into the nineteenth century of ancient forms of human subjugation, which even the new birth of freedom during the late eighteenth century could not quite extinguish. In part, however, it represented something quite different: a large-scale adaptation of the ancient tradition of slavery to the imperative demand of the New World for manpower. Slavery increased rapidly in the seventeenth and eighteenth centuries. With immigration and the transportation of indentured servants, it became one of the basic means for providing enough labor to clear the wilderness in most parts of North, South, and Central America. The colonizing labor force contained indentured white men as well as Negro slaves, especially during the seventeenth and early eighteenth centuries—refugees and scoundrels, followers of the Young Pretender and other lost causes, adventurers, peasants forced or induced to migrate, huge numbers of men who bonded themselves for two to eight years in exchange for passage and support. Until it was outstripped by slavery in the middle of the eighteenth century, indentured servitude was the chief form of labor in the Middle Atlantic and Southern North American colonies, and it continued to exist until well after the Revolution. The best estimate is that in the colonial period half the white population south of New England came to America as indentured servants—men recruited in Europe almost as brutally as the blacks were mobilized in Africa, and treated almost as badly on the journey, and in their places of work.

The status of indentured servants was quite as low as that of black slaves. Their contracts could be sold. They were not allowed to vote, to hold land, to engage in trade, or to serve on juries. They could not marry without the consent of their masters, and they were subject to corporal punishment by the master. The control of rebellious indentured servants was a major problem of public order in most of the American colonies and a major source of humanitarian complaint, both in America and in Britain. Many tricks were used to extend the nominal terms of indentured servants, and they became accustomed to degradation. One of the fascinating hypotheses about social experience advanced in recent years by Rossiter and others is that the indentured servants of colonial times, deeply injured by their experience, became not the sturdy yeomen and independent artisans of Federalist America, but an intractable mass of backward Southern "poor-whites," the ancestors of the Snopes.[11]

Historians seem generally to agree that Negro slavery developed strongly in the North American colonies only because white servitude could not produce a sufficient labor supply, especially for the colonies where plantation crops prevailed. Reports of the treatment of indentured servants reached Europe and made their recruitment more and more difficult. At the same time, the African slave trade became diabolically efficient, often with the cooperation of tribal chiefs. The first Negroes who came, in 1619, were probably not slaves at all. For fifty years or so, most Negroes who arrived or were brought here were indentured servants or free immigrants. The records notice several, perhaps many, who became free landholders, businessmen, and the masters of other servants. Some were given land under the headrights system—that is, they were given land grants of fifty acres for each European or African they brought into the colonies. In early

11. Abbott Emerson Smith, Colonists in Bondage (1947); E. S. Morgan, *Slavery and Freedom: The American Paradox,* 59 J. Am. Hist. 1 (1972); *id.,* American Slavery, American Freedom: The Ordeal of Colonial Virginia (1975). See Rossiter, Seedtime of the Republic 91 (1953). See generally Farnam, Chapters in the History of Social Legislation in the United States to 1860, at 60–70 (1938). The generalization is hardly universal. Taney's ancestors were indentured servants. See Walker Lewis, Without Fear or Favor 7 (1965).

times, slaves and indentured servants were treated equally badly. They lived together, without evidence of race feeling or caste distinction.

Soon, however, the treatment of the Negro became more severe, and the main features of American chattel slavery emerged. Correlatively, the South became attached to the conviction that its economy was unworkable without slavery. For many, this view was transformed into a doctrine justified by what they regarded as the Negro's inherent biological inferiority, by Biblical authority, and by natural right: a kind of "chosen people" doctrine. From the 1660s on—the time of the Restoration in England—slavery became the dominant but not the universal position of the Negro in the United States. Slavery itself took on its characteristic American features, notably different from those in the Spanish and Portuguese colonies. Slavery was perpetual and hereditary, and all sorts of presumptions and restraints developed to limit the possibility of freedom for the slave, even by the will or deed of his master. No official made inquiry about their humane treatment, as was the case in Spanish and Portuguese territory. They could not testify in courts, work for pay, own or inherit land, or obtain much legal protection, even against murder. It was a crime in many colonies and states to teach Negroes to read or to use firearms, or to sell them liquor. Blacks were punished more severely than white men for the same offenses. And running away was of course their ultimate crime.

As the institution of slavery crystallized, it affected the status of all Negroes, even the freed Negroes living in the North. They were a caste apart in the law of almost every state, except perhaps Vermont, with special provisions about voting, the ownership of land, crime, their capacity to give evidence, and so on.

Thus a poison entered our lives and pervaded every aspect of them. The Negro was forced to wear a badge of degradation which only the proudest spirits could totally reject or ignore. Self-hatred, a lack of self-respect and self-confidence, inevitably colored almost every Negro's estimate of himself. The effect of our caste system has been almost worse for the Master Race. Both white and Negro Americans were schooled in habits which grip us still as corrosive memories.

Leading spirits in all the colonies protested against slavery, starting with the Quakers in 1671. Jefferson sought to have a paragraph against slavery and the slave trade put into the Declaration of Independence, and he proposed in 1779 that Virginia abolish slavery gradually. Tom Paine denounced it. George Washington favored emancipation, and his will directed that all his slaves be freed on his widow's death. Judge Tucker of Virginia wrote an early book against slavery. And the Congregational preachers of New England, including Jonathan Edwards, Ezra Stiles, and Leonard Bacon, took the lead in preparing public opinion for the abolitionists of the generation which began with Garrison's first number of the *Liberator* in 1830.[12]

While there was considerable progress toward liberty in the North during the era of the Revolution, the egalitarianism of the Declaration of Independence was only rarely and gradually applied to the position of the slave. Not many saw the paradoxical contrast between the social ideals of the Declaration and the position of the Negro—and of women as well, for that matter. As late as the mid-nineteenth century, the most humane and compassionate opinion—that of Lincoln or Monroe, for example—was that the Negro was an unfortunate person of inferior attainments, treated very badly by the whites, to be sure, but not conceivably the white man's equal. For such men, the right solution for the Negro problem was to return the Negroes to Africa. Few were prepared to act decisively against the weight of custom, and against the increasingly panicky and fearful resistance of the South, convinced as it was that its autonomy, and indeed its freedom, were threatened by the protest against slavery.

Hamilton and many other participants in the Convention believed that the Constitution would never have been made unless its several compromises on slavery were accepted, particularly the provision of Article I, Section 2, adapted from the tax provisions of the Articles, that three-fifths of the slaves, discreetly noticed as "all other persons" to distinguish them from "free persons," should be counted in apportioning representatives to the states. Second, one should recall the Sherman Compromise, giving each state two senators, although many factors other than the problem of safeguarding slavery entered into this rule. Third, there was the fugitive slave provision of Article IV, Section 2, denying the principle of *Somerset*'s case in the law of the

12. A convenient review of the literature, as well as a good deal of original research, appears in KENNETH STAMPP, THE PECULIAR INSTITUTION (1956). A classic on South American slavery (and on the social process) is FREYRE, THE MASTERS AND THE SLAVES (2d Eng. ed. 1956). See also FARNAM, *supra* note 11, at 167–79; J. H. FRANKLIN, FROM SLAVERY TO FREEDOM (1947); LOREN MILLER, THE PETITIONERS (1966).

United States. Finally, the first clause of Article I, Section 9, supported by Article V, denied Congress the power to prohibit the slave trade until 1808. "Without this indulgence," Hamilton concluded, "no Union could possibly have been formed."[13]

The fugitive slave section of Article IV was an increasing source of tension as the nation lurched toward civil war. It provided that "no person held to service or labor in one state, under the laws thereof, escaping into another, shall, in consequence of any law or regulation therein, be discharged from such service or labor, but shall be delivered up on Claim of the Party to whom such service or labor may be due."

The provision—not notably ambiguous as constitutional sentences go—defines one dimension of the constitutional and political conflict which led to the Civil War.

If every Northern state had to yield up fugitive slaves to their masters, could those states abolish slavery in fact? Could they enfranchise Negroes? Could free Negroes living in the North go into slave states, and claim there the privilege and immunities of United States citizenship? Was the Northwest Ordinance valid in banning slavery in that territory? Were the great Whig compromises of 1820 and 1850 valid, in the face of this ominous question? By the same token, could the Congress abolish slavery in the territories? Could a state enslave a free Negro if it could catch him?

In that period, many Southerners, who are usually viewed as advocates of states' rights, strongly defended the Constitution as a national limitation on the authority of the free states. And some of the abolitionists were among the strongest advocates of secession.

The Compromise of 1820, which kept the balance between North and South in the Senate, adjourned the issue of slavery for thirty years as an ultimate test of the institutions of Union. But those thirty years were an era of transformation. Industries, universities, cities, and provinces sprang up. Jackson was one symbol of the change; Melville, Thoreau, Hawthorne, and Emerson were others. Especially after 1830, it was one of those times when a mysterious conjuncture of forces precipitates a change in the moral climate. In every country of the world, suddenly, and without much warning, men of all political temperaments, conservative and liberal, began to agitate for social

13. FARNAM, *supra* note 11, at 125.

action against cruelties and injustices long ignored. The forces of humanitarianism touched every phase of social experience. There were poor laws and factory laws, concern about child labor and the rights of women, prison reform, agitation to prevent cruelty to animals, a radical enlargement of the right to vote. And above all, a worldwide movement, led by Wilberforce in England, fought to end slavery.

The antislavery movement was hardly one of mass sentiment, at least in the United States. The Antislavery Society, and the various other branches and sects of the movement, were led by a tiny dedicated elite. At most, the abolitionist movement, even in New England, did not become more than a small, despised band of prophets until well after the beginning of the Civil War. Their support was a political liability even in the election of 1860.

Yet their work offers a fascinating opportunity to observe the functions of leadership in the formation of opinion, and in the preparations for political action. The abolitionists had friends of influence, and leaders who were heard, even if they were scorned and mobbed. For a long time, they challenged the conscience of the nation, and posed the issues which were seen later, when the crisis came, to offer alternative courses. And, as almost invariably happens in the United States, the issues in the debate were dramatized, and intensified, by recourse to the courts. Over and over again trials raised the *Somerset* issue, forcing communities and regions to confront the presence of slavery, not in distant Georgia, but in their own towns.[14]

The rising vehemence of the abolitionist outcry deepened the sense of fear in the South, as the country expanded to the west, and the even balance of North and South in Congress became more and more manifestly an untenable rule for the future. The controversies over the admission of new states were colored by panic, which was in turn heightened by the lightning flash of John Brown's raids.

In this setting, we see *Dred Scott* as a final attempt to restore the old balance and order to a political system in crisis. One of the main structural elements of the Union, as it had hitherto existed, was

---

14. See Commonwealth v. Aves, 18 Pick (Mass.) 193 (1836), discussed in Leonard Levy, The Law of the Commonwealth and Chief Justice Shaw (1957) chs. 5 and 6; People v. Lemmon, 5 Sanford (7 N.Y. Super. Ct.) 681 (1859). See Lloyd, The Slavery Controversy—1831–1860 (1939); J. M. McPherson, The Struggle for Equality (1964); Robert M. Cover, *Supra* note 5.

disintegrating. The nation had to be rebuilt on a new footing. Could that task be accomplished in peace?

III

It is of absorbing interest to reexamine *Dred Scott* as part of this process. Every schoolboy knows it was Taney's great mistake, a dreadful act of judicial usurpation, a self-inflicted wound which is supposed to have weakened the Court for a long time—although the Court issued one of its most powerful and confident decisions, *Ex Parte Milligan,*[15] less than ten years later. Having recited these clichés, we generally fail to read the opinions in the case, and turn to the next chapter.

Dred Scott repays a modern reading, both as a political effort that failed and as an exposition of the concept of national citizenship, the indispensable basis for contemporary civil rights legislation. The reasoning of *Dred Scott* hardly supports the stereotype image of Taney as a defender of slavery and states' rights, although Taney's opinion is marred by polemic and extravagance. Its flaw was more fundamental than the errors of law and the miscalculations of politics on which it rests. In *Dred Scott,* Taney committed the truly fatal error of judges, that of insight and intuition. He failed where Mansfield succeeded so magnificently in *Somerset,* that is, in perceiving the true condition of public morality, even though it was inchoate and perhaps unconscious before he spoke, and, therefore, in perceiving the possible scope of judicial leadership. In *Somerset,* Mansfield framed the issue for decision by stating a premise so majestic, and seemingly so self-evident, that no one noticed its revolutionary character: slavery, he said, is "so odious that nothing can be suffered to support it, but positive law." Once this sentence was put at the top of the page, the result in the case was assured. There were no statutes with which the slave owner could overcome the presumptions Mansfield put in his path. And Mansfield swept away earlier judicial decisions of contrary import.

But Mansfield's premise was by no means self-evident. As Lord Stowell tartly observed, "ancient custom is generally acknowledged

15. 71 U.S. (4 Wall.) 2 (1867).

as a just foundation of all law." And Parliament had authorized slavery in Virginia, where the relationship of slavery between Stewart and Somerset had been established. With some bewilderment, however, Stowell recognized the binding quality of Mansfield's achievement, in holding that the owners of slaves had no authority or control over them in England, nor any power of sending them back to the colonies in chains.

> Thus fell, after only two-and-twenty years, in which decisions of great authority had been delivered by lawyers of the greatest ability in this country, a system, confirmed by a practice which had obtained without exception ever since the institution of slavery in the colonies, and had likewise been supported by the general practice of this nation and by the public establishment of its Government, and it fell without any apparent opposition on the part of the public. The suddenness of this conversion almost puts one in mind of what is mentioned by an eminent author, on a very different occasion, in the Roman History, *"Ad primum nuntium cladis Pompeianae populus Romanus repente factus est alius"*: the people of Rome suddenly became quite another people.[16]

It is easy to understand Taney's mistake in *Dred Scott.* He was eighty years old, and had just lost his wife and daughter under harrowing circumstances. Reasonable, sober men, devoted to the Union, hoped for a new and sagacious compromise, like that of 1820, which could reconcile North and South, and allow slavery to fade away gradually, as villainage had faded in England. In the troubled decade of the 1850s, the appeal of *Dred Scott's* desperate remedy is apparent. Most moderate opinion hoped the Supreme Court would issue a Solomonic judgment that could achieve magical results. The unthinkable alternative of war distorted judgment. The old Federalist and Jacksonian Chief Justice from Maryland, Catholic, pacific, and devoted to the nation, sought to restore the rule that had harmoniously corresponded to public feeling in 1789 and 1820: the premise of the Negro as a person apart in our law. His intuition failed him. He did not perceive that the social and moral basis for the rule had vanished, so that the rule itself, and all its corollaries, had become obsolete.

16. The King v. Allen, 2 Hagg. 94, 106, 166 Eng. Rep. 179, 183 *Adm. 1827). See also Osborn v. Nicholson, 80 U.S. (13 Wall.) 654, 660–61 (1872); Scott v. Sandford, 60 U.S. (19 How.) 393, 407–27, 534–36, 590–600, 624–27 (1857).

And, above all, he failed to divine, as Mansfield had in *Somerset,* a clarifying hypothesis buried in the integuments of the future, and waiting to be born.

Perhaps there was no such rule. It is generally thought that the conflict was beyond reach of the courts. Surely no solution was conceivable without nullifying at least the fugitive slave provision of the Constitution, which had in all probability been addressed to the decision in *Somerset* in the first place. Within a few years, Taney took a long step in that direction, in holding that the duty of a state under Article IV, Section 2 of the Constitution to deliver up a fugitive from justice, while mandatory, was political, and could not be enforced by the courts.[17] But even if that approach would have been adequate, it came too late.

IV

Dred Scott was a slave owned by an army doctor named John Emerson. Between 1833 and 1836, Emerson was stationed in Illinois, where slavery was forbidden by the Northwest Ordinance and the state Constitution. Scott accompanied his master first to Illinois, and then to Fort Snelling in what is now Minnesota, free territory under the Missouri Compromise. At Fort Snelling, with Emerson's consent, Scott married a slave Emerson had purchased there from another officer. In 1838, Scott, his wife, and two children went with Emerson to Missouri, where Emerson died in 1843. The pleadings in *Dred Scott* establish that Scott and his family had been conveyed as slaves to Sanford, or Sandford, as he is called in the United States Reports, some time before suit was brought.

In 1851 or 1852, as the terrible storm of American history grew darker and more electric, Scott sued for his freedom and that of his family in the state courts of Missouri. His case rested on the *Somerset* theory—that his sojourn in free territory had made him a free man. Whatever might have been the result in Illinois or other free states or territories, the Missouri courts held, the status of the Scotts was determined by the law of Missouri, where they had lived with Emerson as a slave, where Emerson had been domiciled, and died, and where the transfer of Scott and his family to Sanford, as slaves, had

17. Kentucky v. Dennison, 65 U.S. (24 How.) 66 (1861).

taken place. In this decision, the Missouri courts followed the theory
of a recent ruling by the Supreme Court of the United States,[18]
which treated Kentucky law as decisive in determining the status of
Kentucky slaves who had lived temporarily in Ohio, and then returned to Kentucky. The judges, that is to say, followed Lord Stowell
and Story in reading *Somerset* narrowly, as a case which did not
really free Somerset but simply suspended the enforcement of his
servile status while he was in England. At an earlier time, the Missouri courts had recognized the freedom of men taken into free
territory as slaves. But now, the Missouri Supreme Court wrote, "not
only individuals but States have been possessed with a dark and fell
spirit in relation to slavery, whose gratification is sought in the pursuit
of measures, whose inevitable consequence must be the overthrow
and destruction of our government. Under such circumstance it
does not behoove the State of Missouri to show the least countenance
to any measure which might gratify this spirit."[19]

But resistance to Stowell's view of *Somerset* was increasing, and
increasing rapidly. Scott's counsel did not give up. Instead of appealing directly to the Supreme Court, which would obviously have been
hopeless in the face of *Strader,* he started a new proceeding in the
federal court of St. Louis, approaching the issue of Scott's status by
another route. The defendant in the federal suit was Sanford, a citizen
of New York, the administrator of Emerson's estate, and the brother
of Mrs. Emerson, who had meanwhile married a Massachusetts
doctor of abolitionist sympathies, and moved to Massachusetts.[20]

The theory of the new suit was trespass: that Sanford had wrongfully used force to detain Scott as a slave, despite the fact that Scott
had become free by reason of his residence in free territory. Under
the federal statutes, the only basis for the jurisdiction of the federal
court in what seemed to be an ordinary suit for tort—normally a
matter of state law—was the diversity of citizenship between Scott,
the plaintiff, a citizen of Missouri, and Sanford, the defendant, a
citizen of New York. Sanford filed a "plea to the jurisdiction of the
court"—a motion to dismiss the proceedings for want of jurisdiction,
on the ground that Scott was not a citizen of Missouri, as alleged,

18. Strader v. Graham, 51 U.S. (10 How.) 82 (1851).
19. Scott, a man of color, v. Emerson, 15 Mo. 577, 586 (1952).
20. Carl B. Swisher, THE TANEY PERIOD, 1836–64, at 599–601 (5 HISTORY
OF THE SUPREME COURT OF THE UNITED STATES, 1974).

"because he is a negro of African descent; his ancestors were of pure African blood, and were brought into this country and sold as negro slaves."[21] Scott's lawyer responded with a demurrer, a reply which, in law, meant that even if it were conceded for purposes of argument that what Sanford had said in his pleading were true, it could not affect the legal conclusion that Scott had capacity to sue in the federal courts as a citizen of Missouri. The federal trial court held for Scott on this point, deciding that he did have capacity to sue. The case then went to the jury on the basis of an agreed statement of fact, in which Sanford's defense was that he had a right "gently" to lay hands on Sanford, and restrain him, because Scott was his slave. The jury found for Sanford: Scott was still a slave in Missouri.

The case reached the Supreme Court in 1854. It was argued twice, and the result was not announced until March 6, 1857, two days after the inauguration of James Buchanan as President. There were nine opinions, taking up 234 pages in the official Reports of the Supreme Court. For our purposes, we should note certain highlights from the two main opinions, that of Taney, for the majority, and Benjamin R. Curtis' masterly dissent.

Both Taney and Curtis agreed that the jurisdictional propriety of an action by a lower federal court could always be reviewed by the Supreme Court, since the limited statutory jurisdiction of the United States courts represented an important element of balance between the states and the nation in the American system of federalism. The parties could not confer jurisdiction on the federal courts if an appropriate statutory basis for jurisdiction did not exist—that is, in cases of this kind, if it appeared on the record that the plaintiff and the defendant were not citizens of different states. The federal courts could not expand their powers at will whenever the parties, for reasons of their own, acquiesced in such a usurpation.

Was Scott a citizen of the United States, and a citizen of Missouri, with the privilege of bringing suit in the federal courts as a citizen?

The question revealed a deep ambiguity in the American constitutional system, not fully cured even by the first sentence of the Fourteenth Amendment, which was expressly intended to reverse the decision of *Dred Scott:* "All persons born or naturalized in the United States, and subject to the jurisdiction thereof, are citizens of

21. Dred Scott v. Sanford, 60 U.S. (19 How.) 393, 396–97 (1857).

the United States and the State wherein they reside." Before the passage of the Fourteenth Amendment, and since, the relationship between state and national citizenship has presented difficulties which mirror the conflicting political theories of American sovereignty: Are we a nation, made by the constituent act of the people? Or a federation, established by agreement among sovereign states? Is the written Constitution of 1787 a treaty, or something infinitely more fundamental, a code struck off by the people themselves, and therefore as binding on the states as on the nation? It was reasonably clear in Taney's time, and even more clear today, that the "state citizenship" needed to establish the privilege of suing in the federal courts required citizenship of the United States and residence or domicile in one of the states.

In the 1850s, what was American citizenship, and how was it acquired? The Constitution was obscure. The nation came into existence as a full-fledged member of the society of nations with the Declaration of Independence, and the revolutionary war which followed it, that is, through an assertion of sovereignty which finally obtained the full recognition of the international community. Both Taney and Curtis agreed that it was the people of the United States who embodied that sovereignty, and asserted it as a political community, ultimately through the enactment of the written Constitution of 1787, which was composed and ratified in their name and by them, not by the states.

Could Negroes, the descendants of slaves, be constituent members of that sovereign body, and part of the embodiment of the national principle? And is it for the nation or for the states to decide who are the members of the sovereign body, "We, the people of the United States"? The Constitution gives Congress the power to establish a uniform rule of naturalization: a power early held to be exclusively for Congress, since citizenship pertains so directly to the nature and functioning of the national government. But the Constitution says nothing else on the subject, except for the axioms implicit in the requirement that no person except a natural born citizen, or a citizen of the United States at the time of the adoption of the Constitution, could be President or Vice-President, and the provision—of critical importance to the problem of *Dred Scott*—that "the Citizens of each State shall be entitled to all Privileges and Immunities of Citizens in the several States." This clause is the only language in the Constitution itself which comes close to addressing the question of national citizenship. Manifestly, it posits the conception of national citizenship, and rests on it. And it deals with the privileges and immunities of citizens of the United States. But their citizenship is defined obliquely. To be a citizen of the United States, must one also be a citizen of a state? What about citizens born in territories, or the District of Columbia? The children of citizens born abroad? Can a state make someone a state citizen, and therefore a citizen of the United States, if he is not capable of being naturalized?

The states have had—and have still—various rules about their own state citizenship, regulating the right to vote, the right to become members of professions limited to citizens, and so on. For example, several states allowed women to vote in state elections long before the passage of the Nineteenth Amendment.

But, at least since the enactment of the Constitution, state legislation could not confer national citizenship. Whether a person was a citizen of the United States was a matter of national law, inherent to the existence of the nation. It was for the Congress, not the states, to pass laws on the subject of citizenship, immigration, and other problems affecting the size and composition of the national political community. The proposition was deemed nearly self-evident, despite the absence of language on immigration or citizenship in the written Constitution itself. And it was peculiarly important to the delicate compromises on the subject of slavery which permitted the nation to be born in the first place.

Changes on this theme were a fundamental element in the great debate of *Dred Scott* between Taney and Curtis.

Taney approached his argument from the vantage point of the most commonplace, and most dubious, of judicial major premises: "No one, we presume, supposes that any change in public opinion or feeling, in relation to this unfortunate race, in the civilized nations of Europe or in this country, should induce the court to give to the words of the Constitution a more liberal construction in their favor than they were intended to bear when the instrument was framed and adopted."[22]

As a living growth, the law expounded by judges evolves only because changes "in public opinion or feeling" occur, and occur constantly. Such changes in the code of social morality, and experi-

22. *Id.* at 426.

ence with the results of earlier rules, transform the variables whose interaction determines the path of the law. Psychologically, there is no way in which the men of a later generation can "know" what the Founding Fathers intended. It is impossible for them to view the world as their ancestors saw it: they cannot imagine or reproduce the combination of ideas and perceptions which constituted their ancestors' universe, nor guess the relative importance to their ancestors of the several factors and policies which composed it. On the other hand, the democratic character of our society depends ultimately not only on the insight and intuition of the judges, but on their restraint—their capacity, that is, to distinguish those changes in the law which can and should be made by judges in the common law way, and those which the judges should leave to the legislatures and the people.

In *Dred Scott,* Taney plunged forward to delineate what he supposed to have been the position of the Negro in American law at the end of the eighteenth century, and took his stand firmly on that model as the rule which should govern the court's decision in 1857. His argument starts with Jefferson's echoing words from the Declaration of Independence:

> "We hold these truths to be self-evident: that all men are created equal; that they are endowed by their Creator with certain unalienable rights; that among them is life, liberty, and the pursuit of happiness; that to secure these rights, Governments are instituted, deriving their just powers from the consent of the governed."
>
> The general words above quoted would seem to embrace the whole human family, and if they were used in a similar instrument at this day would be so understood. But it is too clear for dispute, that the enslaved African race were not intended to be included, and formed no part of the people who framed and adopted this declaration; for if the language, as understood in that day, would embrace them, the conduct of the distinguished men who framed the Declaration of Independence would have been utterly and flagrantly inconsistent with the principles they asserted; and instead of the sympathy of mankind, to which they so confidently appealed, they would have deserved and received universal rebuke and reprobation.
>
> Yet the men who framed this declaration were great men—high in literary acquirements—high in their sense of honor, and incapable of asserting principles inconsistent with those on which they were acting. They perfectly understood the meaning of the

language they used, and how it would be understood by others; and they knew that it would not in any part of the civilized world be supposed to embrace the negro race, which, by common consent, had been excluded from civilized Governments and the family of nations, and doomed to slavery. They spoke and acted according to the then established doctrines and principles, and in the ordinary language of the day, and no one misunderstood them. The unhappy black race were separated from the white by indelible marks, and laws long before established, and were never thought of or spoken of except as property, and when the claims of the owner or the profit of the trader were supposed to need protection.[23]

Curtis's dissent was equally striking. His opinion is permeated by Mansfield's premise: "Slavery, being contrary to natural right, is created only by municipal law."[24] While he accepts the structure of Taney's argument in order to answer it, he never comments on Taney's thesis that he is bound in 1857 to enforce Taney's conception of the Negro's legal status in 1789.

Curtis first takes up Sanford's plea in abatement—his motion to dismiss the case on the ground that Scott was not and could not be a citizen of Missouri for purposes of bringing suit, because Scott was a Negro of African descent, whose ancestors were brought into this country and sold as slaves. Sanford's plea, Curtis points out, was not a general denial of Scott's citizenship, nor even a claim that Scott was a slave at the time of suit. The fact that Dred Scott was a descendant of slaves does not give rise to an inference that he was then a slave who, Curtis was willing to admit, could not have sued as a citizen. But many descendants of slaves had become free men, by manumission and otherwise. No presumptions should be indulged to help cure the defect in the pleading. In order to sustain his plea in abatement, Sanford had to prove that not one person of African descent, whose ancestors were sold as slaves in the United States, could become a citizen of the United States. If it could be shown that any such person could be a citizen in 1857, or could have been a citizen in 1776 or 1789, Scott would necessarily prevail on this branch of the case.[25]

23. *Id.* at 410.
24. *Id.* at 624.
25. *Id.* at 567–76.

Curtis started with the phrase "a Citizen of the United States, at the time of the Adoption of this Constitution" from Article II, Section 1. Clearly, he argued, the use of the phrase—and common sense in any event—demonstrated that in the first instance the citizens of the United States under the new Constitution were those who were already citizens of the United States under the Articles of Confederation. This was the sovereign political body of which Taney spoke: the people of the United States in whose name, and for whose benefit, the Constitution was promulgated. In 1789, when the Constitution went into effect, the citizens of the United States were surely the citizens of the sovereign states who had entered into the much looser political system organized under the Articles of Confederation. It followed that in 1776 and 1789 "the sovereign people of the United States" did include men, women, and children of African descent, whose ancestors had been brought into the United States and sold as slaves. Curtis's proof was simple: at the time the Articles and the Constitution were ratified, he showed, all free native-born inhabitants of the states of New Hampshire, Massachusetts, New York, New Jersey, and North Carolina, at least, though descended from African slaves, were not only citizens of those states, but, if otherwise qualified, could vote as well. And he pointed out that Congress had refused to limit to white persons the provision of the Articles which provided that "the free inhabitants" of each state, paupers, vagabonds, and fugitives from justice excepted, "shall be entitled to all the privileges and immunities of free citizens in the several states."

Nothing in the Constitution, Curtis contended, could deprive "of their citizenship any class of persons who were citizens of the United States at the time of its adoption, or who should be native-born citizens of any State after its adoption; nor any power enabling Congress to disfranchise persons born on the soil of any State, and entitled to citizenship of such State by its Constitution and laws. And my opinion is, that, under the Constitution of the United States, every free person born on the soil of a State, who is a citizen of that State by force of its Constitution or laws, is also a citizen of the United States."[26]

In this view, Curtis anticipated some of the noblest and most humane of the Supreme Court's decisions on citizenship, although

26. *Id.* at 576.

Curtis's stress on state citizenship as a step on the way to national citizenship has not survived, and was probably close to error even before the passage of the Fourteenth Amendment.

These were facts and conditions, Curtis remarked, of which all the public men of the time were aware. The painful status of Blacks in American society did not prove that the sweeping generalizations of the Declaration of Independence were intended to apply only to white men, or that the Founding Fathers were hypocrites. "My own opinion is," Curtis wrote, "that a calm comparison of these assertions of universal abstract truths, and of their own individual opinions and acts, would not leave these men under any reproach of inconsistency; that the great truths they asserted on that solemn occasion, they were ready and anxious to make effectual, wherever a necessary regard to circumstances, which no statesman can disregard without producing more evil than good, would allow; and that it would not be just to them, nor true in itself, to allege that they intended to say that the Creator of all men had endowed the white race, exclusively, with the great natural rights which the Declaration of Independence asserts."[27]

Taney's response to Curtis's argument was vehement. The Chief Justice delayed the publication of his own opinion until he could revise it in the light of Curtis's dissent. And his irritation with Curtis at the time was one of the factors which led that remarkable man to resign from the Court.[28]

"[W]e must not confound the rights of citizenship which a State may confer within its own limits," Taney said, "and the rights of citizenship as a member of the Union. It does not by any means follow, because he has all the rights and privileges of a citizen of a State, that he must be a citizen of the United States."[29] The states have a wide discretion about allowing aliens or other noncitizens to exercise some or all the privileges of citizenship. But they cannot "introduce a new member into the political community created by the Constitution of the United States."[30] That power is exclusively national.

Abstractly, Taney was surely right in this contention, although it did not meet Curtis's basic argument: at the time the Articles and

27. *Id.* at 574–75.
28. See SWISHER, *supra* note 20, at 631–38.
29. Dred Scott v. Sanford, note 21, *supra,* at 405.
30. *Id.* at 406.

the Constitution were adopted, citizenship was a matter of state law;
therefore the original citizens of the United States, when the Constitution went into effect, were those who were already citizens of the
states, and thus of the United States, including Blacks descended
from slaves in at least five states.

In buttressing his thesis that the Negro was regarded as a race
apart at the end of the eighteenth century, and in no sense a participant in the sovereignty of the nation, Taney was at pains to refer
to legislation of the five states mentioned by Curtis: legislation forbidding intermarriage, confining service in the militia to free white
citizens, and otherwise discriminating against the Negro in a humili-
ating and degrading way. And he noted that some of the states
which allowed a few Negroes to vote were extremely active in the
slave trade itself.

Thus a narrow majority of the Court, led by Taney, decided that
the trial court had no jurisdiction of the subject matter, because
Dred Scott, a descendant of slaves, could not have been a citizen of
the United States, and therefore could not have invoked federal
jurisdiction on grounds of diversity of citizenship. Curtis argued that
the Court should have stopped at that point, ordered Scott's complaint dismissed, and declined to pass on any of the other issues of the
case. Taney and his colleagues disagreed. In an appeal from a lower
federal court, the Supreme Court has the power to correct all the
errors committed in the court below, and should do so here. In this
exchange, Curtis spoke for the better and more prudent practice—
that of declining to pass on constitutional questions unless their
settlement is required by the nature of the case, and no lesser ground
of decision is available. The rule is often violated. But it remains a
basic norm of the American constitutional system, essential to the
balance of power among the three branches of government.

Once launched, however, Taney and his colleagues sought to
refashion the political compromises which had ruled American politics for more than a generation. Scott did not become free by virtue
of his sojourn at Fort Snelling, despite the federal statute prohibiting
slavery in the territory of the Louisiana Purchase north of Missouri,
and north also of thirty-six degrees thirty minutes north latitude. The
Missouri Compromise was unconstitutional, the Court concluded,
going far beyond any powers Congress might be considered to have in
preparing the people of a territory for statehood. The United States
cannot hold colonies, nor create an empire, Taney said. If territories

are acquired—and Taney did not quite say that the Louisiana Purchase, too, was unconstitutional—they can be held and governed only as parts of the United States, and as the territories of prospective states. Congress must exercise its powers in accordance with the Constitution. In passing laws for the territories, Congress could not abolish trial by jury, establish a Church, abridge freedom of speech or of the press, or take property without due process of law. If the statute really purported to free Dred Scott and his family at Fort Snelling, it fell under that prohibition—as a taking of property without due process of law.

To this cycle of argument, Curtis's answer was withering. Whatever the earlier controversies on the subject, Curtis said, it is settled by history that the United States, like any other nation, can acquire territory pursuant to the usual rules of international law. Under the Constitution, the government of the new territory must be organized and provided by Congress, unless and until it is decided to admit the territory as a state. Since the status of slavery, and its incidents, could exist only by virtue of municipal law, Congress could legislate on the subject of slavery in the territories without restriction. In Curtis's opinion, following Mansfield, slaves become free, at least in Stowell's sense, when their owners voluntarily place them permanently within another jurisdiction where there are no municipal laws establishing slavery. Since this is the case, Curtis contends, the power of Congress to pass laws on the subject of slavery in the territories should be considered at least as complete as that of the states, many of which prohibit slavery. The argument that such a prohibition deprives anyone of his property without due process of law, Curtis concludes, simply does not bear examination.

> It must be remembered that this restriction on the legislative power is not peculiar to the Constitution of the United States; it was borrowed from *Magna Charta;* was brought to America by our ancestors, as part of their inherited liberties, and has existed in all the States, usually in the very words of the great charter. It existed in every political community in America in 1787, when the ordinance prohibiting slavery north and west of the Ohio was passed.
>
> And if a prohibition of slavery in a Territory in 1820 violated this principle of *Magna Charta,* the ordinance of 1787 also violated it; and what power had, I do not say the Congress of the Confederation alone, but the Legislature of Virginia, or the Legis-

lature of any or all the States of the Confederacy, to consent to
such a violation? The people of the States had conferred no such
power. I think I may at least say, if the Congress did then violate
Magna Charta by the ordinance, no one discovered that violation.
Besides, if the prohibition upon all persons, citizens as well as
others, to bring slaves into a Territory, and a declaration that if
brought they shall be free, deprives citizens of their property
without due process of law, what shall we say of the legislation of
many of the slave-holding States which have enacted the same
prohibition? As early as October, 1778, a law was passed in
Virginia, that thereafter no slave should be imported into that
Commonwealth by sea or by land, and that every slave who should
be imported should become free. A citizen of Virginia purchased
in Maryland a slave who belonged to another citizen of Virginia,
and removed with the slave to Virginia. The slave sued for her
freedom, and recovered it; as may be seen in Wilson *v.* Isabel, (5
Call's R., 425.) See also Hunter *v.* Hulsher, (1 Leigh, 172;)
and a similar law has been recognised as valid in Maryland, in
Stewart *v.* Oaks, (5 Har. and John., 107.) I am not aware that
such laws, though they exist in many States, were ever supposed to
be in conflict with the principle of *Magna Charta* incorporated
into the State Constitutions. It was certainly understood by the
Convention which framed the Constitution, and has been so
understood ever since, that, under the power to regulate commerce,
Congress could prohibit the importation of slaves; and the exercise of the power was restrained till 1808. A citizen of the United
States owns slaves in Cuba, and brings them to the United States,
where they are set free by the legislation of Congress. Does this
legislation deprive him of his property without due process of
law? If so, what becomes of the laws prohibiting the slave trade?
If not, how can a similar regulation respecting a Territory violate
the fifth amendment of the Constitution?[31]

V

The opinion in *Dred Scott,* which after a time became a target for
abolitionist speakers, dissolved under the pressure of events, adding
to the anxieties of the time. It threw doubt on the Whig compromises

31. *Id.* at 626–27.

of 1820 and 1850, and made the equilibrium of Congress hopelessly unstable. The parties were split into fragments, as the debate between Douglas and Lincoln was reenacted in every village and town.

The election of 1860 mirrored the confusion of the public mind. The Republican nominee was moderate and ambiguous on the Negro question, against slavery and against abolition as well. While some of his supporters—Seward and Andrew, notably—were strongly abolitionist, abolition was avoided in the campaign as warmongering would be avoided today. The abolitionist sentiment as such was weak: Lincoln carried New York by 50,000, but a constitutional amendment easing Negro suffrage lost 2 to 1.[32] Nonetheless, Lincoln represented "an anti-slavery idea," as Wendell Phillips said, and the country understood it.[33]

The firing on Fort Sumter released reservoirs of passion no one knew were there. The mystical notion of the Constitution as an indissoluble union of people, not states, proved its transcendence. For the longest, bloodiest years of war of the century, the people testified to their faith in this instinct for union. As the war progressed, the slavery issue became as vital to the war effort as the idea of union itself. Despite the resistance and hesitations of the politicians, and the strong racial prejudices of the people of the North, the atmosphere toward abolition changed. The abolitionists' meetings were larger and more fashionable. The Republican Party openly sought their help both in 1862 and in 1864. In *Dred Scott,* one of Taney's most telling arguments to show that Negroes were not regarded as part of the sovereign constituent mass of "the people of the United States" in 1789—"the political community formed and brought into existence by the Constitution of the United States"[34]—was that they were often disqualified for military service by the laws of the states.[35] Hence a strenuous effort was made, over bitter resistance, to form Negro regiments and to send them to the front.[36] For the simplest and most

32. McPherson, *supra* note 14, at 25.
33. *Id.* at 27.
34. *Scott v. Sanford,* 60 U.S. (19 How.) 393, 403 (1857).
35. *Id.* at 415. His other argument at this level, equally symbolic, was the mass of laws of the period against marriage between members of different races. *Id.* 409–16.
36. McPherson, *supra* note 14, at 192–220; *id.,* The Negro's Civil War, 143–244 (1965).

direct of reasons, the Republican Party began to press the cause of enfranchising the Negro, North and South.[37]

The impulse for reform, so unwillingly and almost absentmindedly kindled by the circumstances of war, flickered out after eleven postwar years of violent controversy. Three great amendments were passed, and many changes in the position of the Negro began to take place. The abolitionist society was disbanded and split up on the ground that its primary goal, the abolition of slavery, had been accomplished. Legislation to provide land and special forms of education for the freed Negro failed of passage. These two causes, fundamental to the realization of equality for the Negro, were left to weak pilot projects financed and staffed by private groups. The earnest efforts of philanthropy were commendable, and accomplished much. But they could not take the place of massive governmental action commensurate in scale with the magnitude of the problem.

37. WOODWARD, REUNION AND REACTION 94–95 (1951).

Three

The Negro in Our Law—II

          I propose here to examine the influence of our culture's collective aspiration for our law as a factor in the work of the Supreme Court. To illustrate my argument, I shall refer to a phase of the long history of the Negro in America, the period immediately after the Civil War, when the law made certain basic decisions about the legal position of the Negro—decisions which have taken nearly a century to reverse.

I

I can summarize the main point I want to make by reporting a conversation with Professor Takayanagi of the University of Tokyo, the distinguished and astute Chairman of the Japanese Cabinet Commission on the Constitution. The Commission was appointed because of public concern about a dramatic feature of Japan's postwar Constitution, its renunciation of war and of the armed services. One segment of Japanese opinion, restive at Japan's complete dependence on United States protection, favored repealing those clauses so that Japan could reestablish its military forces. Other groups, fearing a revival of militarism, or sympathizing with China or the

In a somewhat different form, this chapter was given as a part of a symposium organized by the Northwestern University School of Law under the auspices of the Julius Rosenthal Foundation, 1965. It was published by the Northwestern University Press in PERSPECTIVES ON THE COURT 53–107 (1967). © 1967 by Northwestern University Press.

Soviet Union, were vehemently opposed. The issue was one quite capable of leading to riots, or worse, and threatening all that had been achieved in Japan since the war.

After making a comprehensive study of constitutions and constitutionalism, and a revealing enquiry into the history of the modern Japanese Constitution, Professor Takayanagi reached this conclusion: the world, manifestly, has not followed the lead of Japan in renouncing military forces and war. Given the condition of international politics, Japan must have some armed services in order to participate responsibly in her own defense. But the anti-war provisions of the Constitution should not be repealed. There are many instances, he pointed out, when a law on the books is not enforced, or not fully enforced. Perhaps it cannot be enforced for a time. Perhaps custom and the minds of the people are not yet ready for the law as it has been declared. Nonetheless, the law may express aspirations to which the legal system and the people themselves are altogether committed. Under such circumstances, he argued, it would be wrong to repeal the law only because at the moment it cannot be carried out.

So it is, he said, with the disarmament provisions of the Japanese Constitution, the first such provisions in the world. They represent an idea in which the Japanese people believe, after their experience with militarism, and they hope that in time other people will join them in their convictions. Until that happens, Japan must be defended by American forces and by Japanese defense forces, for the world is a dangerous place. Disarmament is therefore impossible now, but the disarmament article should remain on the books.

Such was the tenor of his report on this controversial and delicate feature of the Japanese Constitution.

The most persuasive example he offered to support his case was the history of the Fourteenth Amendment as applied to the Negro. While we are not accustomed to thinking of the Fourteenth Amendment in this perspective, Professor Takayanagi was clearly right. The amendment was ignored, or enforced in a most partial and lopsided way, for almost a century. But its presence in our law has been indispensably valuable.

The Fourteenth Amendment was one of the three great post–Civil War amendments, passed at the high point of Union sentiment during the Reconstruction period, to make secure the goals for which the Congress of the day thought the war had been fought. The amendments were passed for a number of reasons.[1] There was constitutional doubt about Congress's authority to protect the rights of Negroes without them, and there was growing apprehension about the depth and intensity of Southern resistance to acknowledging the rights of Negroes and the law of the nation. In one of Justice Miller's remarkable letters to his Southern brother-in-law, William P. Ballinger, he wrote:

> We cannot in the face of the events that have occurred since the war trust the South with the power of governing the negro and Union White man without such guarantees in the federal Constitution as secure their protection. Now you will say this is unjust. Let us see. Of course I do not believe that all the stories I see in the papers about killing, beating, shooting these men are true. If you are fair minded you must admit that many of them are true. You will say that they are done by low degraded men who are found in all communities, and that your leading men disapprove of it. That is always said in reply. Show me how you disapprove of it. Show me a single white man that has been punished in a State court for murdering a negro or a Union man. Show me that any public meeting has been had to express indignation at such conduct. Show me that you or any of the best men of the South have gone ten steps out of their way to bring such men to punishment or to take any steps to prevent a recurrence of such things. Show me the first public address or meeting of Southern men in which the massacres of New Orleans or Memphis have been condemned or any general dissent shown at *home* at such conduct. You may say that there are two sides to those stories of Memphis and New Orleans. There may be two sides to the stories, but there was but one side in the party that suffered at both places, and the single truth which is undenied that not a rebel or secessionist was hurt in either case, while from thirty to fifty negroes and Union white men were shot down precludes all doubt as to who did it and why it was done.

> Now as I feel and think, so large numbers of men who are not politicians think and feel. I am for Mr. Dixon's plan of settlement.

1. A. M. Bickel, *The Original Understanding and the Segregation Decision,* 69 HARV. L. REV. 1 (1955), reprinted in POLITICS AND THE WARREN COURT 211 (1965); J. ten Broek, *The Antislavery Origins of the Fourteenth Amendment* (1951), republished as EQUAL UNDER LAW (rev. ed. 1965); J. B. JAMES, THE FRAMING OF THE FOURTEENTH AMENDMENT (1956); J. P. Frank & R. Munro, *The Original Understanding of "Equal Protection of the Laws,"* 50 COLUM. L. REV. 131 (1950).

I am for your plan. I am for universal amnesty and universal
suffrage, not because any of these are the best in themselves, but
because we are losing what is more valuable than any of these
things in the struggle which is demoralizing us worse than the war
did.[2]

Beyond this sentiment, strongly felt among those, like Miller, who
favored a conciliatory course in the politics of reunion, there was also
a current of opinion seeking to enlarge the Bill of Rights as a limitation on the powers of the states as well as of the national government.
Congressman John A. Bingham, one of the most active members of
the committee which worked on the project of the Fourteenth Amendment, expressed his view of its import in these terms:

There was a want hitherto, and there remains a want now, in
the Constitution of our country, which the proposed amendment
will supply. What is that? It is the power in the people, the whole
people of the United States, by express authority of the Constitution to do that by congressional enactment which hitherto they
have not had the power to do; and have never even attempted to
do; that is, to protect by national law the privileges and immunities
of all the citizens of the Republic and the inborn rights of every
person within its jurisdiction whenever the same shall be abridged
or denied by the unconstitutional acts of any State.[3]

Bingham, and the abolitionist tradition for which he spoke, were
concerned with far more than assuring the equal protection of
Negroes, and perhaps with far more than applying the Bill of Rights
to the states. Professor ten Broek contends that their purpose was to
provide a national protection throughout the country to the "natural
rights" of man, a conception he rightly describes as a "revolution in
federalism."[4]

The first case under the Fourteenth Amendment to reach the
Supreme Court sharply raised the contending views of its scope. The
famous *Slaughter House Cases*[5] dealt with the constitutionality of a
Louisiana statute, passed in 1869 by a Reconstruction legislature,
granting a twenty-five-year monopoly of the slaughtering business in

2. CHARLES FAIRMAN, MR. JUSTICE MILLER AND THE SUPREME COURT,
1862–1890, at 192 (1932). The date of the letter is February 6. 1866.
3. 46 Congressional Globe 2542 (1866).
4. TEN BROEK, EQUAL UNDER LAW 239 (1965).
5. 83 U.S. (16 Wall.) 36 (1873).

the New Orleans area to a corporation formed by an influential group of carpetbaggers.[6] The statute was justified as an exercise of the state's interest in protecting the health of its citizens and, more generally, of its police powers.

The case reached the Supreme Court as the controversies over Reconstruction brought the nation to a condition of disturbed and exhausted paralysis. The zeal of the immediate postwar period was oozing away. The resistance to national authority in the South had proved more violent than had been anticipated, and the effort required to overcome it was more burdensome. Military government in the territory of the Confederacy continued, giving rise to political conflicts which challenged every aspect of the customary constitution. The impeachment of President Johnson threatened one of the three great institutions of government, and Congress had ominously sought to control the independence of the judiciary. As the fevers of the Reconstruction period waned, strong instincts for a compromise of conciliation became a significant theme of public opinion and of public life. When the *Slaughter House Cases* came to the Court for decision, that theme in public opinion was in process of crystallization. Ten years later, at the time of the *Civil Rights Cases,* it had become completely dominant.

In the *Slaughter House Cases,* a majority of the Court took a narrow view, perhaps even the narrowest possible view of the Fourteenth Amendment. The objectors to the monopoly argued that the statute conferred "odious and exclusive privileges upon a small number of persons at the expense of the great body of the community of New Orleans," and deprived "a large and meritorious class of citizens— the whole of the butchers of the city—of the right to exercise their trade, the business to which they have been trained and on which they depend for the support of themselves and their families."[7] They were protected against these injuries, they claimed, by the Thirteenth and Fourteenth Amendments, despite the acknowledged power of the state to regulate slaughterhouses in the interest of the common good.

The butchers' claim of protection was addressed primarily to the conception of national citizenship—that the right to pursue a common

6. Charles Fairman, *Mr. Justice Bradley,* in A. Dunham & P. Kurland, Mr. Justice 81 (2d. ed. 1964).
7. *Supra* note 5, at 36, 60.

calling was a privilege of national citizenship, and that the Fourteenth Amendment conferred upon each citizen an immunity from state regulation depriving him of the right, or at least an immunity from state regulation as unreasonable and confiscatory as the Louisiana monopoly statute.

After two rounds of argument, the divided Court upheld the Louisiana statute. The three great postwar amendments, Justice Miller wrote, were "additional guarantees of humans rights; additional powers to the Federal government; additional restraints upon those of the States," found by the people to be necessary under the circumstances of recent history "fresh within the memory of us all."[8]

The Thirteenth Amendment, however, afforded the objectors no support, he found. It was a "grand yet simple declaration of the personal freedom of all the human race within the jurisdiction of this government—a declaration designed to establish the freedom of four millions of slaves."[9] It did not conceal within its interstices an unanticipated guarantee of the right or privilege to pursue the butcher's trade.

The objectors' case was no stronger, the Court held, under the Fourteenth Amendment. That amendment, like the Fifteenth, was a response of "the statesmen who had conducted the Federal government in safety through the crisis of the rebellion" to the experience of the Negro in the South during the first postwar years. These men came to realize that without the protection of the Fourteenth and Fifteenth Amendments, "the condition of the slave race would . . . be almost as bad as it was before."[10] The "pervading purpose" lying at the foundation of each of the three amendments, therefore, "without which none of them would have been even suggested," the Court said, was "the freedom of the slave race, the security and firm establishment of that freedom, and the protection of the newly-made freeman and citizen from the oppressions of those who had formerly exercised unlimited dominion over him."[11] While "we do not say

8. *Id*. at 67–68.
9. *Id*. at 69. On this phase of Miller's opinion, see Jones v. Alfred H. Mayer Co., 392 U.S. 409 (1968), discussed by Professor Fairman in his classic RECONSTRUCTION AND REUNION, 1864–1888, pt. 1 at 1207–60 (6 HISTORY OF THE SUPREME COURT OF THE UNITED STATES, 1971)
10. *Supra* note 5, at 70.
11. *Id*. at 71.

that no one else but the negro can share in this protection,"[12] ". . . [w]e doubt very much whether any action of a State not directed by way of discrimination against the negroes as a class, or on account of their race, will ever be held to come within the purview of this provision."[13]

The plaintiffs in error relied principally upon the privileges and immunities clause of the amendment, rather than upon its conceptions of due process or the equal protection of the laws. The first part of the Fourteenth Amendment, the declaration of national citizenship, was primarily intended to overrule the *Dred Scott* case, the Court said, and to make certain that Negroes were capable of becoming citizens of the United States, and hence of the state wherein they reside. The sentence recognizes, however, the continued distinction between national citizenship and citizenship of a state. The privileges and immunities of national citizenship constitute a small bundle of rights which "owe their existence to the Federal government, its National character, its Constitution, or its laws."[14] The clause does not provide national protection for the larger part of the civil rights of citizens, which remain the exclusive province of the states, save for the special protection of the Negro.

The experience of the Civil War, Justice Miller observed,

has added largely to the number of those who believe in the necessity of a strong National government.

But, however pervading this sentiment, and however it may have contributed to the adoption of the amendments we have been considering, we do not see in those amendments any purpose to destroy the main features of the general system. Under the pressure of all the excited feeling out of the war, our statesmen have still believed that the existence of the States with powers for domestic and local government, including the regulation of civil rights—the rights of person and of property—was essential to the perfect working of our complex form of government, though they have thought proper to impose additional limitations on the States, and to confer additional power on that of the Nation.

But whatever fluctuations may be seen in the history of public

12. *Id.* at 72.
13. *Id.* at 81 (the context refers to the equal protection clause).
14. *Id.* at 79.

opinion on this subject during the period of our national existence, we think it will be found that this court, so far as its functions required, has always held with a steady and an even hand the balance between State and Federal power, and we trust that such may continue to be the history of its relation to that subject so long as it shall have duties to perform which demand of it a construction of the Constitution, or any of its parts.[15]

Hence, the Court concluded, the Fourteenth Amendment should not be construed to protect the butchers of New Orleans against the slaughterhouse monopoly established by the legislature of Louisiana.

Was it the purpose of the fourteenth amendment, by the simple declaration that no State should make or enforce any law which shall abridge the privileges and immunities of *citizens of the United States,* to transfer the security and protection of all the civil rights which we have mentioned, from the States to the Federal government? And where it is declared that Congress shall have the power to enforce that article, was it intended to bring within the power of Congress the entire domain of civil rights heretofore belonging exclusively to the States?

All this and more must follow, if the proposition of the plaintiffs in error be sound. For not only are these rights subject to the control of Congress whenever in its discretion any of them are supposed to be abridged by State legislation, but that body may also pass laws in advance, limiting and restricting the exercise of legislative power by the States, in their most ordinary and usual functions, as in its judgment it may think proper on all such subjects. And still further, such a construction followed by the reversal of the judgments of the Supreme Court of Louisiana in these cases, would constitute this court a perpetual censor upon all legislation of the States, on the civil rights of their own citizens, with authority to nullify such as it did not approve as consistent with those rights, as they existed at the time of the adoption of this amendment. The argument we admit is not always the most conclusive which is drawn from the consequences urged against the adoption of a particular construction of an instrument. But when, as the case before us, these consequences are so serious, so far-reaching and pervading, so great a departure from the structure and spirit of our institutions; when the effect is to fetter and degrade the State governments by subjecting them to

15. *Id.* at 82.

control of Congress, in the exercise of powers heretofere universally conceded to them of the most ordinary and fundamental character; when in fact it radically changes the whole theory of the relations of the State and Federal governments to each other and of both these governments to the people; the argument has a force that is irresistible, in the absence of language which expresses such a purpose too clearly to admit of doubt.

    We are convinced that no such results were intended by the Congress which proposed these amendments, nor by the legislatures of the States which ratified them.[16]

The dissents of Justice Field and Justice Bradley have had an important influence on the law—an influence by no means exhausted. The Supreme Court has not yet quite accepted their doctrine of national citizenship. But the gospel they preached of judicial protection against state regulations the judges thought outrageous became the basis for two generations of "substantive due process" in the area of economic controls, and then for another round of judicial activism in the protection of civil liberties.

The dissenters in the *Slaughter House Cases* contended that the legitimate interest of the state in regulating slaughterhouses did not authorize it "to encroach upon any of the just rights of the citizen, which the Constitution intended to secure against abridgement."[17] The grant of a monopoly had no reasonable relation to the end of protecting health, or minimizing the nuisance of slaughterhouses. It could not be analogized to the grant of franchises for the conduct of utilities "of a public character appertaining to the government."[18]

While Justice Field found it unnecessary to rest his conclusion on an interpretation of the Thirteenth Amendment, he discussed the intriguing possibility of construing that amendment as a broad protection for all the liberties and privileges of free men, and a prohibition against all unequal privileges and other restraints which might be deemed "servitudes."[19]

---

    16. *Id.* at 77–78. See South Carolina v. Katzenbach, 383 U.S. 301, 359–60 (1966) (Black, J., dissenting on the ground that Section 5 of the Voting Rights Act of 1965 treats states like "conquered provinces").

    17. *Supra* note 5, at 87.

    18. *Id.* at 88.

    19. *Id.* at 89–93. This argument found powerful support in Justice Harlan's dissent in the Civil Rights Cases, 109 U.S. 3 (1883), and has entered upon a new period of active life in the line of decisions which began with *Jones,* note 9, *supra.*

He then turned with great force to a magisterial construction of the Fourteenth Amendment, and particularly to the notion that national citizenship clothes the individual with an armor of immunity against the state with respect to those aspects of liberty which the Court may regard as "the fundamental rights of free men." Justice Bradley enlarged upon the theme. Both relied on Justice Washington's famous opinion in *Corfield v. Coryell,* only now beginning to come into its own.[20] The English inheritance, extending back to Magna Carta, was invoked to give content to this idea. The immunity, they contended, includes the inalienable and imprescriptible freedoms of man in society—his rights to life, liberty, and the pursuit of happiness. Justice Bradley wrote:

> Rights to life, liberty, and the pursuit of happiness are equivalent to the rights of life, liberty, and property. These are the fundamental rights which can only be taken away by due process of law, and which can only be interfered with, or the enjoyment of which can only be modified, by lawful regulations necessary or proper for the mutual good of all; and these rights, I contend, belong to the citizens of every free government.
>
> For the preservation, exercise, and enjoyment of these rights the individual citizen, as a necessity, must be left free to adopt such calling, profession, or trade as may seem to him most conducive to that end. Without this right he cannot be a free man. This right to choose one's calling is an essential part of that liberty which it is the object of government to protect; and a calling, when chosen, is a man's property and right. Liberty and property are not protected where these rights are arbitrarily assailed.
>
> I think sufficient has been said to show that citizenship is not an empty name, but that, in this country at least, it has connected with it certain incidental rights, privileges, and immunities of the greatest importance. And to say that these rights and immunities attach only to State citizenship, and not to citizenship of the United States, appears to me to evince a very narrow and insufficient estimate of constitutional history and the rights of men, not to say the rights of the American people.
>
> On this point the often-quoted language of Mr. Justice Washington, in *Corfield v. Coryell,* is very instructive. Being called upon

20. 6 F. Cas 566 (No. 3,230) (C.C.E.D. Pa. 1823); U.S. v. Guest, 383 U.S. 745 (1966); U.S. v. Price, 383 U.S. 787 (1966).

to expound that clause in the fourth article of the Constitution, which declares that "the citizens of each State shall be entitled to all the privileges and immunities of citizens in the several States," he says: "The inquiry is, what are the privileges and immunities of citizens in the several States? We feel no hesitation in confining these expressions to those privileges and immunities which are, in their nature, *fundamental;* which belong, of right, to the citizens of all free governments, and which have at all times been enjoyed by the citizens of the several States which compose this Union from the time of their becoming free, independent, and sovereign. What these fundamental privileges are it would perhaps be more tedious than difficult to enumerate. They may, however, be all comprehended under the following general heads: Protection by the government; the enjoyment of life and liberty, with the right to acquire and possess property of every kind, and to pursue and obtain happiness and safety, subject, nevertheless, to such restraints as the government may justly prescribe for the general good of the whole; the right of a citizen of one State to pass through, or to reside in, any other State for purpose of trade, agriculture, professional pursuits, or otherwise; to claim the benefit of the writ of habeas corpus; to institute and maintain actions of any kind in the courts of the State; to take, hold, and dispose of property, either real or personal; and an exemption from higher taxes or impositions than are paid by the other citizens of the State, may be mentioned as some of the particular privileges and immunities of citizens which are clearly embraced by the general description of privileges deemed to be fundamental."

It is pertinent to observe that both the clause of the Constitution referred to, and Justice Washington in his comment on it, speak of the privileges and immunities of citizens *in* a State; not of citizens *of* a State. It is the privileges and immunities of citizens, that is, of citizens as such, that are to be accorded to citizens of other States when they are found in any State; or, as Justice Washington says, "privileges and immunities which are, in their nature, fundamental; which belong, of right, to the citizens of all free governments."[21]

The Court was not to assert this sweeping position as the higher law of the Constitution for another twenty-four years, and then it relied on the due process clause of the Fourteenth Amendment,

21. *Supra* note 5, at 116–18.

rather than on the idea of citizenship.[22] But the concept was asserted, and asserted with compelling force.

Meanwhile, the political climate prepared the Court for the further retreat of the *Civil Rights Cases.* The country endured the bitter years of reconstruction and reunion, and slowly became reconciled to "the lesser evil" of the Compromise of 1877, a decisive rule of our polity between that day and 1964. By 1877, the nation had become tired of occupying the South, and tired of the turbulence to which the struggle for Negro rights seemed to lead. A movement symbolized by the Ku Klux Klan, and in many places led by it, had helped to mobilize Southern support for massive resistance to national authority. Those in the South who held other views were intimidated or discouraged. Many left the South altogether.

President Grant's Administration did not undertake to enforce the Civil Rights Acts or the Force Act with any vigor. The Freedmen's Bureau was abolished. The so-called "Radicals" no longer controlled the Republican party. Their place was taken, more and more openly, by men of the old Whig spirit, who wished to reach an accommodation with the Southern "propertied classes" and terminate the era of violence and instability which prevailed in many parts of the South.

The contest over the outcome of the Hayes-Tilden election of 1876 gave men of this persuasion their opportunity. Apparently won by the Democratic candidate, Governor Tilden, the election was so close, and the returns from many states so open to objection, that the result was in doubt until the moment before Inauguration Day, and the country witnessed ominous preparations for the renewal of armed conflict. The Compromise of 1877, which led to the inauguration of President Hayes, still has aspects of mystery, despite Professor Woodward's authoritative study of the subject.[23]

What is certain about the atmosphere of the Compromise, however, is that on one side it involved an acceptance of the Republican candi-

---

22. Allgeyer v. Louisiana, 165 U.S. 578 (1897), and its long line of descendants, castigated by generations as undemocratic and now rapidly resuming their place in our law under the pressures of the quest for equal rights.

23. C. VANN WOODWARD, REUNION AND REACTION (1951); BUCK, THE ROAD TO REUNION—1865–1900 (1937); K. M. STAMPP, THE ERA OF RECONSTRUCTION 1865–1877 (1965); Sister Marie Carolyn Klinkhamer, *Joseph P. Bradley: Private and Public Opinion of a "Political" Justice,* 38 U. DET. L.J. 150 (1960).

date for the Presidency, and the consolidation of a powerful Republican party, based not on abolitionist New England and on Negro votes in the South, but on the agrarian and conservative Middle West and Northwest, where the Copperhead sentiment still flourished. Thus a tacit coalition emerged between Southern Democrats and some Northern Republicans as the normal ruling force in our politics—the ultimate power bloc to which authority always tended to return. On the other side, the Compromise implied an end of military occupation and of Reconstruction government in the South. Its hidden premise was the restoration of white rule in the South, and the disenfranchisement of the Negro. The nation walked by on the other side as riot, massacre, boycott, and lynching were used to deprive the Southern Negro of his vote, and degrade him anew to the caste of helot.[24]

We allowed violence to nullify the Constitution, and condoned a political order based on disobedience to law. The North yielded to mob action and to Southern resistance in the Confederate spirit. The South abandoned its effort to expand to the west. But it clung to white supremacy in the South itself.

Troubled men, North and South, said that "after all, the Negro was not yet ready" for equal citizenship. They comforted themselves with the thought that the disenfranchisement of the Negro and the coming to power of Jim Crow were transitory phenomena, measuring no more than necessary delays in the fulfillment of the promise of the Fourteenth and Fifteenth Amendments. Passion and custom were too strong at the moment for the enforcement of the law, they concluded. But the education and social advance of the Negro and the ultimate egalitarianism of the American people would "gradually" prevail. Such, at least, was their hope.

After 1877, the political life of the country turned away from the Negro problem, and the reforming spirit was absorbed in private efforts to help the Negro through education and social development.

The Fourteenth Amendment was interpreted in a number of relatively minor cases, as the Court sought to adapt its command to the stubborn texture of American habit. Not all cases brought under the amendment were lost. In *Strauder v. West Virginia,* for example, a Negro's conviction of murder was reversed because Negroes were excluded from jury duty by a state statute. Such a statute, the Court

24. See, e.g., C. MAGRATH, MORRISON R. WAITE 154–71 (1963).

said, affixed "a brand" upon Negroes, asserting their inferiority and denying them the equal protection of the laws.[25] It was an error on the part of the state court to deny Strauder's motion for removal of the case to a federal court, the enforcement remedy provided in the Civil Rights Act. But in *Virginia v. Rives,* a conviction was upheld under similar circumstances, because the Virginia statute did not explicitly exclude Negroes.[26] The technique upheld in *Rives* made *Strauder* for all practical purposes a dead letter.

This was the context of the *Civil Rights Cases* of 1883, which settled the position of the Negro in our law for nearly seventy-five years. The cases were decided by eight votes to one, with Justice Harlan alone dissenting. The Court found two sections of the Civil Rights Act of 1875 to be unconstitutional as applied to the factual situations before it. The statute made it a federal offense to deny to any person[27] the full and equal enjoyment of places of public accommodation, except for reasons of law applicable alike to citizens of every race or color. The cases dealt with refusals to serve Negroes in hotels, theaters, and railway cars in the District of Columbia, California, New York, and Tennessee—that is, *not* in the Deep South.

The Court's opinion was written by Justice Bradley, one of the strong justices of a strong bench. His sense of the times is attested by his decisive vote on the Electoral Commission in 1877, awarding the presidency to Hayes. Originally, as his dissent in the *Slaughter House Cases* makes clear, he thought the Fourteenth Amendment authorized the national government to protect the more fundamental rights of man by affirmative action, as well as by preventing unwarranted restraints imposed by the states, or by "outrage, violence and combination on the part of individuals."[28] His opinion in the *Civil Rights Cases,* however, completely accepted Justice Miller's contrary theory, which had become that of the Court and of the country. In large part, Justice Miller's basic view of the amendment has dominated the field, and does so still.

The Fourteenth Amendment, Justice Bradley wrote, should be

25. 100 U.S. 303, 308–9 (1880).
26. 100 U.S. 313 (1880). These and related cases of the period are discussed in LOREN MILLER, THE PETITIONERS 118–35 (1966).
27. The statute uses the terms "person" and "citizen" almost interchangeably.
28. MAGRATH, *supra* note 24, at 120–21.

read negatively, in the light of Justice Miller's premise in the *Slaughter House Cases*—that it was intended to accomplish a minimal and interstitial change in the allocation of power between the states and the nation. The amendment did not declare an independent code of national civil rights, he said, nor did it authorize Congress to establish such a code. It prohibited the states from discriminating against Negroes in their traditional fields of legislative power and empowered Congress "to adopt appropriate legislation for correcting the effects of such prohibited State laws and State acts."[29]

The argument concealed a number of assumptions.

The first was nearly the antithesis of *McCullogh v. Maryland,*[30] where the Court had asserted a comprehensive national power to adopt such means as seemed to the Congress appropriate and proper in carrying out national responsibilities.

The second was closely related to the Court's construction of the first sentence of the Fourteenth Amendment. The limited conception of national citizenship asserted in the *Slaughter House Cases* implied a correspondingly restricted list of the privileges and immunities of national citizenship which Congress could protect by such means as it deemed "necessary and proper."

The third, and most fundamental, was the facile distinction between "affirmative" and "negative" powers, as if the power to prevent denials of "the due process of law" and of the "equal protection of the laws" can on analysis be distinguished from the power to assure due process and equal protection in the modes of law:

> Positive rights and privileges are undoubtedly secured by the Fourteenth Amendment; but they are secured by way of prohibition against State laws and State proceedings affecting those rights and privileges, and by power given to Congress to legislate for the purpose of carrying such prohibition into effect: and such legislation must necessarily be predicated upon such supposed State laws or State proceedings, and be directed to the correction of their operation and effect.[31]

The Court invoked an ancient rhetorical device—a reduction to the absurd:

29. The Civil Rights Cases, 109 U.S. 3, 11 (1883).
30. 17 U.S. (4 Wheat.) 316 (1819).
31. 109 U.S. 3, 11–12 (1883).

That would be to establish a code of municipal law regulative of all private rights between man and man in society. It would be to make Congress take the place of the State legislatures and to supersede them. It is absurd to affirm that, because the rights of life, liberty and property (which include all civil rights that men have), are by the amendment sought to be protected against invasion on the part of the State without due process of law, Congress may therefore provide the due process of law for their vindication in every case; and that, because the denial by a State to any persons, of the equal protection of the laws, is prohibited by the amendment, therefore Congress may establish laws for their equal protection. In fine, the legislation which Congress is authorized to adopt in this behalf is not general legislation upon the rights of the citizen, but corrective legislation, that is, such as may be necessary and proper for counteracting such laws as the States may adopt or enforce, and which, by the amendment, they are prohibited from making or enforcing, or such acts and proceedings as the States may commit or take, and which, by the amendment, they are prohibited from committing or taking.[32]

The Civil Rights Act, the Court said, did not refer to any supposed or apprehended violation of the Fourteenth Amendment by the states. It proceeded directly to impose federally declared obligations on individuals.

If this legislation is appropriate for enforcing the prohibitions of the amendment, it is difficult to see where it is to stop. Why may not Congress with equal show of authority enact a code of laws for the enforcement and vindication of all rights of life, liberty, and property?[33]

By interpreting the Fourteenth Amendment as a minimal change in the old pattern of federalism and subordinating its thrust at every doubtful point to the authority of the states, Justice Bradley easily reached his conclusion of unconstitutionality. As a matter of judicial method, the opinion turns on the absence of specific legislative finding of what everybody knew, namely that the states were in fact violating the Fourteenth Amendment.

It does not profess to be corrective of any constitutional wrong committed by the States; it does not make its operation to depend

32. *Id.* at 13–14.
33. *Id.* at 14.

upon any such wrong committed. It applies equally to the cases arising in States which have the justest laws respecting the personal rights of citizens, and whose authorities are ever ready to enforce such laws, as to those which arise in States that may have violated the prohibition of the amendment. In other words, it steps into the domain of local jurisprudence, and lays down rules for the conduct of individuals in society towards each other, and imposes sanctions for the enforcement of those rules, without referring in any manner to any supposed action of the State or its authorities. . . .[34]

This abrogation and denial of rights, for which the States alone were or could be responsible, was the great seminal and fundamental wrong which was intended to be remedied. And the remedy to be provided must necessarily be predicated upon that wrong. It must assume that in the cases provided for, the evil or wrong actually committed rests upon some State law or State authority for its excuse and perpetration.[35]

The requirement of a Congressional "finding" of state dereliction before the national government could proceed would not apply in an area where the Constitution gave Congress general power to legislate directly, as it does in the field of interstate commerce, patents, bankruptcy, and the like. By characterizing the subject matter of the Civil Rights Act—the assurance of equality in places of public accommodation—as a matter of state law, subject only to the limitation of the Fourteenth Amendment, Justice Bradley chose the premise which guaranteed this conclusion. He was careful to leave Congress another opportunity to act, if it wished to take it. Congress could make the legislative findings whose absence the Court found fatal to the statute —a course it followed in enacting laws to protect the voting rights of Blacks.[36] Or it could pass a statute resting on the commerce power, for Bradley remarked that "whether Congress in the exercise of its power to regulate commerce amongst the several states, might or might not pass a law regulating rights in public conveyances passing

---

34. *Id.* at 14. State action the national government could correct under the Fourteenth Amendment, Justice Bradley indicated, includes "laws and proceedings, and *customs having the force of law,* which sanction the wrongful acts specified," *id.* at 16, and see also 21 (italics added).

35. *Id.* at 18.

36. 79 Stat. 437 (1965); South Carolina v. Katzenbach, 383 U.S. 301, 323–27 (1966).

from one state to another, is also a question which is not now before us, as the sections in question are not conceived in any such view."[37] Following this suggestion, the Congress selected the modern commerce power as the constitutional foundation of its 1964 Civil Rights Act.[38]

II

The Supreme Court's decision in the *Civil Rights Cases* correctly interpreted the inner condition of the law at the time. It is difficult to speculate about how the country would have responded to the challenge had the majority been willing to follow Justice Harlan's bold lead. The five to four division of the Court in the *Slaughter House Cases* had become something quite different—a nearly unanimous position. Consciously or unconsciously, the justices appraised the nation's view of the Negro's status in our society and in our law. They sensed the boundary beyond which they could not go in enforcing the amendments.

In all probability, the justices were right. It is hard to suppose that in 1883 the nation would have girded itself again to a passionate political struggle in behalf of the Negro's equality before the law. The visible reproach of slavery was ended. The nation had wearily survived the turmoil and anguish of the presidencies of Andrew Johnson and Grant. It accepted the end of the military occupation in the South with relief. Strong political instinct pressed us to restore and revive the familiar politics of the old Whig nation. Racial prejudice against the Negro was a fact to be conjured with throughout the country, not least among the immigrants in the cities and factories of the North. The prevailing political mood reflected the equilibrium of the moment among the various forces which constitute the law: the desire for reunion, and an end of civil war; the concept of dual sovereignty in our thought about the nature of the nation, with the surviving distinction between national and state citizenship which only *Dred Scott* and the dissenters in the *Slaughter House Cases* had thus far openly chal-

37. The Civil Rights Cases, 109 U.S. 3, 19 (1883).
38. 78 Stat. 241 (1964); Heart of Atlanta Hotel v. United States, 379 U.S. 241 (1964); Pollak, *The Supreme Court and the States: Reflections on Boynton v. Virginia,* 49 Calif. L. Rev. 15 (1961).

lenged; and the prevailing view of the Black as a man apart, no longer a slave but hardly an equal member of the social order.

Under these circumstances, the Court accepted all that lay behind the political compromise of 1877. At the least, that compromise implied the disenfranchisement of the Negro in the South and the restoration of white man's government in the Southern states, that is to say, a virtual moratorium on the enforcement of the Fourteenth and Fifteenth Amendments as a protection of Negro rights in that part of the country. The government in Washington treated the undeniably constitutional chapters of the Civil Rights Acts—most particularly those dealing with the selection of jurors and with voting —as dead letters. The nonenforcement of the Fourteenth and Fifteenth Amendments in the South became a basic element in the structure of the political system, and a basic, if guilty, expectation of the white South.

But the coalition of 1877 did not rule unchallenged, even in the period before 1914. The industrial and financial revolution of the late nineteenth century and early twentieth century stimulated its counterthesis. The oligarchs and titans of the great new companies aroused fear as well as envy. Small-town independent business and regional leaders rallied against the specter of complete economic control from New York. Agrarian protest swelled and found effective political expression in the Granger movement and in Populism. Trade unions were formed, often led by socialists linked to the various socialist movements of Europe. Journalists and other writers stirred an outcry against the concentration and abuse of economic and political power. And many of our best spirits devoted themselves to protest against the materialism and vulgarity they found to be rampant in American life. Recurring economic depressions invariably fortified the chorus of protest and strengthened political groups concerned with the grievances behind such protests.

Inevitably and invariably, justice for the Negro emerged as an object of all our progressive movements, although not until recently as one of their major goals. Some of the radical Progressive leaders were anti-Negro, anti-foreign, anti-Catholic, and anti-Semitic. But they were exceptional. The spirit of social advance which they expressed and embraced could not resist the rightness of the Negro's claim.

Meanwhile, year by year, the industrial revolution drew people from farms to factories, from rural areas to the growing cities. More and more Negroes joined in the migration. A slowly rising fraction of the Negro population, armed with high school or college diplomas, undertook middle-class vocations and middle-class patterns of life.

The accident of Theodore Roosevelt's unsatisfied ambition played a significant part in the political history of the Negro's cause, as it did in the political history of the Republic. The Republican party never fully recovered from the Bull Moose campaign of 1912, which was followed by the Progressive Party effort led by Senators La Follette and Wheeler in 1924. During his first term, President Franklin Roosevelt was able to speed up the exodus from the Republican party which his republican cousin had begun twenty years before. Senator Norris and many other Progressive Republicans became Roosevelt Democrats during the early thirties and then simply Democrats who supported Presidents Truman, Kennedy, and Johnson, and backed Adlai Stevenson as a candidate in 1952 and 1956. Attracted by the welfare programs and the liberal spirit of the New Deal and the Fair Deal, the growing mass of Negro voters in the North and the scattered Negro voters of some Southern cities were notable among the Bull Moose pilgrims who left the Republican party. The Negro voter became one of the pillars of the Democratic party, along with labor and the urban interest generally, as that party reoriented itself imaginatively to the pattern of underlying change in American society.

III

These political events did not occur in a vacuum. The nation grew. It suffered the pangs of Manifest Destiny and became a participant in world affairs, with commitments in the Caribbean and the Pacific and a growing sensitivity to the balance of power in Europe. It undertook the regulation of railroads and other national utilities, and began to create a national antitrust policy and national policies toward agriculture, labor, and banking. The elections reflected the changing concerns and the changing needs of a small, isolated, homogeneous, agricultural, rural nation which was rapidly becoming a vast, urban, cosmopolitan, and industrial leader in world politics.

The first economic need of the men who tamed the continent has always been manpower—an insatiable and imperious demand which led us to indentured servitude and then to slavery, and later to immigration on a massive scale. The perennial shortage of labor in the American economy has been the source of some of our most difficult social problems—that of the Negro, manifestly; those of the melting pot in our great cities; and, later, the resistance to immigration and the nostalgic desire to restore the Anglo-Saxon or Nordic atmosphere of an earlier America, represented by the Oriental Exclusion Acts and the Immigration Act of 1924. The latter statute, passed under trade union pressure, drastically reduced the flow of immigrants which had made economic growth possible between 1880 and the mid-twenties.

In the course of this far-reaching transformation, the Negro ceased to be the ignorant and forlorn freedman of the 1870s and 1880s, and became more and more visibly a member of the urban melting pot. A large fraction of the Negro population remained in the South as agricultural workers, at least until the decline of cotton in the 1930s and the industrial migrations of the Second World War. But the advance guard of Negro immigrants in the cities of the North began to endure the trials and strains of assimilation as early as the turn of the century, and a significant number of them emerged with success.

The Negro, of course, faced special hazards in the melting pot, and he faces special hazards still. Like other immigrants reared in primitive agricultural villages, the Southern farmhand in a big Northern city, be he white or Negro, suffers the handicap of not being familiar with the skills and habits of modern urban life. The Negro rarely comes into the melting pot as a toolmaker, or mechanic, or welder, or even as a carpenter or plumber, because tight restrictions on apprenticeship have for generations excluded him from training in the basic trades of advanced technology. Sometimes not even the menial jobs are open to him. The curse of slavery has been a terrible burden, both for white men and for Negroes, and it has been felt, and is felt today, in all our arrangements for living, working, and schooling.

Despite our pervasive heritage of racial tension, however, the melting pot worked for the Black as it did the white immigrant—not so quickly, perhaps, as in the case of some white groups particularly well prepared for urban life, but quite as rapidly, in all probability, as the average. In our frustration at the slowness and difficulty of the process of assimilation, we often forget that the Negro immigrant to the North is by far the most recent of our mass immigrants. In many cities of the North, the Negro population has risen from 5 per cent to

20 per cent or more during the last thirty years, almost entirely as a result of migration from the rural South. This vast movement has taken place at a time when other immigration has been largely confined to middle-class or near-middle-class refugees, or to the relatives of citizens enjoying special advantages on the social ladder. We have forgotten what the immigration of the late nineteenth century was like, with its "huddled masses" of the poor and ignorant, its alien atmosphere, and its often disorderly circumstances. Large-scale white immigration came to an end before World War I and was never resumed in the same way again.

As soon as they were able to do so, the successful early Negro migrants in the North began campaigns to protect the rights of Blacks and to improve their position. These voluntary societies, many of which trace their lineage back to the abolitionist and Negro welfare groups of the nineteenth century, have been indispensable factors in organizing and directing the campaigns which prepared the way for the Civil Rights revolution of the postwar period and particularly for decisive national action in 1964 and 1965. Such groups have worked in many areas and at many levels. Some have pursued quiet programs of persuasion in individual communities, arranging with those in authority to have private or public barriers to equality removed. Others have functioned in the realm of opinion and of politics, seeking support for the idea of progress.

In retrospect, the most important and effective of these groups— the organ whose achievement made that of all the others possible— was the Legal Defense and Education Fund of the National Association for the Advancement of Colored People. That organization conceived and applied the bold and simple idea of appealing to the law to enforce the law. Their original plans were by no means a systematic blueprint for the campaign which emerged, case by case, from the process of their experience. But the germ was there, based on the realization that the ultimate moving power in American society is the body of ideals expressed in the Declaration of Independence and the Constitution, enforced by the courts as law. All the rest followed—the prodding, restless demonstrations on the streets, the meetings, the marches, the sit-ins, and the petitions. For the purpose of the protests was to stir a nation to obey its own law, even when the law required, and imposed, a political and social revolution.

To realize why their program of change through law accomplished

so much, and how it aroused the nation to respond, we must go back
to the 1880s again and recall the way the law developed.

IV

While the inauguration of President Hayes began a period of self-
deception and discreet silence on the problem of Negro rights, the
Supreme Court did not openly suspend all attempts to apply and
interpret the Fourteenth and Fifteenth Amendments. On the contrary, for two generations the Fourteenth Amendment was one of
the most fashionable provisions of the Constitution, being invoked
repeatedly as the basis for striking down state laws regulating business. And, starting before the turn of the century, the due process
clause of the Fourteenth Amendment, and the equal protection
clause as well, began to be applied as tests for the legality of criminal
trials in the state courts, including trials conducted in the shadow of
force and the threat of force. Somewhat later, the amendment was
also invoked in another important line of cases to protect freedom
of speech and of the press, freedom of religion, and other personal
and political rights.

Before 1930, then, the Supreme Court had established two positions of central importance to the Civil Rights Revolution of the last
thirty years: first, it had made the Constitution, and the process of
constitutional adjudication, a far more active and continuous force
in American public life than had ever been the case before, and it had
won general acceptance for its role as the active protector of constitutional rights; and secondly, it had built a corpus of precedents
from which the modern law of personal liberty emerged naturally
and with the invaluable sanction of past authority.

The true turning point in the recent history of the Court is the
Chief Justiceship of Charles Evans Hughes. The moral temper of the
country was changing under the impact of the Great Depression and
the experience of war and the threat of war. The law reflected that
change, and played a considerable part in bringing it about. Each
decision applying a principle of constitutional order opened a debate
in the legislatures, the press, and the classrooms of the nation—a
debate which often reached the country stores and the political campaigns as well. Each case also suggested new possibilities to lawyers

and, therefore, tended to invite further tests of principle through further litigation.

During the 1930s, the constitutional law of personal and civil rights began to grow. The Supreme Court dealt with a surprising number of problems, from freedom of speech and of religion to martial law, the right to vote, and the concept of due process in the criminal trial. And, in case after warning case, it began to enforce the Fourteenth Amendment to protect Negroes against discrimination. The justices seemed to be alerting the nation to the fact that the old moratorium of 1877 was crumbling away and would not long endure.

The civil liberties and Negro organizations responded to the Court's lead and began to bring cases far more frequently than ever before. And, in the normal manner of a common law court, the Supreme Court dealt with the questions brought before it, sometimes upholding and sometimes denying the claim of right.

The struggle for equality has transformed American society in the last thirty-five years. While justice for the Negro has been its central theme, the effort has not been confined to the problem of the Negro. Once released, the "gospel of liberty" is contagious. In clearing up one wrong, men notice others. They see old habits of injustice, long taken to be the order of nature, with new eyes. So it has been with the flowering of the Jeffersonian spirit in our time. Once we concluded, for example, that it was wrong to deny the Negro a vote, it became impossible to tolerate old systems of apportionment that gave white men and women in rural districts double or triple votes, and citizens in urban centers only half a vote, or a tenth of a vote.

Thus, the social and political experiences that altered the moral climate of the country also altered the law. In turn, the decisions and opinions of the courts, and notably those of the Supreme Court, exerted a powerful and far-reaching influence on the national mind. The renewed protection of Negro rights in the courts during the 1930s emerged as an integral part of a wider development, a fresh, confident assertion of the spirit of liberty and equality in many realms and at many levels of American life: in Washington and in the states, in the universities and in the churches, in business, in law, in politics, and in social life. It was one of those remarkable moments when the impulse for improvement was strong and made itself universally felt. The progressive feeling naturally embraced the question of Negro rights.

V

These then were the main forces behind the breakthrough in Negro rights represented in part by the Civil Rights Act of 1964 and the Voting Rights Act of 1965. Changes in the outlook and experience of our people, shaped and brought into focus as changes in law, have forced the nation at last to realize that we have tolerated hypocrisy or worse in the surviving resistance to the Fourteenth and Fifteenth Amendments and in the political arrangements based on the Compromise of 1877.

The intensity of the yearning for progress was greatly heightened by World War II and by the strains and pressures of the period of Cold War. So far as the rights of the Negro are concerned, it has become more and more visibly absurd to require him to serve in the armed forces abroad and then to deny him full equality as a citizen at home. Race has taken on altogether new dimensions as a political and social problem, with the end of empire in the world, the rising importance of the nations of Africa and Asia, and the revulsion of the modern spirit against Hitlerism in all its forms.

On the question of Negro rights, we have lived through what can be described as a political symphony of democracy in action.

In the first movement, the Supreme Court declared the theme with great force and in terms which finally demanded a political response. For a generation or more, the Supreme Court had challenged the nation to make good its promise of equality to the Negro. Recognizing the changes which have occured in society, in the status of the Negro, and in other parts of the law of the Fourteenth Amendment, the Court decided case after case in favor of the Negro—cases dealing with the use of public parks; the right to vote in primary elections; the right to attend state-supported schools, colleges, and other institutions; the selection of jurors; and many cognate problems.

The process of challenge reached its culminating point in *Brown v. Board of Education,*[39] in 1954, dealing with segregation in elementary schools. That case stirred the country as none of its predecessors had done, for it touched the daily life of all the people and put the issue in a form which politics could no longer ignore.

39. 347 U.S. 483 (1954); R. Kluger, Simple Justice (1976).

Congress then declared the second movement of the symphony. Slowly, reluctantly, it considered the implications of the problem for a decade, while the reapportionment movement began to alter the historic balance of political power within the states and to sap the walls of old forts and citadels.

In this period, Southern resistance to the law became quite frantic. Officials avoided open contempt of court orders, but used every other device ingenious and often desperate men could think of to circumvent them. Violence against the civil rights petitioners was endemic and went almost entirely unpunished, even when it was murder. The movement of civil disobedience to law, led by men who had taken oaths to uphold the Constitution, spread throughout the South and reached into other parts of the nation as well. The United States was at last forced to recognize, in a series of clashes with Southern officials closely analogous to the revolt of the French officers in Algeria, that it faced something approaching an insurrection.[40]

Southern leaders, mindful of the lessons of 1877, made strenuous political efforts to reestablish the old bargain which had permitted them to postpone the consequences of Appomattox for almost a century. Starting in 1948, some of them sought to precipitate another electoral deadlock in which they could hope to determine the choice of a president on their own terms. In Congress, they fought to preserve their historic alliance with leading members of the Republican party.

Finally, after ten years of deliberation, Congress responded, and responded with overwhelming force, in the Civil Rights Act of 1964. Many factors converged to produce its fully considered action in that year, despite the fact that it was an election year, and a year when many congressmen faced disturbing hazards at the polls. There was the majestic civil rights demonstration of 1963 in Washington, and other unmistakable manifestations of deep public feeling. The zeal and skill of President Johnson's leadership and the poignant memory of President Kennedy's death played significant parts in the timing of the event. The country came to sense the nature and gravity of the crisis—a crisis of legality as well as one of justice in law. Television brought into every home the spectacle of police brutality

40. FRIEDMAN, SOUTHERN JUSTICE (1965): CHARLES MORGAN, A TIME TO SPEAK (1964).

toward peaceful civil rights demonstrators and of Southern officials and Southern mobs defying the law. There was somber realization, too, of what was implicit in the reluctance of Southern juries to convict men of crimes linked to the civil rights movement. In the end, for most senators and congressmen, their vote for the Civil Rights Act of 1964 was an act of conscience and of duty. They were receiving masses of hostile mail. They could not estimate the extent of the so-called white "backlash" they faced at the elections in the fall. But they knew that the Supreme Court was right in seeking to enforce the Fourteenth Amendment against racial discrimination. And, having seen the face of anarchy, they voted to put the full power of the federal government behind the judges' quest for lawful order.

The overwhelming vote of the Congress for the Civil Rights Acts of 1964 and 1965 in effect ratified the work of the Supreme Court in this field during the long generation since Chief Justice Hughes's appointment in 1930. And, by an accident of history, both the substance of the civil rights law and the historic and juridical legitimacy of the Supreme Court's conception of its role were placed squarely in issue by the Presidential campaign of 1964. The election of 1964 was, among other things, a referendum of both subjects, because the candidates took explicit and altogether different positions on them.

Thus, with a symmetry and clarity rarely found in the political life of democracy, the people themselves ratified what the Court and Congress had done. Their vote, the ultimate reservoir of sovereignty, gave renewed life to the Constitution and a renewed mandate to the Court.

And, at long last, it interred the Compromise of 1877.

VI

My purpose in chapters 2 and 3 has been to consider law not as a static body of rules, but as a way of making decisions of policy. I have sought to direct attention to the sources of the law, and to the methods it uses in making policy decisions—methods based on certain modes of thought and certain rules of procedure. Their goal is to help the actual approach the ideal posited in our minds by history and by our sense of justice, and to contribute to the gradual evolution of the ideal itself.

I began by recalling the position of the Negro as a degraded slave, entitled, in the famous phrase of *Dred Scott,* to no rights the white man was bound to respect. The burden of that history is not easy to escape, either for the white man or the Black. In quick review, I then tried to evoke the several chapters of the story: the rise and fall of movements of reform; the compromises engineered by the great Whigs, as the nation flowed westward, and the collapse of their work in the tragedy of the Civil War; the period of reconstruction, and that of quiescence after 1877, while the nation concentrated on building cities and industries; the response of the Progressive movement, which began again to stir the nation's conscience; the wars of the twentieth century, the Depression, and now the extraordinary age in which we live—one dominated by a social revolution so pervasive and so familiar we scarcely notice it.

In our country, the Supreme Court has been a major source of our concept of the ideal as the interpreter of the Constitution in a wide area of social policy. Over a generation, and with increasing insistence, the Court has appealed to the country by reminding us that we have made promises to the Negro we have not kept, and that those promises represent our highest aspirations. For the Court, this is not a usurpation of function, but a fulfillment of its peculiar and particular function as a spokesman of law. The Court has thus helped to maintain a creative tension in our minds between social actuality and our shared notion of what society ought to become. In the intellectual and moral climate of our time, the Court has proposed and the nation has accepted great strides forward both in actual law, and in the prevailing ideal for law—strides intended to help achieve liberty and equality, and to make fraternity more nearly conceivable.

For us, the Civil Rights Acts of 1964 and 1965 are the final skirmishes of our Hundred Years' War for Liberty and Equality. That war has forged a loose and uncertain union of states into a nation. And it has rededicated the nation irrevocably to the proposition that all men are created both free and equal. Steeped in the passion of our history, the civil rights statutes of the sixties are something more as well. They mark the end of one quest, but they begin another—the search for Fraternity, an idea with even deeper roots in human experience than those of Liberty and Equality, strong as they are.

In all modern democratic cultures, Fraternity has thus far been the neglected goal of social action. We have too easily assumed that if men were free they could fulfill their need for meaningful and cooperative association with their fellow men through the processes of voluntary choice alone. We define the obligation of government toward each citizen as a duty to assure him life, liberty, and the right to pursue his own notion of happiness in his own way. This belief, so characteristic of eighteenth-century rationalism, was an important feature of its revolt against the restrictive tradition of medieval society.

But man has had to pay a price for the famous shift from status to contract. Liberty is a lonely creed, as Croce remarked. In the course of our effort to make good the promises of liberty and equality on which the nation stands, we have discovered the power of an older truth, too long neglected—that all men are indeed brothers. The maxim is not a pious sentiment, but a social fact. Cain's behavior was as "brotherly" as Joseph's.

Man is a social creature, not a hermit, and his life is hopelessly incomplete unless he has a respected and useful place in the life of a community. The conditions of modern urban life have deprived many people of an acknowledged task and an acknowledged position in their villages and tribes, without providing equivalent satisfactions. They may lack the skills or the psychological strength to deal with the bewildering choices of contemporary society. For them, liberty and equality are simply not enough. Unaided, a considerable fraction of our people—a fifth, a quarter, perhaps even a third of the nation—sink back into the morass of poverty and alienation. Their plight is analogous to that of many new nations in Asia and Africa which have not yet mastered the secrets of modern wealth.

Imbued as we are with the Puritan spirit, we have come to accept as a moral duty the obligation to welcome the excluded, both at home and abroad, as integral members of a more fraternal society. And we have gradually realized that unless the barriers to such integration are overcome, the rightful protests of the excluded will become more desperate and more bitter, until they threaten the general peace.

There is no way of knowing whether the condition of depressed poverty among us is now more widespread than was the case in times past. We do know that it is less tolerable and less easily ignored today than ever before, because the moral climate of our public life has changed, and changed for the better, in the years since Theodore Roosevelt and Woodrow Wilson gave new impetus to the progressive forces in American history.

The Supreme Court has been a significant participant in that process of change. And the Negro's call for justice under law has been a moving force—in many ways the decisive force—in stirring the Court to act.

The need to face the challenge of the Negro's claim, and its manifest rightness, led first the courts and then the political arms of government to inaugurate movements of social action which have transformed the country.

This transformation, touching the quality of every part of our social life, permits us to watch and judge the proper constitutional role of the Supreme Court in the making of social policy. This aspect of the Court's work is not peculiar to constitutional cases, and is not peculiarly "political" in that realm, as compared with other parts of the law. Judges understand the interplay of custom and policy, and they make policy choices when they decide cases of torts or bills and notes. But the policy element in constitutional litigation tends to be more sensitive and more explosive than in cases of negotiability or of liability without fault.

The judges' function in this regard needs to be carefully defined. In a democracy—or at least in American democracy—the Supreme Court speaks in the name of the people, the ultimate body politic from which the Constitution derives. The Court acts as the people's representative in enforcing constitutional rules for the governance of power. But the Court's decisions are not final—and the point is crucial to the theory of democracy. They can be reversed by the process of amendment. And, to be effective, they often require the concurrent action of other branches of government, which may or may not be forthcoming.

The decisions of the Court are therefore appeals quite as much as they are commands—appeals to principle and to aspiration. The authority of the Court depends ultimately on qualities even more important than the dialectic skill of judges in what Coke called our "artificial" modes of reasoning—that is, on their wisdom and sense of strategy, their sensitivity to the state of public feeling, and their insight into the dynamics of social action. Without the guidance of perceptions of this order, the Supreme Court cannot play its part in the long, slow, historical process through which the actual approaches the ideal in the movement of social experience. Only in such terms can its justices help as magistrates to form society's notion of the ideal, which changes too in the light of time. For to be worthy of their task, the judges must be more than mediators in resolving clashes between the nation's conscience and its history, between the higher law of the American Constitution—Jefferson's "law of nature and Nature's God"—and *ius gentium*. Unless a sufficient number of the justices possess the gift of prophecy, and the gift of tongues, the Court will flag in its ultimate task as a legal institution— that is, its responsibility to speak for the values of law as an integral part of the process of making social policy.

In part, the strange and disturbing history of the Negro in our law is no more than a special instance of the conflict between custom and positive law, and between the positive law at any moment and the goal of law which is the "compass" of our policy, in Lord Radcliffe's arresting phrase. In part, however, it has been something more: a clash between authority and anarchy, a crisis not of law but of legality itself. When governors and legislators and state police openly or secretly resist the plain command of law, our system of law is challenged as it has not been challenged for a century. In this clash, those who advocate and practice civil disobedience defy what Ortega y Gasset called the *concordia* of society—the indispensable concord and agreement, the universal consensus on the fundamental procedural rules and norms of the civil order, which alone make it possible to enjoy a social life ordered by law.

Part Two

Of Obligation

The Citizen and the Law

Since the early part of this century, men and women of insight have sensed a process of disintegration at work within the liberal Western democratic societies—a process at once structural, moral, psychological, intellectual, and political. Artists and poets often perceive such movemeents before less gifted mortals. In this period, all branches of art, literature, and philosophy have been marked by visions of dissonance and withdrawal, and by a growing anxiety about the fate of man in an alien universe, nearly out of control. Are these changes symptoms of a disease fatal to the civilization of Rationalism, Liberalism, and Enlightenment? Or are they no more than normal outward signs of change, accenting the rise and decline of styles in the reassuring rhythm of nineteenth century history?

The climate of opinion in nineteenth century Europe and America was dominated by what J. B. Bury called the Idea of Progress. Against the background of all that has happened since August 1914, no one today can be as confident as nearly everyone was two generations ago that the Gospel of Liberty is about to triumph over Despotism and Reaction—everywhere.

One of the most striking aspects of this transformation has been the rise in the relative importance of the state among the institutions of modern societies. Both in liberal and in illiberal societies, the state has many more functions than was the case a century ago, and therefore pervades society far more deeply and continuously than ever before. Does this accumulation of functions in the state necessarily imply the end of human freedom?

In his remarkable book, "Power, the Natural History of its Growth," written during the Second World War, Bertrand de Jouvenel envisages a steady increase in the authority of the Minotaur state, made nearly inevitable by the opportunities modern society offers to man's insatiable appetite for Caesarism. "The only obstacle that Caesarism has to fear," M. de Jouvenel writes, is "a movement of libertarian resistance," governed by law as "a system of civil and political liberty."* A legal order of this character and quality, Jouvenel contends, cannot develop except among peoples whose folkways respect the principles of liberty, and whose leaders are genuinely devoted to them. Under such circumstances, and only under such circumstances, can one hope for institutions of law strong enough to prevail as a limitation on the cancerous growth of power, and the basis for the balanced harmonies of true civilization.

Part 2 deals with two aspects of the relationship between the individual and the modern state. Chapter 4 originated as a response to the waves of protest, riot, and civil disobedience which swept over every nation of the Western world, except beleaguered Israel, during the decade 1963–74—a movement

* BERTRAND DE JOUVENEL, POWER, THE NATURAL HISTORY OF ITS GROWTH 283, 277 (1945, 1948; rev. Am. ed. 1952).

which has not yet run its course. That movement was most strongly manifest in the universities, and was often led and always much
influenced by university students. Chapter 5
deals with a related phenomenon—the obligations of the lawyer to unpopular clients. It was
stimulated by the difficulty I experienced in
retaining lawyers to represent students and
others who participated in the Yale Freedom
Rides of the early sixties. Those Freedom
Rides were a peaceful demonstration conducted to challenge the resistance described in
chapter 3, which involved the civil disobedience of many citizens and public officials in
the South to the Fourteenth Amendment.

Four

The Rightful Limits of Freedom in a Liberal Democratic State

Of Civil Disobedience

I

As Geoffrey Woodhead points out, any book is "the child of its time." Even classical scholarship invariably reflects not only the preoccupations of the scholar's world, but also his own reactions to that world.[1] If, as Woodhead shows, this is the case for the study of Thucydides, it is hardly remarkable that the focus of concern has recently shifted in the literature of liberty. The contributors to that literature are usually men and women devoted to the expansion and protection of personal freedom. For many centuries, they have written almost exclusively about the obligation of the liberal state to respect the moral autonomy of the individual. They have preached toleration, and attacked beliefs which they thought had become superstitions, restraints which no longer deserved the support of opinion. In this turbulent final third of the twentieth century, for the first time in modern history, there is widespread interest in the recip-

This paper draws on *The Consent of the Governed,* a Fourth of July oration delivered at Monticello under the auspices of the Thomas Jefferson Memorial Foundation in 1968 and printed in the Autumn 1968 VIRGINIA QUARTERLY REVIEW; on *Chief Justice Warren and the Gift for Action,* a speech given in 1968 and printed in the Spring 1969 issue of the YALE LAW REPORT; and on a memorandum prepared for the National Commission on the Causes and Prevention of Violence in 1969. It was presented in approximately its present form at the Centennial Convocation of the Association of the Bar of the City of New York on April 30, 1970, and appeared in the proceedings of that convocation, Is LAW DEAD? (ed. E. V. Rostow 1971). © 1971 by Eugene V. Rostow.

1. GEOFFREY A. WOODHEAD, THUCYDIDES ON THE NATURE OF POWER ix–xii (1969).

rocal issue: the rightful obligation of the individual to the liberal society in which he chooses to live.[2]

The reasons for the change are self-evident. All the world over—at least in societies which have or wish to achieve liberal governments—difficult problems have arisen in defining the boundary between individual freedom and public order. It could hardly be otherwise in a world which challenges the presuppositions of liberalism more and more insistently.

The tension between order and liberty is perpetual, and insoluble. The words represent principles which are equally indispensable, and equally valid, at least in the hierarchy of American values. Sometimes we conceal the conflict between them by talking of "ordered liberty." The differences among people on how to balance the claims of order and of freedom may depend as much upon personality as upon political philosophy. The old antinomy has vexed every generation in every country: every judge; every philosopher of politics or law; every liberal; every conservative. The way in which society

2. Among recent articles and books, these exemplify the resurgence of interest in the problem of obligation: M. WALTZER, OBLIGATIONS: ESSAYS ON DISOBEDIENCE, WAR, AND CITIZENSHIP (1970); H. W. JONES, THE EFFICACY OF LAW (1969); A. FORTAS, CONCERNING DISSENT AND CIVIL DISOBEDIENCE (1968); J. P. PLAMENATZ, CONSENT, FREEDOM AND POLITICAL OBLIGATION (2d ed. 1968); G. WOODCOCK, CIVIL DISOBEDIENCE (1963); H. A. BEDAU, ed., CIVIL DISOBEDIENCE: THEORY AND PRACTICE (1960); W. O. DOUGLAS, POINTS OF REBELLION (1970); H. L. NIEBERG, POLITICAL VIOLENCE (1969); C. Cohen, H. A. Freeman, & E. Van Den Haag, *Civil Disobedience and the Law*, 21 RUTGERS L. REV. 1, 17, and 27 (1966); C. L. Black, *The Problem of the Compatability of Civil Disobedience with American Institutions of Government*, 43 TEXAS L. REV. 492 (1965); M. Keeton, *The Morality of Civil Disobedience*, 43 TEXAS L. REV. 507 (1965); P. Freund, *Civil Rights and the Limits of Law*, 14 BUFFALO L. REV. 199 (1964); J. Goldstein, *Psychoanalysis and Jurisprudence*, 77 YALE L. J. 1053 (1969), esp. at 1064–71; H. Pitkin, *Obligation and Consent*, 59 AMER. POL. SCI. REV. 990 (1965); and 60 AMER. POL. SCI. REV. 39 (1966); F. A. Allen, *Civil Disobedience*, 36 CINCINNATI L. REV. (1967); H. Prosch, *Towards an Ethics of Civil Disobedience*, 77 ETHICS 176 (1967); Kent Greenawalt, *A Contextual Approach to Disobedience*, 70 COLUM. L. REV. 48 (1970); W. T. Blackstone, *Civil Disobedience: Is It Justified?* 3 GEORGIA L. REV. 679 (1969). The three collections of value-oriented papers PHILOSOPHY, POLITICS, AND SOCIETY, ed. Peter Laslett, then Laslett & W. G. Runciman (1956, 1962, 1969) represent the movement, and have given it momentum. R. S. SUMMERS, ed., ESSAYS IN LEGAL PHILOSOPHY (1970), should also be noted, as should JAMES FINN, ed., A CONFLICT OF LOYALTIES: THE CASE FOR SELECTIVE CONSCIENTIOUS OBJECTION (1968).

Two widely read books published since this paper was given, JOHN RAWLS, A THEORY OF JUSTICE (1971), and ROBERT NOZICK, ANARCHY, STATE, AND UTOPIA (1974), carry forward the discussion, but add little to its substance. All the problems they discuss are analyzed in this chapter.

draws the boundary between liberty and order is critical to its quality, and to its atmosphere.

In drawing that boundary, cultures like ours tend to resolve most doubts in favor of individual liberty. We are still dominated by the optimism of the Enlightenment, and its faith in the perfectibility of man. And we believe that the continuity of American society, and of our constitutional system, is the order of nature. We never really doubt their toughness and tenacity, and their capacity to brush off any threat. Still, though our law goes to great lengths to protect the individual against the state, it has hardly abandoned its inherent right to protect the state against the individual, or the hostile group, and to insist on some deference to the prevailing code of social morality.

Cultures of pessimism, on the other hand, tend to give greater weight to the claims of order. They start from a Hobbesian view of human nature. They never confuse men with angels, and they live with nightmare memories of civil war, revolution, and tyranny. Their instinct is to keep the dark side of mankind in tighter rein, and, if choice be necessary, to sacrifice some individual freedom to the hope of social peace. Men of this temperament often fear liberty as the entering wedge of chaos.

If men live together in society, the fact and the mode of their cooperation necessarily limit their individual freedom. How a society fixes these inevitable outer limits of individual freedom is one of the few issues of public policy on which it is legitimate to distinguish a "liberal" from a "conservative" position. The terms are so fashionable, and are invoked so often, that they have lost nearly all their meaning. But in this area—that of marking the zone of toleration and of freedom protected from the state—these cherished words do apply. I should make it clear that I approach the subject as a liberal who believes in the widest feasible zone of personal freedom for the individual as a good in itself—indeed as one of the highest goals of law in human society. I approach it also as a student of the social process who is convinced that the law of a society must reconcile the claims of liberty and of order in accordance not with my personal norms of social justice, and my vision of the future, but with its own —the spirit of its law, in Montesquieu's phrase, its superego, in effect, and the compass of its quest for the grail.[3] If the law deviates from

---

3. The phrase is Lord Radcliffe's, from THE LAW AND ITS COMPASS (1960). I have commented on the problem in *The Enforcement of Morals*, CAMBRIDGE LAW JOURNAL 174 (1960), reprinted in THE SOVEREIGN PREROGATIVE (1962).

that course, society is subjected to severe and potentially dangerous tension.

American constitutional law has witnessed a remarkable enlargement of the realm of personal freedom during the last forty years. Viewed in perspective, the growth of our law of civil liberty and of civil right, starting about 1915, and gaining momentum steadily after 1930, is an achievement of merit, however much remains to be done. Now, like other open societies, we are being forced to reexamine the rightful limits of personal freedom—rightful, that is, for our society, living in harmony with the code of its particular, and particularly libertarian, constitution.

The reexamination of the problem of social peace has been precipitated throughout the Western world during the last twenty years by an extraordinary increase in the amount and vehemence of social protest, which has often become riot, and occasionally approached the boundaries of civil war. Genuinely revolutionary political movements have of course sought to take advantage of the phenomenon of protest. The Cultural Revolution of the West has been as important in Japan, Germany, and France as in Uruguay or the United States. The same symbolic revolutionary costumes, hair styles, music, and vocabulary parade everywhere. The sans-culottes of our time, however, wear levis. The tide has waxed and waned. But it is felt as a presence and a potentiality—for many, an ominous restraint. The experience has transformed the atmosphere of every city and every university of the West.

The degree of stress in this process of reexamination is notably acute for the United States, as compared with other democratic societies. Our society is being subjected to the pressure of deep and difficult psychosocial transformations. Several are unique to the American scene. And in the United States, as in other countries, social protest is being expressed and dramatized in new and sometimes disturbing styles.[4]

In the spring of 1970, when this chapter was given at a public meeting in New York, the tide of protest was at its apogee in the

---

4. The creation and development of the twentieth-century style in social disruption is brilliantly reviewed by NORMAN F. CANTOR in THE AGE OF PROTEST (1969), and GEORGE DANGERFIELD in THE STRANGE DEATH OF LIBERAL ENGLAND (1936). These themes are traced more deeply in NORMAN COHN, THE PURSUIT OF THE MILLENNIUM (1957) and JOHN PASSMORE, THE PERFECTIBILITY OF MAN (1971).

United States. Its themes were articulated almost daily. A story in the *New York Times* for April 22, 1970, recalls the thesis. The story reported local reactions to events at Isla Vista, California, a college town beset by nights of rioting, culminating in the death of a student who had been helping other students put out "fires set by bands of maurauding demonstrators." Some of the militants were said to advocate street fighting as a way of radicalizing the community. "Basically, the issue is how to build a mass movement," one said. "The mass of left liberals are not ready for street fighting." A fresh-man is quoted: "When I saw the kids trying to burn the bank, I thought they were insane. But then the cops came in and they were obviously looking for trouble. . . . Later they used tear gas on campus. I just can't support a government that sends in troops to do things like that." Another student commented, according to the re-porter, "I don't go in for this window breaking and violence. But maybe there isn't any other way to get changes. Maybe the only way to end the war is to burn down all the Bank of America buildings."

At New Haven, my own university faced the test which so many others have had to endure in recent years. The nominal occasion was a murder trial. Several members of the Black Panther party were charged with killing one of their number on the ground that he had informed the police about a series of bombings carried out by Black Panthers. A brilliant campaign had generated an epidemic of anxiety, fear, guilt, and concern within the University, and elsewhere. There were rumors that Yale and New Haven would be invaded by organized militant groups, and stormed. Some thuggery and several episodes of arson had already occurred. Once again, we saw that these contagious fevers do not respect the generation gap. Otherwise serious scholars wondered whether it is wise or moral to try men duly charged with murder, and whether possible error on the part of a judge warranted burning a few buildings, or jail delivery.

We know, of course, that moods and events of this kind are phe-nomena from the realm of mass hysteria, like the Tulip Mania, the Dance of Death, and the South Sea Bubble. We know also that the driving force behind many of these episodes is not social protest but the attractions of violence, adventure and excitement as sport— the powerful and fundamental lure which has drawn men for cen-turies to hunts, wars, crusades, and expeditions of exploration or of conquest. Perhaps it is quixotic even to try, through disciplined in-tellectual effort, to examine what Mill called "the necessary limits of individual freedom arising out of the conditions of our social life,"[5] that is, the idea of "civil liberty" within organized society, in Rousseau's phrase, as distinguished from "natural liberty" in a state of nature.

The City Bar Association consists of worldly lawyers, beyond surprise at man's capacity for folly, sin, and irrationality. It says much about the ultimate idealism of the legal mind that the leaders of the Association did not respond to the prevailing atmosphere with a shrug of sardonic resignation. On the contrary, they based their centennial program on a premise of unabashed faith in the potentialities of reason, and in the goodness of man. They assumed that most men desire to be upright citizens, but that they are confused and uncertain in the face of arguments like those reported in *The New York Times* story I have just quoted. It followed, in their minds, that a careful analysis of what lies behind these assertions is not only possible, and worthwhile, but indispensable; and that the most practical contribution the Association could make to the peaceful resolution of that time of troubles would be to seek coherence—and, conceivably, even a degree of consensus—at the level of first principles.

Those who planned the Centennial Convocation soberly recognize that our credo and our institutions are being tested with a vehemence the nation has not known since the Civil War. They understand, and understand with sympathy, that in many sectors of our national life angry men say the pace of change is too slow. The peaceful methods of law and of democratic politics, these protesters assert, have failed as an instrument for the ordering of progress. Some deny the idea of law itself as the compass of our social system.

Five turbulent upheavals are occurring simultaneously. Each by itself could well require the best efforts of a generation; their confluence strains the sinews of society.

The first and most fundamental is our vast national effort—more than a century after Appomattox—to make good, at long last, our promise of equality for the Negro. This process has been gaining momentum for a generation. It has been given a powerful new impetus by the judicial decisions, the legislation, and the social experience of recent years. It touches every aspect of our law, our politics and

5. J. S. MILL, ON SOCIAL FREEDOM 31 (ed. Dorothy Fosdick 1941). See also 35–36, 37–40, 61–66.

our settled patterns of habit. And it provokes dangerous conflict, especially in our cities where so many Black citizens now live.

The second is the accelerated pace of urbanization—the immense movement of people to cities, and to urban areas. Many are the rural poor, and especially the Black poor, ill equipped for the requirements of urban life. Their presence has led to countershifts of population, tending further to divide communities on racial lines. The pressures arising from these processes have precipitated a mounting urban crisis, which seems beyond the reach of our traditional methods of local government in many large cities.

The third is the renewal of doubt about the foreign policy the nation has followed since 1945. That policy has imposed burdens unfamiliar to our history: thirty years of conscription, a succession of costly military campaigns, the prospect of apparently endless crisis ahead. We are living through another intense round of the debate we have pursued at intervals since President Wilson urged his countrymen to ratify the Covenant of the League of Nations, more than fifty years ago. This round of the debate, like its predecessors, has sharply divided the country. In 1970, it had a special quality of urgency, because of the anguish of Vietnam, the condition of international politics, and the shadow of the nuclear weapon.

Fourth, the demand for higher education, and for better education of all kinds, has outstripped the capacity of our educational system. Since our people know that education is the key to their advancement, and to the advancement of their children, the many shortcomings of the educational system produce widespread bitterness.

And finally, a fraction of our youth, like their counterparts in other countries, feel frustrated or alienated by their experience. They are the first generation of a world in which the authority of the family, the church, and the nation-state has been radically diminished; the fear of unemployment has been weakened or destroyed as a sanction for work; and the consciousness of good and evil has faded. The idealism of many young people is aroused by injustice, by the malfunctioning of institutions seeking to meet the challenge of change, and by the specter of war. All too often, their education has not prepared them for the world as it is. Many are shocked and bewildered to discover that their society is not Utopia, and that, in the nature of societies, it cannot be made over into Utopia quickly. Few are trained to understand why war and near-war have come to be the dominant feature of the human condition in our time. And a considerable number tend to dismiss the experience of history as the misguided chronicle of people less moral, less idealistic, less humane, and less civilized than the youth of today.

The stress of these linked processes of change has produced waves of riots and of disobedience to law which have become the most critical social problem of our time. Their character was highlighted by a series of assassinations which shocked the nation. Furthermore, many believe there may be significant connections between such social and political phenomena and the increase in ordinary crime, and especially in crimes of violence.

These social storms, and the violence they have generated, have created a climate of doubt about the most basic issue a free society ever confronts: the citizen's moral relation to a valid law.

The nation has had a long and bitter experience with civil disobedience. For more than a century the South openly resisted the commands of the Fourteenth and Fifteenth Amendments.

The resistance of the South was justified by moral claims, asserted with passionate conviction: the Amendments had been ratified by coerced legislatures—that is, by legislatures voting under the pressure of military occupation; they were contrary to the word of God, which declared Blacks to be "hewers of wood and drawers of water"; and it was against conscience in any event for the majority of the nation to impose its will on a considerable dissenting minority, and to disregard the strongly held mores and beliefs of a region.

The civil disobedience of the South to the Fourteenth and Fifteenth Amendments was carried out by political means, reinforced by mobs, arson, murder, lynching, and intimidation. These tactics "succeeded" in a pragmatic sense—that is, they produced a state of policy which could not have been achieved by political means alone. But Jim Crow and the Ku Klux Klan have left behind a poisonous legacy, which will require the best efforts of a generation to clear away.

In the late sixties, as the South moved to accept the law of the nation, the practice of civil disobedience, and the jurisprudence invoked in its behalf, suddenly spread. Earnest men claimed that the citizen has a right—even a duty—to refuse military service for a war he disapproves, and, more generally, that his own feelings of injustice and unfairness, if strongly enough held, justify illegal action on his part. The precedent of Nuremberg, and Gandhi's example, were invoked in support of draft resistance and cognate acts of disobedience to valid law. Some defended arson, trespass, and other forms of violence as protest, on the ground that they might hasten the reform of institutions and policies. Such methods were justified as means by the fact that they might produce desirable ends. A few embarked on campaigns of subversion or "confrontation" designed, they said, to weaken or destroy important institutions of society, and society itself, on the ground that they, or others, were aggrieved, excluded, or unfairly treated, and that society itself must be deemed hopelessly and inherently unjust.

Taken together, this is a formidable array.

The phenomenon raises two issues: first, the citizen's moral relation to the law in a society of consent; and, second, the capacity of the American legal and political order to meet the felt needs of our people for social justice.

The two problems are reciprocal. They cannot be studied in isolation from each other: The idea of order without justice is odious.

The first of these issues is one of the oldest and at the same time most novel dilemmas in legal and political philosophy. The American constitutional order rests on an explicit answer to the question—the theory of the social contract, dear to the men of the Enlightenment who made the nation. In their view, the Constitution was made by people, not by the states, through a unique constituent act. "We the people of the United States," in their memorable phrase, meeting in special assemblies, entered directly into the covenant of the Constitution, committed to the proposition that the just powers of government derive from the consent of the governed. It follows that in the kind of society they wanted to achieve, the citizen was bound—morally bound—to obey the law he helped to make.

Where does their theory stand today, in a vast pluralistic society, far less homogeneous than the thirteen British colonies of the Atlantic seaboard in the late eighteenth century? What are its alternatives? Can it, should it, be used to explain the citizen's moral relation to the law of the United States in the last third of the twentieth century?

But even if we renew agreement on the proposition that the citizen of a free society owes his fellows a moral obligation to obey the law, the problem of disobedience and violence would remain. Moral rules and principles, however universally accepted, are never universally obeyed. Life and literature would be more tranquil, but less interesting, were this not the case. Antigone's dilemma has parallels in every generation. Whatever one's school of philosophy may be, we know that when our society, by a considerable margin, fails to satisfy the mores of our people, violent and illegal protest has occurred in the past, and will continue to occur in the future. We have had a long history of protest going beyond the limits of law—rebellions by tenants, debtors, and taxpayers, the Ku Klux Klan, labor conflicts, farmers' protests, and draft riots, to say nothing of the Civil War itself—as antecedents for the diverse phenomena of protest we endured during the last fifteen years.

The philosophical problem of obligation cannot therefore be studied in isolation. It must always be concerned with another theme: Can our political and legal system satisfy the legitimate demands of modern society for social justice in peace, and without regression or collapse?

Thus the question must be not simply to justify the ways of law to the community, but to vindicate the law as a means of achieving justice—not merely to defend the law, but to help make it worthy of defense, as the supreme and all-embracing instrument of social progress, and of social peace.

It is an old and harsh social truth that unless the leaders of a society lead, there is little hope either for the institutions placed in their trust, or for society itself.

In the late sixties and early seventies, wherever men looked, they witnessed happenings which affronted their sense of the right order of things—bombings, strange increases in the common crimes, turbulence at the universities, draft resistance, the rhetoric and sometimes the pantomime of revolution. In turn, these storms have stirred an intense preoccupation with the ancient philosophical problem of man's moral relation to the law.

I should make it clear at the start that the subject of this paper is the model for right behavior which should prevail in a liberal civilization, and particularly in the United States. A generally accepted model for exemplary behavior has a profound influence on the pattern of actual behavior, although even the most upright and responsible citizen doesn't always succeed in living up to it. The influence of legal and moral norms on society does not depend on whether laws are fully enforced or fully respected at any given moment. The critical issue, as Weber pointed out, is "the 'orientation' of an action toward a norm, rather than the 'success' of that norm."[6]

In this perspective, and for this purpose, how should we evaluate the claims put forward in the name of civil disobedience?

II

The Case for Civil Disobedience

Is the highest form of moral liberty, as Rousseau contended, "obedience to self-imposed law," which alone makes man truly his own master?[7]

Or is there an inalienable right of civil disobedience which citizens of conscience possess because they are moral beings—a right to disobey valid laws they do not approve, and to engage in organized programs of unlawful conduct (including some recourse to violence) by way of protest against such laws?

There are, of course, now as always, cynics, immoralists, and criminals among us, and genuine revolutionaries as well—romantics with a burning desire to destroy society in the name of anarchy, communism, nihilism, or even vaguer doctrines of purification and rebirth through the purge of fire. But their efforts rally significant support only because many people are in doubt about the extent of their duty to obey valid laws they oppose. The pervasiveness of such doubts has been a factor leading to violence, or weakening the restraints against it, particularly in the cycle of troubles which have beset our universities at intervals during the last fifteen years, and spread from the universities to other areas of society.

An extensive literature asserts that there is a right of civil disobedience, and that the more disturbing features of the movements of protest to which society has been subjected—the turbulence, the violence, the shouting down of speakers, the campaigns to discredit authority and even due process of law—are all moral, legitimate, and indeed legal exercises of a kind of personal freedom which the law should now recognize as subsumed within the idea of liberty protected by the Constitution.

6. MAX WEBER, ON LAW IN ECONOMY AND SOCIETY 13 (ed. Max Rheinstein 1954).

7. THE SOCIAL CONTRACT, bk. I, ch. 8 (1762).

Some proponents of civil disobedience contend that even if some of the occasions on which this "right" has been exercised have involved acts which in their view should be recognized as "excessive," and therefore "technically" illegal, society should be wise enough not to prosecute the men, women, and children of superior virtue who are responsible for them. They do no more, it is urged, than apply the tactics of the civil rights movement, and the philosophy of Martin Luther King, Jr., in other settings. If it was right, and legal, for Black students to sit at the counter of a lunchroom in North Carolina twenty years ago, and ask for food despite a state law forbidding its sale to them, it is argued, then it must be also right, and legal, for Harvard students to sit in the dean's office and demand an end of ROTC, the abolition of grades or the employment of more Blacks on Harvard construction projects.

Besides, it is said, even if some of the manifestations of civil disobedience go "too" far, one should put the blame not on those who have committed the "excessive'" acts, but on the society whose callousness to injustice has driven morally superior persons to such extreme behavior. In any event, they contend, the "excessive" protests are redeemed by their beneficent effects. They dramatize the views of the protesters for the media, and thus jar our stolid and harassed institutions into reform.

Other arguments and analogies are advanced to justify the recognition of at least a limited legal and moral right of civil disobedience. The Nuremberg trials are often invoked to support the contention that in the United States men are bound to disobey laws they believe to be unjust, and to organize illegal protests against them. Similarly, one finds many references to Gandhi, Thoreau, and George Washington as proponents and exemplars of civil disobedience.

Finally, some of the more analytical supporters of the idea contend that society should recognize a limited and entirely nonviolent right of civil disobedience for men who disobey the law to advance not their own moral principles but those of society itself, when in fact, or at least in the firm and sincere judgment of the demonstrators, the laws have deviated from the community's sense of justice.

In a few cases, philosophers advance norms of their own, rather than those they conceive to be implicit in the moral code of American society, as the proper test for the citizen's obligation to the law in a society of consent. A few would make obedience to law a prudential matter for the individual, an issue of convenience, of balancing the advantages and risks for him, rather than an ethical question. Others argue that the individual does face an ethical problem in determining his relation to the law, but that the ethical problem must be resolved—by the individual, or perhaps in the end by the lawmaking agencies of society—on utilitarian grounds ("the greatest good for the greatest number"). Another group would claim a right of disobedience for the individual because in practice the law does not reach a standard of tolerance and perfection which is advanced as the only true test and bench mark of justice.

Others argue that while the social-contract theory is morally persuasive as to laws the free citizen has helped to make himself, it cannot bind the citizen to laws made by his elected representatives.

Finally, a few would contend that while the social-contract argument is unassailable in its own terms, the United States is not a society of consent—that power is so concentrated, politics so corrupt, opportunity so limited, and freedom so illusory, that America must be regarded as the equivalent of Hitler's Germany, or the Soviet Union.

These are the main themes of the case for civil disobedience which have impressed and shaken public opinion without quite persuading it. Many of the writers, clergymen, professors, judges, and philosophers who support these views command wide respect. For our culture, there is deep resonance, calling up the memory of heroes and martyrs, in the comment of one of the leaders of draft resistance that what he did "may be a crime, but it is not a sin."

III

The Obligation to Obey Valid Law in a Society of Consent: The Major Premise

It is the thesis of this paper that our society—as a society of consent —should not and indeed cannot acknowledge a *right* of civil disobedience; that the moral and philosophical arguments advanced in support of such a right are in error; and that the analogies invoked in its behalf are inapplicable.

The major premise of my argument is the corollary of Jefferson's powerful sentence, which echoes Locke, Rousseau, and a long line of philosophers stretching back to Plato at least: the "just powers" of government derive from "the consent of the governed." It follows, I should contend, that in a society of consent the powers of government are just in Jefferson's sense: that is, they are legitimate, because authorized and renewed by procedures of voting all must respect. As a consequence, a citizen of such a society owes his fellow citizens, and the state they have established together, a moral duty to obey *valid* laws until they are repealed or fall into desuetude. I stress the word "valid" in the preceding sentence, to distinguish situations— of the utmost importance for our legal order—where the citizen is testing the constitutionality of a statute, an ordinance, or an official act. In our complex constitutional system, such tests are not in fact regarded as acts of disobedience to law, but as appeals from positive law to the Higher Law of the Constitution.

For me, this proposition is the beginning, not the end, of the problem. It does not of itself permit us to resolve all the questions which are necessarily involved in defining the citizen's obligation to the law in a society of consent. But, I should contend, it is the right place to start such an analysis.

The individual owes other moral duties in his life—to his God, his family, his work, his conscience. Sometimes—often—there is conflict among the moral claims upon a man. But if man lives in a society of consent, and above all in a society of equality and of liberty, his relation to the valid laws of that society should be regarded as moral in character, and entitled to great weight in the hierarchy of moral claims he must face in the course of his life. If a man decides to commit an act of civil disobedience—for example, because he feels that what the law requires would breach his obligation to God— our culture would acknowledge at most his power, but not his right or privilege to do so. In such cases, the citizen faces a moral dilemma —he may resolve it in one way or another. But I can find no basis for saying that society has acknowledged, or must acknowledge, or should acknowledge his "right" to decide to violate the law. If the citizen should violate the law, then he should in turn acknowledge that he thereby breaches a covenant with moral dimensions, and is not committing a purely technical offense. To be sure, he would contend that he is breaking the law in order to avoid what he would regard as a greater sin. But the law too has a moral content; it represents the moral judgment of the majority, and its sense of justice. Under such circumstances, the individual should at least respect his duty to the law he has helped to make by accepting its penalties.

Most philosophers have concluded that the citizen's relation to the law in a society of consent is a moral obligation, and not simply a matter of convenience, of habit, or of fear. Different theories have been put forward to account for the moral element in the citizen's obligation to the law in such societies. On analysis they turn out to be contractual in character, if not always in language. The moral obligation to obey the law, they say, is in the end an instance of the moral obligation to keep one's promises, particularly one's important promises, on which others have relied. Some writers stress the importance of an explicit promise, like a formal oath. Others, like Professor H. L. A. Hart, infer a promissory obligation, either from the citizen's voluntary participation in a society he is free to leave, or from the reliance of other citizens, who have obeyed the law in the expectation of his obedience in turn. The citizen, these men say, has accepted the benefit of the laws, and of the obedience of others to them. Therefore he owes his fellow citizens, and the law, a reciprocal obligation.

Professor Hart's benefit theory of the social contract, while perfectly familiar as contract doctrine, proves too much. It does not permit a discrimination between the citizen's obligation to the law in a tyranny and in a democracy. But that distinction is surely the heart of the matter. The citizen accepts some benefits—i.e., fire protection or education—from the most despotic regimes, and may be deemed to have consented, or at least submitted, even to slavery. The essence of Jefferson's thesis, however, is that unless the citizen can participate responsibly in the making of the laws, he is not morally bound to obey them.

It may be more direct, and more realistic, to draw the moral element in the citizen's obligation to the law from the necessary conditions of social cooperation within different kinds of societies. The obligation to the law of a citizen in a liberal, democratic society is necessarily greater than that of a citizen under conditions of tyranny. The spacious tolerance of a free society is possible only if the laws are generally accepted and respected voluntarily, so that the role of force and coercion in the society can be kept to a minimum. The idea of a free society posits a much higher degree of civic responsibility on the part of each citizen than the concept of a tryanny or a system of paternalism. When a man elects to be a citizen of a society of consent, he necessarily undertakes a personal and far-reaching obligation to the laws, and his fellows do likewise. No such society could fulfill its aspirations, nor indeed remain free very long, unless this obligation were respected.

Thus the substantive content of the social contract is not the same in all societies, although in all—even in prisons—there are some links, some rules which define the relations of members to each other, and to the whole. For a society of consent—and particularly for the liberal and egalitarian democracy of the United States— Jefferson's axiom demands that the citizen take a high degree of responsibility for the law. In the words of the famous first sentence of Montesquieu's *Spirit of the Laws,* this approach defines the citizen's duty to the law of a free society as "a necessary relation derived from the nature of things," that is, in its broadest sense, a law.

The modern, secular world has long since rejected the divine right of kings. The proudest claim of the legal tradition we inherited is that the king is under the law. The eighteenth century theory of the social contract has become the prevailing political theory of modern times, and the only modern rival for the doctrine that power proceeds from the barrel of a gun. I agree with Professor Rawls that it is the appropriate basis, both in ethics and in political theory, for the concept of political obligation in a democracy.[8] As Professor d'Entreves has said, "The principle of equality, together with the related notion of consent as the foundation of power, is the essential component of the idea of legitimacy in the modern world."[9]

The notion of the social contract is of course a metaphor. The social contract is hardly a formal document to be interpreted like a deed. But the phrase embodies the idea of an understanding nonetheless, a core of quintessential ideas, values and customs, defining the ultimate norms of the society, and binding all who share its culture. That body of shared values—what Cicero called the Concordia of society—is the foundation on which any community is built. It involves a commitment on the part of each citizen to play the game according to the moral code of the community as a whole, and to respect the equal rights of all his fellow citizens.

8. John Rawls, *The Justification of Civil Disobedience,* in BEDAU, *supra* note 2, at 241. *Id.,* A THEORY OF JUSTICE (1971), enlarges but does not modify the thesis significantly. See 333–94.

9. A. P. D'ENTRÈVES, THE NOTION OF THE STATE 199 (1967). He warns, and warns wisely, that "equality has its perils, and . . . consent is no sufficient guarantee of the preservation of the basic values of democracy, since it is possible to consent to anything, even to being no longer equal or free."

The social contract binds the state as well as the citizen. The two sets of obligations are reciprocal. Neither can exist without the other. But the citizen's obligation continues as long as the state remains faithful to the fundamental rules.

The social contract is the organizing principle of society. It does not vanish when either party—the state or the citizen—breaches one or another of its covenants, so long as the basic pattern remains vital. Even the most perfect of democratic societies is capable of error, and indeed capable of error which violates its own code of social morality, or higher ideals urged by individuals in the name of moral advance. But unless such errors breach the essential terms of the social contract itself, and destroy the capacity of democracy to correct its errors, they do not weaken the citizen's moral obligation to obey valid law, nor do they dissolve the social contract.

The question is always one of degree. If, for example, a President should dismiss the Supreme Court and the Congress, and attempt to rule by decree, all would concur, I should suppose, that the United States had become a different country, and that the social contract itself was in gage. But an individual is not justified in concluding that the state has abrogated the social contract because he feels, and feels passionately, that injustices are unremedied, or not remedied fast enough. Human society has never achieved all its ideals, and it is not likely to do so soon. The test proposed by Jefferson is still persuasive. Governments are instituted among men, he argued, to secure the unalienable rights of man. It follows, he said, that men are justified in altering the form of their government when it becomes destructive of these ends, and in revolution itself when "a long train of abuses and usurpations, pursuing invariably the same Object, evinces a design to reduce them under absolute Despotism."[10]

As Professor Rawls has written, "Even under a just Constitution, unjust laws may be passed and unjust policies enforced. Some form of majority principle is necessary but the majority may be mistaken, more or less willfully, in what it legislates. . . . Assuming that the Constitution is just and that we have accepted and plan to continue to accept its benefits, we then have both an obligation and a natural duty (and in any case the duty) to comply with what the majority enacts even though it may be unjust. In this way we become bound

---

10. The Declaration of Independence.

to follow unjust laws, not always, of course, but provided the injustice does not exceed certain limits."[11]

The moral duty to obey valid laws is expressed and explained in somewhat different ways.

The purely legal tradition is that each person is bound by ties of allegiance to the sovereignty of a nation, to its laws and to its social code, by the fact of residence or citizenship. Allegiance, the lawbooks have said for centuries, is the reciprocal of the protection each person receives through living in an organized community.

The nature of a citizen's adherence to the social contract of a free society is expounded as a matter of consent by Plato in the *Crito*.

The most famous and most influential denial of Socrates' argument is that of Thoreau. His essay "Civil Disobedience" and his "Speech in Defense of John Brown" assert the theory that a citizen of superior virtue—the rare man of conscience, a member of the "wise minority," in Thoreau's phrase—has the right and indeed is under a duty to disobey valid laws—like tax laws—when his conscience, and his conscience alone, tells him that important policies of the society are wrong.

The *Crito* presents Socrates on his last day. Crito had come at dawn, to offer Socrates a chance to escape so that he could live safely in exile. In answering his friend's urging that he should leave prison, despite the decision against him under the laws of Athens—a decision he regarded as erroneous and unjust—Socrates speaks for the laws, in declaring man's ultimate duty to obey the decisions of a reasonable legal system he has voluntarily accepted, when he has failed to convince the authorities of law that they are wrong.

Since the literature of the subject contains little beyond a few grace notes that are not dealt with in these essays, I can summarize the debate by presenting an imaginary dialogue between Socrates and Thoreau.

> SOCRATES In leaving the prison against the will of the Athenians, do I not wrong those whom I ought least to wrong? Do I not desert the principle that we are never intentionally to do wrong, and that injustice is always an evil and dishonor to him who acts unjustly?

11. THEORY, *supra* note 8 at 245.

THOREAU   But the mass of men serve the state not as
           men mainly, but as machines, with their
           bodies. In most cases there is no free exer-
           cise whatever of the judgment or of the moral
           sense; but they put themselves on a level
           with wood and earth and stones. Such com-
           mand no more respect than men of straw or
           a lump of dirt. They have the same sort of
           worth only as horses or dogs. When power is
           in the hands of the people, a majority con-
           tinues to rule not because they are most
           likely to be in the right, nor because this
           seems fairest to the minority, but because
           they are physically the strongest. Can there
           not be a government in which majorities do
           not virtually decide right and wrong, but
           conscience?

SOCRATES   Suppose I do play truant, and the laws and
           government come to interrogate me. "Tell
           us, Socrates," they say, "what are you about?
           Are you going by an act of yours to over-
           turn us—the laws, and the whole state so far
           as in you lies? Do you imagine that a state
           can subsist and not be overthrown, in which
           the decisions of law have no power, but are
           set aside and trampled upon by individuals?"

THOREAU   In fact, I quietly declare war with the state,
           after my fashion, though I will still make
           what use and get what advantage of her I
           can. The authority of government, even such
           as I am willing to submit to, is still an im-
           pure one: To be strictly just, it must have
           the sanction and consent of the governed. It
           can have no pure right over my person and
           property but what I concede it. I please my-
           self with imagining a state at last which
           would not think it inconsistent with its own
           repose if a few were to live aloof from it, not
           meddling with it nor embraced by it.

SOCRATES   "And was that our agreement with you?" the
           laws would answer, "or were you to abide by
           the sentence of the state? For, having brought
           you into the world and nurtured and educated .

you, and given you and every other citizen a share in every good which we have to give, we further proclaim to any Athenian, by the liberty which we allow him, that if he does not like us when he has become of age and has seen the ways of the city, and made our acquaintance, he may go where he pleases and take his goods with him. But he who has experience of the manner in which we order justice and administer the state, and still remains, has entered into an implied contract that he will do as we command him. And he who disobeys us is, as we maintain, wrong, because he has made an agreement with us that he will duly obey our commands; and he neither obeys them nor convinces us that our commands are unjust, and we do not rudely impose them, but give him the alternative of obeying or convincing us; that is what we offer, and he does neither."

THOREAU   But there are nine hundred and ninety-nine patrons of virtue to one virtuous man. All voting is a sort of gaming, like checkers or backgammon, with a slight moral tinge to it, a playing with right and wrong. A wise man will not leave the right to the mercy of chance nor wish it to prevail through the power of the majority. There is little virtue in the action of masses of men. Any man more right than his neighbors constitutes a majority of one already. Why is the government not more apt to anticipate and provide for reform? Why does it not cherish its wise minority? It is not a man's duty as a matter of course to devote himself to the eradication of even the most enormous wrong; but it is his duty at least to wash his hands of it.

SOCRATES   But I of all men have acknowledged the agreement, made at leisure, not in haste or under any compulsion or deception. If I flee, the laws will say, "Consider, Socrates, that if you do escape you will be doing us

	an injury. You would be breaking the covenants and agreements which you have made with us, and wronging those whom you ought least of all to wrong, that is to say, yourself, your friends, your country, and us, the laws, whom you would be doing your best to destroy."
THOREAU	Any man knows when he is justified, and all the wits in the world cannot enlighten him on that point. The murderer always knows he is justly punished; but when a government takes the life of a man without the consent of his conscience, it is an audacious government, and is taking a step toward its own dissolution.
SOCRATES	Who would care about a state which has no laws?

Professor Rawls, who approaches this subject very much as I do, would however, justify narrowly limited forms of civil disobedience "in a reasonably just (though of course not perfectly just) democratic regime"[12] when they are entirely peaceful; when the actors fully accept the rightness of their punishment; when acts of disobedience are limited to dissent on fundamental questions of internal policy, and especially to "the liberties of equal citizenship"; and when they consist of political action which addresses "the sense of justice of the majority in order to urge reconsideration of the measures protested and to warn that, in the sincere opinion of the dissenters, the conditions of social cooperation are not being honored."[13]

In Professor Rawls's sense of the term, civil disobedience is "disobedience to law within the limits of fidelity to law"—that is, disobedience as a means of appealing to the majority, or to the courts, in the name of the sense of justice of the community as a whole.

I have one fundamental difficulty with Professor Rawls's definition. How are we to determine whether the "firm" and "sincere" minority

12. *Id*. at 240.
13. *Id*. at 246–47. Although Professor Rawls's book is carefully called A THEORY OF JUSTICE, he repeatedly assumes that his own views on justice— egalitarian, democratic, and humane as they are—constitute in fact the moral code of the American community as a whole. See, e.g., 363–77.

is right in its view that the measures adopted by the majority violate
the sense of justice of the community as a whole? Presumably, the
majority has already decided the contrary. It has not as yet been
persuaded by the arguments of the minority. Professor Rawls seeks
to distinguish the grounds for civil disobedience he would have
society respect from purely individual views of social justice, or
views based on considerations of interest. I can find no substance
in his distinction.

I can understand the difference between the opinions of an individual about the morality and justice of a given measure, and the
view of it that would be taken under the code of morality of society
as a whole, as applied and interpreted by mass public opinion, by
elections, by the President, by governors, by legislatures, by customary procedures of bargaining and informal adjustment, by courts,
and ultimately by twelve men in a jury box. I can also understand
that the dissenting individual would claim—with complete sincerity
—that he was interpreting the community's sense of justice more
correctly than the majority. Indeed, I often reach such conclusions
myself about particular laws, policies, and judicial decisions. But
if the majority does not come to agree, how can Professor Rawls's
distinction justify civil disobedience in the one case, where the
minority appeals to the community's sense of justice, but not in the
other, where dissent rests on explicitly individual ethical views?
Aren't the minority views quite as "individual" in the one case as
in the other? I can find no halfway house, or Third Thing, between
the two concepts. I conclude that while Professor Rawls would not
allow civil disobedience to go as far as Thoreau, he would, like
Thoreau, condone civil disobedience when the individual, and the
individual alone, firmly, earnestly, and sincerely decides that he
is right, and the majority wrong, in interpreting the community's
sense of justice. Such arguments confuse "is" and "ought"—that
is, they confuse the law (and morality)-that-is at any time with the
law (and morality) an individual thinks preferable.

Professor Wolff's admirably clear essay on obligation accepts
the social-contract theory of obligation, but only for a limited case
of no practical significance.[14] His argument merits careful examina-

14. E. V. Rostow, ed., Is Law Dead? 110 (1971). Professor Wolff's
paper in Is Law Dead? fairly summarizes his other writings on the subject. See
R. P. Wolff, ed., The Rule of Law (1971). Save in minor detail, Professor
Nozick's theory of obligation is identical with Professor Wolff's. Nozick,
supra note 2.

tion, for it is scrupulously put, and helps to define the philosophical difference between anarchism and all other theories of social life. And Professor Wolff's confession of doubt, at the end of his essay, highlights its moral and intellectual significance.

Wolff starts from a most particular premise. Using Rousseau's language, but not his analysis, Wolff says that when men submit to laws they have made themselves, they are "as free as before." Thus he would acknowledge a *moral* obligation to obey the law only for small communities where every citizen votes on all the laws, and a single negative defeats any measure. Even if the principle of majority rule is built into the social contract—as is surely the case for the United States—he argues that a free man who promises to obey the decisions of the majority forfeits his freedom, and his moral autonomy, exactly as if he had promised to obey "a king, or a priest, or a slave-master." He concludes therefore that in a representative democracy the citizen has no moral obligation to obey the law, although he may generally do so on grounds of convenience, prudence, and deference to the correlative interests and rights of his fellow citizens. For Wolff, the citizen is morally bound by a promise to obey a law only if he has himself formally voted for it, and, presumably, for each application of it as well. Then, but only then, does a moral obligation to obey the law flow from the promise of a morally autonomous man—a promise freely and directly given.

But should we—must we—accept Wolff's formula as the only valid test for determining when the citizen has a moral duty to obey the law?

Wolff starts with Kant's idea that the moral autonomy of the individual is both the end and the means of a just society. He agrees with Kant and Rousseau that a morally autonomous and responsible man ought to keep the promises he has made to those with whom he shares the benefits and burdens of social life. But tentatively, at least, he rejects Kant's view, and Rousseau's, that the idea of moral autonomy within a just society is compatible with the practice of representative government, based on the majority principle. Instead, he insists that the citizen who lives in an organized society retains his moral autonomy only if he is "as free as before": that is, as free as Robinson Crusoe.

I agree with Wolff that the citizen "loses" some freedom—as compared with Crusoe—by promising to obey majority decisions on matters which the society has committed by agreement to its government. I should go further. He would "lose" quite as much freedom, in Wolff's sense, in a society where every citizen had a veto over policies desired by a majority, even a large majority, of his fellows. I should suppose that the individual can never be as free as Crusoe in an organized society, however libertarian.

What follows?

Rousseau's metaphor is hardly a usable standard for so fundamental a discrimination. It is a romantic fancy dear to the vocabulary of the Enlightenment, and integral to the task of turning men's hearts from God to Nature's God. The notion of man living in a state of nature was a step toward liberation from theology, Reason's substitute for the Garden of Eden.

But for all its charm, this whimsy cannot provide a convincing ethical criterion by which to measure man's obligation to the laws he has helped to make.

In the first place, as Hobbes showed with devastating force, the state of nature is hardly an idyll, once there are two Robinson Crusoes trying to adjust to each other's freedom, but a brutish condition of war and chaos in which the individual can never live tranquilly, confident that his rights will be respected. Methods for adjusting competing claims of freedom and autonomy would be needed even in Wolff's ideal state of natural anarchy, in order to avoid dominance by one citizen over another. If the citizens of the anarchy agree upon an acceptable method for reconciling conflicting claims, and establish limits for conflict, so that one will not be able to indulge his autonomy at the expense of the autonomy of another, won't they be smuggling the social contract in at the back door, in the sequence of constitution-making which all the classic political philosophers described as the process of transition from the state of nature to commonwealth? And if they agree on a majority principle, or on judicial protection of individual rights, in order to assure each citizen an equal or an optimal degree of freedom, won't they necessarily cross the line Wolff has drawn so clearly?[15]

But these refinements of the concept of Robinson Crusoe's autonomy are the least important aspect of the problem.

---

15. These problems are examined in K. J. ARROW, SOCIAL CHOICE AND INDIVIDUAL VALUES (1951), esp. at 30 ff.; J. ROTHENBERG, THE MEASUREMENT OF SOCIAL WELFARE (1961), Ch. 13, and *Conditions for a Social Welfare Function,* 61 J. POLIT. ECON. 389 (1953); R. Wollheim, *A Paradox in the Theory of Democracy,* in P. LASLETT and W. G. RUNCIMAN, eds., PHILOSOPHY, POLITICS, AND SOCIETY, 2d ser., at 71 (1962); and in the papers of Professors Dyke and Riker in E. V. ROSTOW, ed., IS LAW DEAD? 134, 370 (1971).

By living in society, man is necessarily less free than if he were living in a state of nature. This is what Rousseau meant by his distinction between "natural" and "civil" liberty. One should qualify this comment by recalling that there are many freedoms, and other amenities, which can be enjoyed only in organized society, so that it is by no means obvious that the sum total of freedom and of moral autonomy is necessarily less in society than in the woods; in large societies than in small; in cities rather than in the provincial villages of the countryside. It is hard, after all, to exercise one's moral autonomy save in facing the dilemmas, and making the choices, which arise from the presence of others, each also seeking to use his freedom.

Living in society, men enact laws in order to make freedom and serenity possible for all, and to secure other ends as well: decency, amenity, and social justice, for example. Each society will differ, as I remarked earlier, in its aspirations with respect to the degree of freedom and serenity to be sought for the citizen, and in its conceptions of decency, amenity, and social justice as well. Assuring the individual the moral autonomy of Robinson Crusoe is not the only concern of society and its government which should be considered to have moral validity.

In this connection, the phrases of the American social contract are striking. The Declaration of Independence states the theme, with great but not exclusive stress on the protection of individual rights:

> We hold these Truths to be self-evident, that all Men are created equal, that they are endowed by their Creator with certain unalienable Rights, that among these are Life, Liberty, and the Pursuit of Happiness.—That to secure these Rights, Governments are instituted among Men . . .

The Constitution enlarges and qualifies the thesis:

> We the People of the United States, in Order to form a more perfect Union, establish Justice, insure domestic tranquility, provide for the common defence, promote the general Welfare, and secure the Blessings of Liberty to ourselves and our Posterity, do ordain and establish this Constitution . . .

·The real problem in judging the ethical quality of social arrangements is not whether they achieve for the citizen the degree of moral autonomy which Robinson Crusoe possessed. Such a test would be chimerical, to say the least. Society must fulfill many functions and accommodate many jarring claims. In human societies, individual freedom and moral autonomy cannot be viewed as absolutes, but as matters of more or less. Valid provisions made by the majority to provide for the common defense, for example, may well qualify individual freedom. A valid law establishing conscription surely reduces the citizen's liberty well below Crusoe's norm. It is not reasonable to judge the moral rightness of such accommodations by an absolute standard, however appealing.

Jefferson's standard—the standard of the American code of social justice—is drawn from two aspects of the idea of "consent." First, the individual has consented to the social compact: he has given his Platonic promise to obey the laws of the state where, as an adult, he has freely decided to stay. And, second, the society to whose code he has adhered is itself a society of consent.

The first meaning of the word "consent" in the previous paragraph would apply to the individual in any kind of society—tyrannical, oligarchic, or dictatorial—if he had freely accepted its rules, and the benefits of living under its institutions. This is H. L. A. Hart's theory of obligation, discussed earlier.[16] But "consent" in that sense is not enough to explain Jefferson's doctrine that the consent of the governed confers "just" powers on the government. Jefferson was talking about a particular kind of government, and a particular ideal for government—a vision of the enlightened republic as it emerged from the pages of Locke and Montesquieu, and the American experience. That ideal contemplated special arrangements to secure liberty—a wide dispersal of authority, and an independent judiciary to protect "the unalienable rights" of man, and to enforce other agreed limits on power against abuse by a transient majority. The citizen was free to come and go, with all his property. And, equally, he could participate actively in the public life of society, through rules and systems which assured its democratic equality, and minimized the risk of tyranny. Both aspects of the idea of "consent" are fundamental.

In the theory of American democracy, then, "consent" is more than a ritual acceptance of the social contract, done once in a lifetime. It is not, in Wolff's phrase, equivalent to accepting the rule of "a king, or a priest, or a slave-master." On the contrary, it is consent to the initiation of a process of continuous citizen involvement in government, through which the mandate of government is regularly

16. See p. 93 *supra*.

renewed from the only rightful source of its authority—the consent of the governed.

That theory, then, answers both the questions Sir Isaiah Berlin regards as fundamental to the definition of liberty: "By whom am I to be governed" and "How much am I to be governed?"[17] Other modern democracies differ from the United States somewhat in the way these two questions are answered. But all such differences among the societies of consent are within a narrow range on the spectrum. All provide for procedures of lawmaking by elected representatives of the people, and all assure the individual an extensive zone of privacy, and a degree of protection against coercion by the state or by private groups.

For Jefferson, for the ethical code of American society, for most philosophers of law and politics in the liberal tradition, and indeed for most philosophers in all but the anarchist tradition, the case for accepting the idea of majority rule as morally valid in this context—that is, as an appropriate foundation for the citizen's moral obligation to obey the law—has seemed persuasive. Must we reject it, as Professor Wolff contends, because it does not leave the citizen "as free as before"? I cannot. The moral autonomy of Robinson Crusoe does not strike me as an operational idea—a concept with sufficient content to be used as a norm. And, even in less poetic form, the moral autonomy of the individual is not a sufficient test for the purpose, standing alone.

Men seek many goals by working and living together in society. As Berlin says, "The extent of a man's or a people's liberty to choose to live as they desire must be weighed against the claims of many other values, of which equality, or justice, or happiness, or security, or public order are perhaps the most obvious examples. For this reason, it cannot be unlimited.[18] The theory of liberty on which the argument here is based accepts "the fact that human goals are many, not all of them commensurable, and in perpetual rivalry with one another."[19]

For me, the key question in judging the moral quality of a society—that is, in deciding whether its laws merit obedience—is how it reconciles these conflicts, whether under stress it genuinely remains

17. I. Berlin, Four Essays on Liberty xlvii (1969).
18. *Id*. at 170.
19. *Id* at 171.

a society of consent, with a powerful internal gyroscope capable of restoring its equilibrium and holding it to its course. To say that such questions are questions of degree, not matters of yea or nay, is not to deny the possibility of distinguishing between freedom in Denmark or Britain, for example, and freedom in the Soviet Union. Drawing the line is sometimes difficult, although it is easy in the case I mention. But making important judgments is generally difficult. I cannot believe it is wise to approach the task by trying to apply a single rule, even the magnificent standard of moral autonomy, at least as Professor Wolff has defined it.

Professor Dworkin also asserts that in a society of consent the citizen has the right to disobey valid law, or at least certain classes of valid law.[20] While Professor Dworkin's theory of obligation purports to differ from Professor Wolff's, on analysis it appears to be the same, although it is not nearly so lucid.

Professor Dworkin prefers to analyze these problems of right and obligation without reference to the idea of a social contract. I do not believe, however, that he has succeeded.

Professor Dworkin takes the institution of individual rights—the focus of his essay, as given—as a "practice," he says, not "a gift of God, or an ancient ritual, or a national sport." Without referring either to custom or to covenant, he then accepts, equally as given, the profession, put forward by those who would describe American society as generally but not perfectly moral, that our legal system recognizes certain basic human rights, and enforces them in behalf of the individual against the government. The existence of these rights, he says, is "in part" the basis of the claim of such men that the law deserves respect (and perhaps obedience as well), although Dworkin dissociates himself from their views.

Rights of this kind—rights like freedom of speech, equality, and due process—Dworkin says, can be considered "strong" when one has a right to do something—for example, to gamble—and it would be wrong for anyone to interfere without special grounds, even though he (and the community) thought the actor was morally wrong to gamble.

Both the legal system and the prevailing moral code of the United States claim to regard basic civil rights as "strong" in Dworkin's sense. Legally, we say that the government bears the burden of

20. Is Law Dead? *supra* note 15, at 168.

proof in justifying the constitutionality of legislation or executive action that affects civil liberties protected by the Bill of Rights, and that such legislation or executive action does not come before the courts with the advantage of a presumption of constitutionality. On the contrary, modern cases treat such laws as almost presumptively invalid. And morally, the pattern of our silences reveals the depth of ingrained habits of tolerance, and the vast patience of society with words and acts which arouse, offend, and disturb.

But Professor Dworkin says something more. I am not sure, however, after analyzing his writings on the subject, and discussing them with him at length, exactly what his next step means.

His argument follows this course: A citizen has a moral (and I believe he also means a legal) "right" to do an act even though the act is against the law, when he would have had the right to do the act, in Dworkin's "strong" sense, if it were not unlawful.

His text suggests two possible sources for such a right—Natural Law or the Social Contract. He speaks often of an individual "having" rights of this order, or of his "having" them except for, or despite, the contrary claim of a valid statute. This language must reflect an inarticulate Natural Law premise—that man is endowed with certain "unalienable rights" by his Creator, or by a code of pure reason, and not by the constitutional customs of his society, embodied in its social contract. On the other hand, Dworkin also calls the protection of individual rights against the state a "practice," not a gift from God—language indicating that he regards man's rights against the state, and the extent of their protection, as a particular attribute of a particular society: that is, as derived from the customs and embraced within the mores or the social contract of that particular society. This, I take it, is the import of what he means when he says that the source of the individual's right is the fact that the society professes to take rights seriously, and should be urged by concerned citizens to live up to that profession.

I should put the latter point in this way: in a secular society, the source of a citizen's civil rights can only be the social compact of his society, which assures the citizen that this or that class of rights, and his personal freedom generally, will be respected by society and the state, and protected by the courts even against legislation or executive action violating the contract. Indeed, I should go further and class the putative abolition of the Bill of Rights as so basic a change in the social contract as to alter the foundation of society.

"If a man believes he has a right to demonstrate," Dworkin writes, "then *he* must believe that it would be wrong for the government to stop him, with or without benefit of law. If *he is entitled to believe that,* then it is silly to speak of a duty to obey the law as such, or of a duty to accept the punishment that the state has no right to give" (emphasis added).

I made the same point, in the vocabulary of my own analysis, in urging that in American society constitutional test cases, and the conduct necessary to initiate them, should not be regarded as acts of civil disobedience, or breaches of the social contract.

But when, in Dworkin's analysis, is a man "entitled" to believe he had a right, for example, to demonstrate, despite a law or an interpretation of law that says his demonstration is a riot? Dworkin says the right survives "contrary legislation or adjudication." So the issue that emerges—and the issue on which Dworkin's case turns— is to define circumstances which "entitle" a man to believe that the government is wrong in trying to prevent him from demonstrating, even though the Supreme Court has said it is right to do so. Dworkin's answer is that the individual is sometimes "right" to reach this conclusion, sometimes "wrong," but that "usually" the government should not prosecute in such cases, even if the actor is "wrong," provided he does not use or incite violence. Dworkin does not take the view that even basic civil liberties are absolutes and can never be validly qualified by the assertion of other morally valid social interests. For example, Dworkin says that censorship may be morally and legally justified in wartime, and that the law of defamation is morally right, according to his own moral standards.

In terms of what standards, and what processes of reasoning, does Dworkin reach this conclusion, and treat it not as a matter of his own moral convictions, but as exemplifying the moral standards of society?

Taking rights seriously, he says, is important to any society which wishes to respect the dignity of the individual, and his moral autonomy, in Kant's sense. Dworkin does not comment on Kant's argument that in a society which does respect the moral autonomy of the citizen, the citizen has a moral duty to uphold the promises he has freely made, and to obey valid laws enacted by representatives he has chosen, under a procedure he has accepted. In the passage I have just quoted, however, to the effect that the right survives "contrary adjudication," Dworkin inferentially rejects Kant's reasoning, although he nowhere explains why.

The ultimate paradox of Professor Dworkin's paper is that he does not identify the source of the rights whose protection he is discussing, unless his reference to the enforcement of personal rights against the government as a "practice" is a clue. He offers a theory of rights (and, presumably, of obligations as well) which he says is an alternative to the social contract theories he regards as inadequate. But he never tells us directly what his alternative is, nor does he set out the propositions with which it is built.

Dworkin says we should take rights seriously, in his "strong" sense, for two reasons: (1) because we claim that taking rights seriously is a desirable feature of American mores, and one which some philosophers (but not Dworkin) believe to justify a general rule of obedience to law; and (2) because taking rights seriously respects the moral autonomy of man, a goal for government to which Dworkin himself attaches great importance, although he carefully points out that in his view it is not the sole legitimate goal for social action.

I can identify only two sources for moral principle: the code of morality of a given society at a given time; and the opinions of individuals who are more or less effectively detached from the attitudes of the society in which they live. Individual views may be put forward in the name of revelation; reason; instinct; prejudice; the good-faith opinion of reasonable men, or men of superior virtue; a vision of natural law and natural rights, existing above and apart from the code of social morality, but somehow manifest, at least to an elect; or one or another of the great philosophical traditions—idealism, utilitarianism, positivism, and so on.

Dworkin concludes that a citizen has a "right" to disobey a law, or at least a law which he thinks interferes with one of his "strong" rights against the government, even though he may be "wrong" in thinking that the law does in fact interfere with his "strong" right. For example, the citizen may regard the state as wrong in prosecuting him for rioting, because in his view he was doing no more than exercising his right of freedom of speech with a vigor that suited his own personality and life style, and the passion of his convictions. Although the citizen may be "wrong" in concluding that the state is "wrong" to prosecute him, Dworkin argues, the citizen still has a "right" we should regard as absolute to disobey the law, at least as long as he doesn't engage in violence, or much violence (or otherwise interfere with the personal rights of others), and as long as he is sincere. That is, to use a terminology I prefer, the citizen has a right to disobey a law, in Dworkin's view, even though the Supreme Court has declared it constitutional, as applied to him, because in the citizen's opinion the law violates a code of natural rights which is independent of the Constitution (or the social contract, or the code of social morality) shared by the society, and even though Dworkin believes that the citizen is wrong, and the Supreme Court right, in interpreting that code in the citizen's case. Dworkin would qualify the anarchist absolutism of this claim with a little mild utilitarianism. The disobedient person should not use violence, or disturb his fellow citizens "too much."

By what standard can we conclude that the citizen and Professor Dworkin are "right" or "wrong" in their respective judgments? Dworkin is clearly not applying standards which purport to be those of the code of social morality of the society; if he were doing that, he would have to be bound, though not persuaded, by the Supreme Court's conclusion that the citizen was not making a speech, but rioting. His criterion is thus necessarily a personal philosophical opinion, shared with many or a few, as the case may be, but not yet adopted by society as a principle governing its law—an opinion based on his own theory of reason, or natural rights, from which he deduces the proposition, several times repeated, that at least where rights against the state are concerned, a citizen has a "right" to decide for himself when disobedience to law is morally (and, I believe Dworkin means, legally) justified, even though for the moment the Supreme Court disagrees, and even though Dworkin himself believes the citizen to be wrong and the Supreme Court right.

Many of Dworkin's arguments on particular points seem more like appeals to the Supreme Court than reasoning that would justify an individual in ignoring the Court: passages of utilitarian analysis, tracing the impact of an act of disobedience on the freedom or sensibility of others, or on the level of obedience to law. Perhaps his assumption that man has a "duty" to obey the voice of his conscience is a clue to his position. At several points, he remarks that both the "liberal" and the "conservative" social-contract view of rights accept the notion that society should defer to the individual's "duty" to his conscience, even if it requires the individual to disobey the law. I can find no support for this statement in the literature to which Professor Dworkin refers.

On analysis, then, Professor Dworkin's position comes down to that of Wolff, Rawls, and Thoreau. Dworkin asserts another version of the anarchist philosophy: that the individual must be allowed to decide for himself which valid laws he will obey, and which he will disobey, provided he is led to his decision by sincere philosophical convictions, and not by greed, avarice, pride, envy, or aggressive impulses, or by motives even less worthy, in Professor Dworkin's code.

The objections to Dworkin's formulation of the anarchist thesis seem to me quite as weighty as those to the others. Like them, Dworkin confuses "is" and "ought" by assuming that his personal "ought" has been accepted as an operational rule of society.[21]

The American community, permeated by Jefferson's ideals, can never stress enough the need to respect the autonomy of the iconoclast, or do too much to protect freedom of thought from repression at the will of the majority.

But no society of consent could live according to Thoreau's principle, and no other society would care enough about the rights of a nonconformist to consider it. It would allow each man to decree himself elect—a claim at odds with the rule of equality which is the essence of democracy.

IV

The Implication of the Major Premise: The Case for Civil Disobedience Reviewed

If the premise I have just stated is accepted—and even Thoreau conceded its moral force, although he sought to carve out an exception to it for himself—then the arguments for civil disobedience fall into place.

---

21. Several political theorists prefer to derive the citizen's moral obligation to obey the law not from a putative contract, made at some real or imagined constituent assembly, and ratified by each individual thereafter at a ceremony of maturity—when he votes, or swears on oath, or decides not to emigrate—but from his moral assessment of the methods of social decision used by the society, and his acceptance of those methods. See, for example, BENN & PETERS, THE PRINCIPLES OF POLITICAL THOUGHT 385 ff. (1959). I can detect no difference between this formulation of the problem—that is, the moral consequences of individual adherence to a system, i.e., consent—and the one I have used here, nor do I believe it would lead to a different resolution of the problems which arise when the polity reaches decisions the individual believes to be wrong. The difficulty of allowing social decisions to be made in accordance with ideas which an individual considers to be the dictates of his conscience is examined by E. VAN DEN HAAG, *supra* note 2, at 30 ff., and by H. A. Bedau, *On Civil Disobedience,* 58 J. PHILOS. 653 (1961).

Manifestly, the example of Gandhi has no bearing on the moral problem of obedience to law in the United States. The laws of British India did not derive from the consent of the Indians. Gandhi's program of nonviolent resistance was planned and carried out as a device of disruption and revolution, an alternative to armed conflict. But it broke no contract voluntarily accepted by the people of India.

The philosophical point is confirmed by a comment Prime Minister Nehru once made to Ambassador J. R. Wiggins, when he was a journalist. At the time of their interview, Nehru was contending with the fast-to-death of a Jan Sangh leader in the Punjab. Nehru was protesting against this form of civil disobedience in a democracy. Wiggins observed that it was about the same kind of thing that he and Gandhi had done against British rule. Nehru said that this was so, but that the decisive and distinguishing difference was that he and Gandhi were dealing with an occupying power, and not with a self-governing country. To use civil disobedience against an occupying power, he explained, "was to act in behalf of the people; to use it in a self-governing society was to use it against the people, who themselves run the government."[22]

Arguments based on the experience of Nazi Germany stand on the same footing. Whatever obligation the German owed to his government in that period, it was hardly the proud duty of the citizen to the laws of Athens which Socrates proclaimed. Nazi Germany was a dictatorship sustained by terror. It did not even allow its citizens to leave. The state had no authority the citizen was bound to respect as legitimate.

Similarly, those among us who preach a right of civil disobedience or even of revolution often invoke the precedent of 1776. But the men of 1776 rested their case not on a universal right of revolution, but on the claim that the British government had broken its promises of local self-government made in the colonial charters. This act, they argued, breached the social contract between Britain and the American colonies, and left the colonies free.

Our tradition recognizes no general "right" of revolution. On the contrary, we rejected that claim on the battlefields of the Civil War. Like every other nation, the United States claims, possesses, and

22. Letter from Hon. J. R. Wiggins. F. A. Allen, *supra* note 2, discusses Gandhi's argument, and its position in India after independence, in an illuminating passage.

occasionally asserts an inherent right of self-defense against internal as well as external threats, a claim fully recognized as just by international law, and by the law of the Constitution. For a society of consent, there can be no claim of a "right" to revolt, unless and until the social compact itself is threatened by destruction.

Nor is the case for civil disobedience supported in any way by the experience of the civil rights movement and the philosophy of the Reverend Martin Luther King, Jr.

By far the larger and more significant part of the struggle for Negro equality was and is an invocation of law, and an appeal to it. The civil rights movement did not engage in civil disobedience to a significant extent, despite its rhetoric, but in campaigns to require the whites to obey the law of the Constitution. Conduct which made it possible to bring cases to test the constitutionality of state statutes or local ordinances cannot be considered breaches of the social contract, or acts of disobedience to law. They are, on the contrary, an exercise of one of the most precious legal privileges of the American social order —the right of any person in an appropriate case to appeal from the positive law to the standards of the Constitution. Such conduct is not an act of war against society, but one of faith in its moral code, and in the law which seeks to express and fulfill the aspirations of that code.[23]

A

Is the Negro Bound by the Social Contract?

There is, however, a more difficult problem in the relation of the Black citizen to the social compact of the United States.

For nearly a century after 1868, the Negro was effectively disenfranchised in the South, and subject to harsh discrimination in most parts of the United States. He still suffers almost everywhere from the burden of deeply established customs which handicap him in his quest for equality. Voting by Negroes has now been generally achieved, under the judicial decisions and statutes of the last twenty

---

23. See, among other papers on this aspect of the subject, C. L. Black's essay, *supra* note 2, and B. R. Curtis, 2 A Memoir of Benjamin Robbins Curtis, LL.D. 363–64 (1879). M. R. Kadish & S. H. Kadish, Discretion to Disobey (1973) argue in large part that this accepted feature of the American legal system justifies a somewhat broader zone of legally permissible civil disobedience.

five years—an immense victory for the Constitution over the long and often violent war of civil disobedience waged against it in the South. Other gains have been made. But no one can yet say that equality for the Black—even equality before the law—is as yet a reality. Socrates spoke of the laws of Athens as having given him "a share in every good which . . . [they] had to give." That statement could not come from a Black man in America, without sharp qualifications.

Does the burden of the past exempt the Negro from the obligations of the social compact?

This, I think, is the most difficult problem of social theory in American life, as it is the most onerous of our moral dilemmas.

Today the Negro helps, more and more genuinely, to make the laws.

We are living in the midst of a convulsive national effort to fulfill the promise of equality for the Black.

But no man can say with conviction that we have yet.come half, or quarter, of the way. It is true that error and the presence of injustice do not of themselves void the social compact. But when error and injustice become the rule, not the exception; when the democratic process itself is suspended; when minority rights and personal freedom are denied—then, surely, the society ceases to be one of consent; the social contract could be regarded as breached; and the power to wage war against society could be claimed as right.

I do not believe the Black American today is in this position, or believes himself to be. It is apparent that society, led by its system of law, is seeking to achieve and guarantee his equality. The resistance is great. Three hundred years of experience have crystallized customs and attitudes which are hard to change. The American people are not saints. Nor are they immune from the disease of group and racial hostility which plagues every nation on earth. But American society is trying, and trying now on a massive scale. Before that effort, can it be said that the social compact is a nullity so far as the American Negro is concerned?

I do not believe that the American Negro can or should be regarded as exempted from the obligation to obey constitutionally valid laws. Nor do I believe that the dark history of America's treatment of the Negro justifies violence or revolution by Black citizens. On the contrary, I should contend that the progress toward Black equality achieved in recent years is primarily the achievement of the law, and the sense of justice of the American community which gives content to the law. It is the achievement, too, of primarily peaceful methods of political and social action which have stirred the nation to rally to the law, and attack the inertia and resistance which have for so long tolerated disobedience to the law of the Fourteenth Amendment.[24]

The moral of that conclusion, for me, is that the entire American community should redouble its efforts, through public and through private action, to vindicate its pledge of equality for the Black. Nothing less could justify the conclusion I have just stated.

B

Are Students Bound by the Social Contract?

There are parallel contentions, though at a far less moving level, in the arguments about university rioting—that students have a right to disobey the rules of their colleges or universities, or to disrupt their operations, because they do not participate in their management. The argument has two heads—one, that no one below the legal voting age is bound to obey the laws, even under Jefferson's theory, because he has not "consented" to them; the second, that students are not bound by university rules because they do not help to make them.

I, for one, cannot find either contention persuasive.

As for the first argument, every society has customary rules recognizing the moment of adult responsibility. Those rules may be unjust to precocious children like John Stuart Mill. But rules on the subject are a necessity. There is, after all, an objective difference between children and adults, and society has to establish a general line between them for many purposes. It can hardly be said that the prevailing practice, based on custom and legislative judgment, is without visible basis in reason. Here, surely, is an area where the minority is bound to accept the moral rightness of the majority's right to decide, without necessarily agreeing with the decision itself. Those deemed children under such rules have always been regarded as members of the community, protected by its law, and bound by them as well. So were women, during the centuries without number before they were accepted legally as the equals of men.

The second contention—that students are not bound by university

---

24. Walzer reaches the same conclusion, *supra* note 2, in ch. 3, 46–73.

rules because they do not help make them—I find equally unpersuasive.

Colleges and universities are established as trusts, largely under state laws, to serve important public purposes—the advancement of knowledge, and the education of young men and women. These goals are fundamental to the quality of our culture as a civilization. And they are of legitimate concern to society as a whole, and not only to the university community.

Universities and colleges are generally organized in the autonomous, self-governing pattern of the university tradition, as it has been adapted to the experience of the United States. Like other professional specialized agencies in society—those charged with licensing doctors and lawyers, for example, or those entrusted with responsibility for the banking system—colleges and universities are governed by specialists, chosen largely on the basis of professional qualifications. Custom, and the courts, have recognized a considerable zone of academic freedom and autonomy, especially in recent years, and have protected universities more and more effectively from political interference, and from interference by private groups. But the authority of those who govern universities derives in a clear line from the laws under which the universities are organized, those of a state or of the nation, as the case may be.

While there is surely ground for reexamining such arrangements, and there will always be room for improving them, it can hardly be contended that the existing pattern of statutes and customs under which our institutions of higher learning are established lacks "legitimacy" in Jefferson's sense. The colleges and universities are institutions in which the community as a whole has vital interests. The laws under which they function have been passed by the state legislatures and by Congress—the institutions of society which exist to determine broad questions of public policy, especially in the field of education. Until those laws have been changed, the arrangements for the governance of our colleges and universities have democratic legitimacy.

Popular theories of "participatory democracy" would challenge this thesis. These doctrines urge that no social institutions can be truly "legitimate" unless all those affected by their functioning participate in making their rules.

The short answer to this contention, for the purposes of our problem here, is that no majority of the American people, in any state, or in the nation, has as yet adopted the theory of participatory democracy, or any variant of it, to replace or modify its general practice of representative democracy, or, in this case, to rewrite the statutes under which colleges and universities are administered. Without such a step there can be no claim that democratic principle requires, or perhaps even permits, the doctrine of participatory democracy to be applied as a rule for action, so long as we adhere to the principle of equality. The Constitution, Justice Holmes once said, does not embody "The Social Statics" of Herbert Spencer. One might add that it has not yet been extended to include the works of Herbert Marcuse.

Universities suffer the ailments of other institutions: bureaucracy, conservatism, timidity, and occasional failures of responsibility. Some university administrators are doubtless too weak to discharge their responsibilities for planning and initiating new ventures beyond the interests of particular schools or faculties, or for reinvigorating those which have fallen into decay. Others are too active and authoritative for the health and autonomy of their faculties.

But these are the normal problems of all organized social life. The shortcomings of a particular university at a particular moment of its history, however irritating, can hardly be put forward to justify illegal programs intended to destroy the university, or to bring about reform, or what claims to be reform, by methods of coercion rather than of democracy.

The experience of labor is sometimes invoked as a precedent in discussions of the crisis in the universities. Students are disturbed, it is contended, as workers were once disturbed—because they do not deal as equals with the faculties and administrators who fix their tasks. The normal American practice, and the basis of our labor law, is that workers bargain with their employers only about wages and working conditions. Problems of engineering, industrial method, or business policy are not submitted to the collective bargaining process. But in many colleges and universities students are seeking a voice not only in fixing the conditions under which they live and study—in dormitory rules, and the lighting of libraries—but in the curriculum appropriate to their training, in the establishment of the standards by which they are to be deemed qualified, and in the choice of those selected to instruct them. I can see no basis in labor experience to justify claims of a right to share in such professional decisions.

The difficulty with the labor analogy goes deeper. Students, after all, are men and women, or boys and girls, at an early stage of their training, seeking to acquire knowledge and skills through study under the guidance and direction of an expert faculty. In relation to their calling, they are much more like apprentices than experienced miners or steelworkers in a labor dispute.

It may be that the next few years will witness the spread and expansion of present practices of organized student participation in some aspects of university policymaking. Our university systems developed, after all, in a period when students were treated paternalistically as schoolboys, and subjected to rules which no longer correspond to the mores of the community.

This is not the occasion for me to express my views about the wisdom of such developments as a matter of educational policy. I happen to sympathize with formal and informal participation by students in the governance of universities, so long as such consultative participation does not dilute the responsibility of faculties and administrators. But I should say that I can find nothing in the idea of the social contract which in the United States requires government to be organized in accordance with the principles of representative democracy, to preclude laws which authorize the organization of specialized professional institutions under professional control. The Supreme Court and the Federal Reserve Board are not "illegitimate" because all those affected by their decisions do not participate directly in making them. Nor does democratic principle require candidates for degrees, or for the licensed professions, to share in setting the standards for their own training, or to participate in grading their own examinations. Such claims would deny the propriety of distinctions of function in the organization of society based on distinctions of training, ability, interest, and experience. The theory of democracy does not support such a claim.

C

Does the Citizen Have a Right to Disobey Laws Which Require Him to Perform Acts He Regards as Immoral?

The last two sections dealt with the claim that Blacks or students may not be bound by the laws or regulations in a society of consent because they do not participate fully in making them.

Now I should like to take up certain problems which arise when citizens who do participate in the making of laws claim a right to disobey some which they believe require them to perform acts contrary to their own religious or personal beliefs, or which they regard as otherwise immoral. This issue arises in a number of situations—in naturalization cases, for example, where the applicant for citizenship, who under the statute must prove his attachment to the principles of the Constitution, says that his religion, or his deepest moral convictions, make it impossible for him to engage in military service which requires him to kill another human being, except perhaps in a war he himself deems just. The same issue arises in another form in draft cases, and in the cases dealing with statutes that require schoolchildren whose parents are Jehovah's Witnesses to salute the flag.

It is inherent in the nature of the United States as a nation, and as a member of the society of nations, as well as in the war powers prescribed by the Constitution, that the national government has authority adequate to protect the nation's security. As the Supreme Court has remarked, the war powers of the national government authorize it not only to wage war, but to wage war successfully—to perform and to require whatever actions may in its judgment be necessary and proper to that end. Chief Justice Marshall said, "The wisdom and the discretion of Congress, their identity with the people, and the influence which their constituents possess at elections, are, in this, as in many other instances, . . . the sole restraints on which they have relied to secure them from its abuse."[25]

From the eighteenth-century beginnings of the republic, the military power of the United States has been used by the President on more than one hundred and thirty occasions and in a great variety of situations, from the Mediterranean to China, in small engagements and in large, pursuant to formal Congressional authorizations and without them, in situations which international law would classify as coming under the Law of War, and those which it would regard as hostilities in time of peace.[26] The Supreme Court decided early in its

25. Gibbons v. Ogden, 22 U.S. (9 Wheat) 1, 197 (1824).
26. This experience is reviewed in A. D. SOFAER, WAR, FOREIGN AFFAIRS AND CONSTITUTIONAL POWER: THE ORIGINS (1976); J. G. ROGERS, WORLD POLICING AND THE CONSTITUTION (1945); H. W. Jones, *The President, Congress and Foreign Relations*, 29 CALIF. L. REV. 565 (1941); C. Mathews, *The Constitutional Power of the President to Conclude International Agreements*, 64 YALE L.J. 345 (1955); R. H. HULL & J. C. NOVOGROD, LAW AND VIETNAM (1968); 2 R. A. FALK, ed., THE VIETNAM WAR AND INTERNATIONAL LAW

history that Congress's power to declare war was not exclusive, but that lesser hostilities could be authorized. Those decisions have governed constitutional doctrine and practice ever since. It has always been assumed, and often said, that Congress has the power to conscript men to serve in the armed forces in times of peace, of war, and of national emergency, when it decided that conscription was an appropriate means for carrying out national policy.

But the states and the Congress, and the colonies before them, have always excused from the military service those whose religious convictions oppose it. By the time of the Revolution, at least, the Quakers were a respected and accepted part of the national community. And our statutes on military service had deferred to their convictions, and to the convictions of other sects holding to pacifist principles. Chief Justice Hughes said in 1931:

> Much has been said of the paramount duty to the State, a duty to be recognized, it is urged, even though it conflicts with convictions of duty to God. Undoubtedly that duty to the State exists within the domain of power, for government may enforce obedience to laws regardless of scruples. When one's belief collides with the power of the State, the latter is supreme within its sphere and submission or punishment follows. But, in the forum of conscience, duty to a moral power higher than the State has always been maintained. The reservation of that supreme obligation, as a matter of principle, would unquestionably be made by many of our conscientious and law-abiding citizens. The essence of religion is belief in a relation to God involving duties superior to those arising from any human relation. . . .
>
> The battle for religious liberty has been fought and won with respect to religious beliefs and practices, which are not in conflict with good order, upon the very ground of the supremacy of conscience within its proper field. What that field is, under our system of government, presents in part a question of constitutional law and also, in part, one of legislative policy in avoiding unnecessary

---

(1969); J. N. Moore, *International Law and the United States Role in Vietnam: A Reply* 76 YALE L.J. 1051 (1967), and R. A. Falk, *International Law and the United States Role in Vietnam: A Response to Professor Moore,* 76 Yale L.J. 1095 (1967); J. N. MOORE, LAW AND THE INDO-CHINA WAR (1972); W. T. Reveley, *Presidential Warmaking: Constitutional Prerogative or Usurpation?* 55 VA. L. REG. 1243 (1969); Bas v. Tingy, 4 U.S. (4 Dallas) 37 (1800). My own views on these problems appear in *Great Cases Make Bad Law: The War Powers Act,* 50 TEXAS L. REV. 833 (1972); Review, 82 YALE L.J. 829 (1973).

clashes with the dictates of conscience. There is abundant room for enforcing the requisite authority of law as it is enacted and requires obedience, and for maintaining the conception of the supremacy of law as essential to orderly government, without demanding that either citizens or applicants for citizenship shall assume by oath an obligation to regard allegiance to God as subordinate to allegiance to civil power. The attempt to exact such a promise, and thus to bind one's conscience by the taking of oaths or the submission to tests, has been the cause of many deplorable conflicts. The Congress has sought to avoid such conflicts in this country by respecting our happy tradition. In no sphere of legislation has the intention to prevent such clashes been more conspicuous than in relation to the bearing of arms. [27]

The Supreme Court has ruled that the obligation to bear arms is a fundamental principle of the Constitution, and a fundamental duty of all who owe allegiance to the nation, citizen and noncitizen alike. The cases declare that the exemption of conscientious objectors from this obligation is an act of grace and prudence on the part of Congress, not a constitutional right[28]—a "happy tradition," in Chief Justice Hughes's phrase, intended to avoid deplorable and unnecessary conflicts. But the unvarying practice of our legislatures from the beginnings of our history establishes a pattern not readily altered, even if conscientious objection is deemed not to be a constitutional right. That history is a fact of significance in evaluating the character and quality of our social order, and its tolerance of individual diversity, in not requiring men to commit acts which violate their own religious convictions.

The statutes now permit the naturalization and the exemption from combat service under the draft of men whose conscientious objection to war derives from religious training and belief, if they accept the obligation to perform noncombat service when called upon to do so.

The legal literature, and cases now before the courts, raise fascinating questions, whose examination would divert this paper from its theme of obligation: whether Congress can conscript men to serve in the absence of a declaration of war, or a declaration of national emergency; whether the right of exemption from the military service

27. United States v. Macintosh, 283 U.S. 605, 633–34 (dissenting opinion) (1931).
28. Hamilton v. Regents of the University of California, 293 U.S. 245, 266 (concurring opinion of Cardozo, J.) (1934).

is constitutional or statutory in character; whether there are constitutional objections to the long-standing practice of Congress in confining the exemption to those whose scruples derive from religious training and belief; and whether men who objected to the campaign in Vietnam have a constitutional right to decline to serve when conscripted.[29]

These issues illustrate the depth and delicacy of the problem of accommodating two vital characteristics of our constitutional system —the undoubted capacity of the nation to use all means Congress and the President deem necessary and proper to protect its security and minimize the risk of nuclear war, and the equally undoubted policy of society to assure maximum freedom for individual autonomy.

The analysis from which this conclusion derives, however, does not go so far as to suggest, and far less to require, that the Constitution, or the fundamental principles which underlie it, be interpreted to reserve to the individual a right to decide whether he will fight in a war he may not approve, or refuse to pay taxes, as Justice Cardozo wrote, "in furtherance of a war, whether for attack or for defense, or in furtherance of any other end condemned by his conscience as irreligious or immoral. The right of private judgment has never yet been so exalted above the powers and the compulsion of the agencies of government. One who is a martyr to a principle—which may turn out in the end to be a delusion or an error—does not prove by his martyrdom that he has kept within the law."[30]

D

When the Individual Believes Valid Laws
Are Immoral or Unjust, Does He Have a
Legal or Moral Right to Employ Civil
Disobedience as a Tactic of Protest?

Related, but different, problems arise when the citizen—confronting a law or policy he regards as immoral—contemplates tactics of

---

29. See United States v. Sisson, 294 F. Supp. 511, 515, 520 (D. Mass., 1968), 297 F. Supp. 902 (D. Mass., 1969), appeal dismissed, 399 U.S. 267 (1970).

30. Hamilton v. Regents of the University of California, 293 U.S. 245, 268 (1934); Gillette v. United States, 401 U.S. 437 (1971).

opposition which go far beyond a simple refusal to obey the law as applied to himself. He has failed to persuade the majority that the law to which he objects is indeed unjust and immoral. Equally, he has failed to persuade the Supreme Court that it is unconstitutional. It may be, to recall Aristophanes' acid comment, that he has succeeded in persuading, but not in convincing, the majority.

What then? Under the circumstances, is he entitled to disobey the law as of right, and live by his own view? Is he entitled to go further, and seek to impose his views on the community not by the vigorous exercise of his constitutional rights of freedom of speech, of the press, and of peaceable assembly, but by tactics of demonstration and coercion which involve planned disobedience to valid laws, interference with the rights of others, and often violence as well? If so, by what authority? Unless one is willing to rely on Divine Revelation— and no society today can accept the idea—or on the anarchist principle, only two possible sources have been suggested for treating the individual's naked power to break the law as a right or privilege: variations on Thoreau's claim of special privilege for individuals of superior conscience, or of superior intellect or sensitivity; and variations on the utilitarian theme, that such conduct will, or may, or might, do more good than harm.

I shall examine some of the implications of Thoreau's thesis first.

As a matter of moral principle, as I remarked earlier, it is not compatible with the political ethics of democracy. No democratic society, and no other society based on the idea of equality, could recognize Thoreau's claim as valid, even for an aristocracy of conscience. No matter how sincerely we honor learning and wisdom, and the diversity of learned views, we have not yet made philosophers kings, nor are we likely to. If the just powers of government indeed derive from the consent of the governed, that consent can be measured and registered only in accordance with the principle of equality.

But, we have been told, the principle of the Nuremberg trials authorizes the citizen to disobey the commands of the state—and to undertake campaigns of wider civil disobedience as well—when his own conscience, and his own conscience alone, tells him that the state is wrong.

Such a claim betrays little knowledge of the Nuremberg proceedings, which I, for one, supported at the time, and would support again. Most of the cases conducted under the agreement which authorized the trials were directed to situations in which individuals accused of violating the Hague Convention and other accepted laws of war claimed as a defense that they were carrying out the orders of a superior officer.

In the first place, as I have pointed out, Nuremberg dealt with Germans under the control of a state in which authority was utterly divorced from consent.

Second, with respect to the defense of superior orders, our own Code of Military Justice gives full protection to the individual soldier who refuses to obey invalid orders—for example, if his superior should order him to kill or torture prisoners, or otherwise violate the laws of war. The Supreme Court established and applied the principle as long ago as 1800.

Finally, the Nuremberg trials examined the novel charge of waging aggressive warfare in violation of international law—that is, of the Kellogg-Briand Treaty. This charge was confined to a few persons in positions of high responsibility in the German government—those directly associated with the decision to wage aggressive war. It was not regarded as a charge universally available, nor yet as a universal solvent of individual responsibility.

There is therefore nothing in the jurisprudence of Nuremberg to support the claim by an American that he is morally or legally entitled to disregard valid law because he disagrees with it, or regards it as immoral, in accordance with his own creed or his own interpretation of the community's creed.[31]

Such reasoning does not, of course, fully answer the question posed when an individual living in a society of consent disagrees with the wisdom or morality of a course legally adopted by the society and supported by a majority of its citizens.

An issue of this kind arose for many of us when American citizens of Japanese descent were arrested, removed from the Pacific Coast, and interned during World War II, under procedures approved by Congress and the President, and later upheld as constitutional by the Supreme Court of the United States.

Were those who remained convinced, as I was, that the Japanese-American removal programs were immoral and unconstitutional,

---

31. W. V. O'Brien reaches the same general conclusions in his article *The Nuremberg Principles* in JAMES FINN, ed., A CONFLICT OF LOYALTIES: THE CASE FOR SELECTIVE CONSCIENTIOUS OBJECTION 140 (1968).

despite the reasoning of all three branches of the government,[32] entitled to express their views through violence, or by engaging in general acts of civil disobedience, or were they required, by the ethics of responsible democratic citizenship, to engage in reasoned efforts to persuade their fellow citizens to confess error and make amends?

If you will accept for the moment the hypothesis, which I believe to be correct, that the nation did violate its own standards of justice in removing citizens of Japanese descent from the West Coast during the war, I conclude that such an act, done immediately after Pearl Harbor, under the stress of war, was not a complete breach of the social contract, which would justify revolution, or tactics of violence which represent the same idea, but an error—a major error—which could be cured—and was cured—by the normal procedures of democratic law and politics.

In this instance, the Congress of the United States ultimately concluded that injustice had been done, and the Congress and the President sought to remedy the injustice through the payment of damages and the restoration of citizenship.

I conclude that similar considerations should govern the behavior of those who remain convinced, as many are, that the nation's course in Vietnam was illegal, immoral, and unwise.

This is not the occasion to examine the legal justification for our policies in Vietnam, either constitutionally or under international law.[33] I note, however, that our legal order provides peaceful procedures through which these issues can be tested, both in the courts and through the possible action of Congress in repudiating the SEATO treaty and repealing the Tonkin Gulf Resolution. The availability of such procedures for determining the legality of our policy in Vietnam distinguishes the problem fundamentally from that facing a German dissenter in Hitler's Reich. And the fact is, of course, that Congress finally acted to terminate our participation in the Vietnam War in 1973 and 1974.

---

32. E. V. Rostow, *The Japanese-American Cases—A Disaster,* 54 YALE L.J. 489 (1945), reprinted in THE SOVEREIGN PREROGATIVE 193 (1962).

33. My own views on the subject are summed up in LAW, POWER AND THE PURSUIT OF PEACE 60–67 (1968); PEACE IN THE BALANCE 154–74 (1972); Review, 82 YALE L.J. 829 (1973); and in *The Justness of the Peace,* 67 AM. J. INT. LAW: PROCEEDINGS AM. SOC'Y INT. LAW 263 (1973). For a discussion of the constitutional base for the war in Indochina, see the Appendix to this chapter, and pp. 287–91, *infra.*

Those who disagreed with the nation's policy in Vietnam had every right to employ all the methods of democratic political freedom to persuade their fellow citizens to accept their views. But, I should contend, they had no moral right to disrupt the draft; to interfere with the freedom of those who believed they were preaching national suicide; to break up universities or public meetings; to burn the files of draft boards; or to engage in other acts of violence and illegality.

The same issues arise, with far less color of right, when the ends sought in demonstrations are changes in university policies, or welfare policies, or policies with regard to the administration of educational systems. In the conflicts which have so profoundly disturbed and weakened our universities in recent years, for example, demonstrators have claimed a "right" to engage in tactics of disruption, the occupation of buildings, and even more extreme forms of coercion. They do not claim that the laws governing the organization of universities are unconstitutional. They undertake such tactics, and undertake to justify them, simply as means to persuade those who could not be persuaded otherwise to change policies about ROTC, university research programs, and the internal organization of universities, or to prevent audiences from hearing speakers whose views the demonstrators disapprove.

What is the possible source of such a right? Not the laws which establish the authority of university officials. Not the Constitution, which defines the rights of freedom of speech and of the press, and of peaceable assembly to petition for the redress of grievances. Not divine right, surely, or some impalpable right of man not articulated in the Constitution.

A number of suggestions have been made as to the legal or moral source from which the "right" to use such illegal tactics might be drawn.

Society should recognize the moral and legal propriety of such tactics, it is urged, when the violations of law are "minor" ones committed by men who are loyal to our own political and moral traditions, and who are sincerely convinced that in pursuing a particular policy the nation has not kept faith with the principles on which its legal and political system purports to rest.

But the law cannot and should not distinguish between the rights of protest of those who do and those who do not generally accept the rightness of our constitutional system. The history of attempts to condemn or to restrict the civil rights of those deemed "disloyal" or "un-American" is not a happy one, and I cannot believe it is wise or practicable for this purpose to distinguish between appeals to the conscience of the nation made by those who in their hearts are attached to the fundamental principles of the Constitution, and those who would gladly destroy it. The distinction is subjective. Ample and depressing experience attests to the difficulties of applying such a test. Our legal order has generally—and, in my view, rightly—addressed itself in large part to actions, and sought to avoid distinctions as to legal rights based on distinctions of attitude. Good men and bad men, anarchists and conservatives, men of all faiths and of no faith, are equally protected by the Constitution and its Bill of Rights, and equally bound by valid laws enacted through constitutional procedures. All are equally free to appeal to the conscience of the nation, and to its traditional values, whether their appeal is made in good faith or in bad.

This argument in behalf of men of good will echoes Thoreau's plea for the special privileges society should, he thought, be deemed to owe to an elect. It too is incompatible with the principle of equality under law, and unworkable and unsound in theory.

Three more general arguments have been put forward to justify illegal action, including some use of "minor" violence:

(1)   that violating laws, and some recourse to violence, should be regarded as a permissible way to dramatize a point of view, and gain access to newspapers and television that would otherwise have been difficult to obtain; an illegal and violent act, it is urged, can shock into a state of reflection some men who would not otherwise consider the problem;

(2)   that such tactics induce desirable changes in policies or institutions that might not have come, or come so soon, through democratic persuasion alone; and

(3)   that violence is sometimes "forced" on militants by the stubbornness and inactivity of those who direct legitimate institutions, and who have not been persuaded by arguments in which militants passionately believe.

These contentions all rest, in effect, on the thesis that the end does indeed justify the means, at least if the means are not "too" damaging.

Convinced of the rightness of their own views, men of this outlook claim the right to seek changes in society against the will of the majority through tactics of planned disobedience which sometimes include the use of force. Thus in 1972 a group of ministers in New York issued a statement which called for some violence if that was necessary to achieve what they regarded as justice for disadvantaged persons in our society.

But the failure to persuade a majority is hardly in itself evidence that the majority is wrong; nor is intensity of feeling sufficient proof that one is right.

I can find no justification in political philosophy, in law, or in morals for this thesis as the basis for social action in a society of consent. It is the argument which has been used to justify every tyranny in history. And it offends a principle of ethics confirmed by the experience of all men—that moral ends cannot justify the use of immoral means. Methods of civil war and of insurrection can be defended ethically in societies like that of Nazi Germany, or other tyrannies, where power rests on force alone; where the social compact of freedom has been breached, as in the America of 1776; or in situations where that compact is threatened with destruction by a coup d'état. But there is no ethical case for revolution in a working and effective democracy, however beset it may be with the difficult problems of social transition. In such societies, laws can be changed legitimately only by the deliberate processes of elections and of parliamentary action: by votes after hearings, reports, and debates, not by the shouts of mobs in stadiums—or on tennis courts. Recourse to illegal methods of political and social action can have the most corrosive effect on society, especially if they are employed by the well-educated and the well-established in the name of moral right. Violations of law by the leadership of a community have more impact on society than ordinary crime.

As for the thoughtless argument that tactics of violence and coercion have forced change at a more rapid pace than could have been achieved by persuasion alone, they recall the classic justification of fascism: that Mussolini made the trains run on time.

Furthermore, those who justify acts of disruption and coercion in the name of a utilitarian theory of civil disobedience have no way of knowing, or predicting, that their behavior has a reasonable chance of achieving more good than harm. By acting on their own decision, without the backing of any majority, they necessarily function not as rational utilitarians, but on impulse and instinct. They cannot find a ground for denying the same privilege to others who feel quite as strongly about the rightness of their views. Thus they degrade the quality of public discourse, from which public opinion flows, for they necessarily reduce the level of rationality, and increase the level of passion and violence, in the process of making decisions of social policy.

The arguments used to justify illegality as a political tactic in contemporary controversies parallel those employed in the worst and most prolonged experience of the nation with civil disobedience: the resistance of the South to the enforcement of the Fourteenth Amendment for nearly a century after 1868. It is worth returning to that experience once more, in connection with the debates over the use of civil disobedience addressed to Vietnam, the crisis of the universities, and the struggle to achieve full equality for Blacks in employment, education, and housing in the North.

The hardest task for law, always, is to achieve a change in custom. And the most difficult task our society has ever undertaken is the enforcement of the Fourteenth Amendment. There is always some difference between positive law and the living law of customary behavior. Sometimes the written law lags behind custom, as it does when laws become obsolete, like statutes proscribing contraception. Sometimes the law collides with custom and has to retreat—the case of Prohibition comes to mind. Often the law seeks to effect a change in custom. The Fourteenth Amendment is the most ambitious example of such an attempt in our history. Another is the field of labor relations, where, after years of frustration and of struggle, the law declared the right of workers to organize and bargain collectively.

The growth of the law normally reflects a complex process of interaction between behavior and the norms of law. The history of the law regarding the Negro in American life is the supreme instance of this process. Its rhythm was influenced by the persistent effort of dedicated and persuasive men, led in modern times by the Legal Defense Fund of the NAACP, and later by the Reverend Martin Luther King, Jr., as well, to persuade the law to fulfill its promise of equality for the Negro, and the slow and uneven response of the people to the urgings of the law.

I take the view that the long resistance of the South to the Fourteenth and Fifteenth Amendments was morally wrong, and I reject and repudiate the philosophy which sought to justify it as a program of civil disobedience backed by violence. As a matter of theory and of experience, I believe that the ideas represented by that campaign have no legitimate place in our national life, although, as I remarked earlier, their defenders can say, with some justice, that they "worked" pragmatically—that is, that they produced a state of policy which could not have been achieved by political means alone.

The same lesson, on a smaller but no less ominous scale, is illustrated in some of the recent experience of our universities.

In the university riots, no claim is made that illegality is undertaken to test the constitutionality of existing positive law. Nor are claims advanced that the enforcement of the law would require a man to do an act morally offensive to his religious convictions. In most cases, these episodes are not directly associated with the struggle for rights for Blacks.

They are simply controversies about ordinary issues of public policy—the status of ROTC training is an example—in which men claim a right to impose their own views by force, because those entrusted by law with the responsibility for decision do not agree; that is, they assert a right to raise themselves above the law and its democratic procedures by their own *ipse dixit* and by the strength of their conviction of the rightness of their cause.

It is of course also true that motives other than a deep interest in the issues animate many who have organized the riots and confrontations of recent years in the universities. Some of the most active precipitators of these events are in fact revolutionaries of one sect or another. Sometimes student demonstrations have the quality of exciting student pranks, undertaken as sport, or of collective hysteria, contagious and mysterious, spreading like a frenzy around the world. Often they become more sinister, involving coercion by storm troopers, interferences with the rights of others, and procedures which resemble those of People's Courts. And it is generally forgotten that intermittent rioting, sometimes serious rioting, has been a feature of university life for many centuries. One difference between the past and the present, of course, is that a much large fraction of our youth now attends universities.

The turbulent demonstrations of recent years at many of our universities, and the cults and fads associated with them, are viewed differently by different members of the university communities. And these differences have wounded and divided faculties, and student bodies, in ways which have accomplished irreparable injury. Some professors find them appealing as revolutionary activities, or as manifestations of high spirits, and of a new and vital life-style. For others, the movement is a new name—fascism—for the ancient social disease of tyranny. They oppose the practice of riot as morally wrong and socially destructive. They deplore the anti-intellectualism, and the contempt for rationality, found so often in university disturbances. They are convinced these events have lowered the quality of education and scholarship. And they can no longer respect—or often even talk to—colleagues who defend what the rioting students have done.

Exactly the same irreparable divisions occur among students. The condonation of tactics of disruption and riot has breached the sense of community and trust among students in ways which will forever color the influence of their educational experience in the lives of this student generation.

There is a fact often ignored in the background of the university riots. The primary responsibility for the preservation of order within a university, and for the enforcement of university rules, is vested in the universities themselves. During the period of the Vietnam war, the normal university sanctions of suspension or expulsion for breaches of the rules were not applied at most universities, save in the most extreme cases, because of the draft. The pattern has survived the end of the draft. Faculties and administrations are reluctant to expel or suspend students for many reasons, including fear of arousing protest. They never lose faith in the perfectability of men. There would be tragedy, too, in expelling any of the few Black students, whose presence represents such strenuous efforts and such high hopes. And closing the universities before the tactics of riot would be the greatest defeat of all for those whose trust and duty is education.

The result of this abdication of responsibility by the universities has been a license to riot, and a transfer of the burden of preserving order to the police. Because of the ancient tradition against having police on university grounds, which is regarded with feeling in all universities, although the rationale for the feeling has long since disappeared, this step is always disturbing. And in many recent instances it has proved disastrous.

Why have the police reacted so often to student rioters with considerable brutality, and sometimes with extreme brutality? It may well be that the motivating factors are deeper than imperfections of police training and discipline. In these cases, students and those associated with them have deliberately breached the prohibitions of the law against violent and coercive behavior. Often their defiance of law is accompanied by words and acts intended to provoke the police to violence in turn. The reaction of the police, all too often, is "If *they* can do it, why can't we?" In short, the violence of the students triggers the release of impulsive and instinctive aggression on the part of some policemen—their class feelings, their hostility, their resentment of what they regard as the privileged position of a spoiled and disturbingly radical group of different outlook, different values, and a different life-style. The effect of the invocation of violence by the students is thus to dissolve, for the moment at least, the network of restraints which the law has laboriously established to confine and contain universal impulsive forces of aggression and hostility, to guide and govern those forces, and to direct their outlet only through the agreed procedures of democracy for resolving social conflicts in peace.

In turn, well-meaning and moderate students often respond to the episode not by rallying to the law but to those who would destroy it. Thus they become accomplices.

These tragic consequences of illegality are among the factors which should be taken into account in evaluating the common attempts to justify such events on the ground that illegal and coercive tactics are more effective than legal ones in obtaining results the demonstrators regard as desirable.

As I have sought to show earlier, the argument does not withstand analysis as a moral justification for such conduct. It is no more than another version of the proposition that moral ends justify the use of immoral means. And even in the perspective of utilitarianism, it suffers from the vice that each man must make his own felicific calculus for society, and act on it, while conceding the same privilege to everyone else.

But I am also persuaded that, at least in our recent experience with the process of social reform, the claim is not correct.

The issue is important. A Socratic theory of the citizen's moral obligation to law, however devoutly believed, would not survive if the social order crumbled all around us. No society can expect the loyalty of obedience to law if it fails consistently to meet the challenge of changing ideals of social justice. And the pressure for change has never been more insistent within the American community.

The question to be examined therefore is whether the society, the economy, and the legal and political system we have inherited can be adapted to these pressures wisely and justly, in time, and in peace.

The answer to these questions is far from self-evident. Our loose and flexible social and political order is dominated by the principle of divided power as a bulwark against tyranny. As Justice Brandeis once remarked, an efficient government is not the primary goal of the Constitution. Its purpose, rather, is to maintain a state of tension within society, through the inevitable friction of its various parts, as the safest and most favorable setting for personal freedom. In that perspective, the Constitution has been an immense success. We have friction galore—between cities and states, between states and the nation, among the three branches of government at every level. No single center of power can possibly seize command. But no political machinery requires more of its votaries, or can be paralyzed more easily by determined and well-placed opposition.

This strong, slow, resilient, and deeply rooted political order, spun out of an eighteenth-century parchment by practical men in the heat of a thousand crises, now faces a difficult agenda of social action—equality for Blacks, rational government for our swollen cities, rethinking and renewed agreement on foreign policy, full employment without inflation, control of the welfare state, educational reform, address to the disaffection of some young people.

Hard as these problems of tangible policy are—and they are very difficult indeed—they impose less stress on those who must decide than the changes which are taking place in the climate of opinion. I find it hard to think of a period in our history when the prevailing outlook changed so quickly. Was the gap between 1850 and 1870, or between 1910 and 1920, as wide as the gap between President Eisenhower and President Nixon? I wonder.

Whether the pace of change in ideas is unusually rapid at this stage, it is surely rapid. Consider just one factor in the process, as an example. The experience of war has always been a prodigious catalyst of social change, and America has been at war, almost without relief, for more than thirty years. It is not surprising that ideas and taboos about dress, sex, language, and many other familiar habits have been transformed. The code of social justice has not been exempted from the storm. The notion of a minimal income as a legal right, for example, would have seemed a fantasy from the realm of science fiction to President Hoover, and even to his successor.

Nonetheless, during the last forty years we have lived through an immense and an immensely rapid change in the prevailing American code of social justice. A review of that experience is indispensable, I think, in considering whether our social order has the capacity to meet and master the new tides of change which are pressing in upon us now, in their appointed turn.

If the social revolutions of the last forty years are viewed in perspective, they appear as among the greatest historic achievements of our political system. The bitter years of depression and war, and the political leadership of President Roosevelt, galvanized the progressive impulses of American life into a moral and political force that transformed the nation. Later Presidents of both parties accepted the basic rightness of what had been accomplished, and built on it.

What have we done?

First of all, I should say, we have developed and accepted a theory and practice in economic planning which should guarantee society against great depressions, and hopefully against great inflations as well, even under the pressure of war. These methods are not much more than a quarter-century old. They are still crude and imperfect. They do not solve all economic and social problems, nor do they guarantee capitalist societies prosperity, growth, and stable prices without thought and effort. But they indubitably work. At a minimum, they have eliminated the specter of a Great Depression, like that of the thirties, from the expectations of man. And they have been supplemented by measures against fraud in finance, by special policies with regard to transportation, agriculture, power, and the provision of credit, which have helped (and sometimes hindered) the responsiveness of the economy to the stimuli of fiscal and monetary controls.

Secondly, we have undertaken other experiments in planning— not the detailed, overall fixing of employment and production quotas, but experiments in regional and urban planning, where again, through trial and error, we have confirmed the promise of such methods in enabling us to solve the problems generated by the prodigious movements of people which have so altered the life of the nation. Perhaps in this area we should state our hopes more modestly. The social costs of the free movement of our people— from rural areas to cities, from South to North, from East to West— are so enormous, and the human dislocations so deep, that perhaps we should be content not to "solve" these problems, or to "master" them, but simply to cope with them.

Third, in this generation the national government has assumed primary responsibility in education, in the provision of medical care, and in social welfare. These titanic steps are remaking the social order, and the universe of men's minds.

Fourth, in the area of law itself, the Supreme Court has led a far-reaching movement for law reform which has involved Congress, the bar associations, the state legislatures, and the political process as well. That movement has steadily gained in momentum, despite the opposition it has provoked. It has accomplished much, although, naturally, even more remains to be done. Our concepts of individual liberty have been broadened. Criminal law administration has been improved, and the use of the third degree reduced as a method of law enforcement. The guarantees of the Bill of Rights have never been more intensively enforced. Stirred by the Supreme Court, and those who brought cases before it, the nation was aroused at long last to insist on the enforcement of the Fourteenth and Fifteenth Amendments in behalf of the Negro.

Responding to the stresses of its experience with depression and war, the nation deeply altered its conception of social justice, through programs conceived in terms which confirmed and fulfilled its own aspirations, and carried out by judicial and parliamentary means. Violations played a minimal part in these events, and often a negative one. The most open act of political coercion of the entire period was President Roosevelt's court-packing plan. It failed. The Supreme Court emerged from that trial, as it has emerged from all its historic trials, stronger than ever as the guarantor of the Constitution. The great social legislation of the last forty years, from AAA, SEC, and social security to poverty, housing, and education, was not easily achieved, and it was often resisted. Its enactment, however, was the achievement of virile democratic politics, not the threats of armed mobs, or the equivalent. The agony of prolonged depression stirred the country not to massacre, or to suicidal violence, but to effective and constructive political action.

In the field of Negro rights, the civil rights movement brought about a profound and continuing process of change in custom and in outlook not, in the main, by using tactics of civil disobedience, but by a full use of lawful methods of peaceful assembly and of protest, and·above all by calling on the courts and the nation to enforce the Constitution against the civil disobedience of those who had resisted the law for a century. The nation responded positively to court decisions, and to peaceful and legal demonstrations against unconstitutional laws or practices. It was aroused to righteousness by the spectacle of men of law in the South, who had sworn to uphold the Constitution, using force to resist its command and the orders of United States courts.

But the response of the nation to the more recent riots and disorders in the ghettos of our cities has been troubled, and, on the whole, negative. Congressional appropriations for poverty and urban programs have been adversely affected by outbreaks of violence. People and business enterprise move away from the areas of violence, making the disease worse. Small tactical improvements may occur here and there, stirred by the threat of violence or disruption. But the strategic lesson, I believe, is clear. The social progress of the nation during the last forty years has been the achievement primarily of democratic law and politics, not of revolutionary methods. In the course of that titanic social effort, the violent and revolutionary resistance of a minority to the valid command of the nation was overcome, not by force, or by force alone, but by the repeated assertion of the nation's political will. Over and over again, the nation showed its distaste for tactics of violence and coercion, and its capacity to be stirred by the active but peaceful methods of its own politics.

It is often claimed, as a justification for violence as a political method, that in the struggle for labor's rights, illegal and sometimes violent tactics were justified in the end by their success in raising the status and rewards of labor, and bringing labor relations within the reach of law.

The transformation of labor law in the century before 1935, and the changed public attitude toward trade unions, was a process which surely included recourse to violence, illegal coercion, and other forms of illegality both by labor and by employers. A limited right to strike was recognized in some states toward the middle of the nineteenth century. And doubt was cast on yellow-dog contracts in the same period, or somewhat later. But the legal rights of labor were cloudy and uncertain. Judicial opinions were not followed up by statutory codes. Practice often failed to recognize even rights about which the courts were clear. And modern statutes did not begin to take shape much before the Clayton Act in 1914.

Under these circumstances, the struggle for labor's rights took place in large part without real guidance from the positive law. The more violent episodes in labor history—going well beyond what custom regarded as reasonable—were almost invariably counter-productive in immediate effect. Progress occurred when labor respected boundaries public opinion could accept. Often, labor made progress when it was the clear victim of violence or unfairness on the part of employers. And it lost ground when it resorted to tactics the public regarded as wrong.

The moral of labor history, I believe, is not that violence and disobedience to law on the part of labor were justified by the passage of the Wagner Act and the recognition of labor's rights, but that those goals were achieved in the main by political means, after violence and counterviolence had produced nothing but bitter exhaustion. In labor, as in civil rights, those who relied primarily on force and coercion lost in the end—the southern segregationists in the field of civil rights, and the anti-union employers in the field of labor.

This is not to suggest that all is well with our society, and that the social tensions we feel all about us are an illusion. Not at all. As in every other period of rapid progress in history, hope based on the experience of progress has generated a deep and urgent restlessness —a desire to press forward more rapidly still, for more progress. Explosive and even revolutionary impatience in societies, as many students of the phenomenon of revolution have remarked, usually develops not in situations of hopelessness, of poverty, and of hunger, but at times when social conditions are improving.

The agenda for social action in the United States is formidable. The process of change has generated its own momentum. Many institutions and arrangements have been left behind by the uneven pace of change in different sectors of society.

But nothing in our experience should lead us to suppose that the agenda is beyond the capacity of our social order. It surely is less formidable than the perspectives which faced us in 1930.

It is bracing to recall 1930. We were in the midst of a depression, which most of us regarded as a phenomenon of nature, beyond the reach of impious man. Economic orthodoxy—and even most economic heterodoxy—did not offer politicians the intellectual tools with which they could hope to devise a policy to end the Depression. And we lived in a constitutional universe which would have denied the government power to carry out a full employment policy, even if at that point we could have devised one.

As these words are written, in December 1976, it is obvious that we are in trouble again. The industrialized nations of the capitalist world are caught up in a series of problems which have triggered worldwide inflation and staggering balance of payments deficits. For three years, they have been mesmerized and paralyzed by the shock of events, and have done almost nothing to master them.

I venture to guess, however, that rationality will break through before long, and that policy will not be as feckless and as stupid as it was during the thirties. My basic reason for that conclusion is not the optimism of Candide, but the fact, vivid in everyone's memory, that inaction during the thirties accomplished nothing, but that some well-considered actions worked well.

V

Conclusion

I started by recalling the view that law was the necessary condition and predicate of individual liberty. That is a proposition which unites "liberals" and "conservatives"—that is, those who prefer somewhat more to somewhat less individual freedom from official restraint. Personal freedom within organized society is made possible, this view holds, only by law—that is, by the influence of generally accepted rules and principles which satisfy the sense of justice of the community and assure the capacity of the citizen to live and seek fulfillment without being afraid of his fellows or of the state.

I examined the case for civil disobedience against the background of the strenuous and difficult processes of social change through which we are living, and in the perspective of Jefferson's thesis that the just powers of government derive from the consent of the governed. I have tried to show that on analysis the case for recognizing a right of civil disobedience can rest on only two grounds, apart from the argument of anarchism: first, Thoreau's claim that an elite within the society is exempted from the moral sanction of majority rule, and that its members should therefore be allowed to decide for themselves which laws to obey and which to disobey; and second, that citizens are justified in conducting demonstrations which violate valid positive law in order to dramatize their cause, and to precipitate change which might not otherwise come about, or come about so soon.

Thoreau's argument denies the moral premise of democracy—that of equality among citizens as citizens.

The second set of arguments, popular at the moment, amounts to no more than the claim that it is right to seek moral ends through the use of immoral means. The arguments that are advanced to justify such claims are usually utilitarian in character—that a "little" violence, surely "not too much," might encourage those who govern us to mend their ways. But there can be no showing that such tactics do more good than harm. And there is a great deal of evidence that progress has come in the United States only when the community as a whole accepts both the rightness of the ends sought and the rightness of the means used to achieve them.

To accept civil disobedience as a right would make concord within society impossible. In times of stress, Thoreau's quiet war could hardly remain a limited war, confined to a few eccentrics at the fringes of society. Different groups would join him in claiming the right to dissociate themselves from society. Presumably they would be as convinced of their superior virtue as he was of his own. Competition in violence and in intimidation would become more open and more intense. The taboos with which democracy has sought to control and redirect our aggressive impulses would weaken. Despite our profound and nearly universal instinct to avoid such a course, we could all too easily find ourselves far beyond the accepted democratic limits of social conflict. As a people, we know the horror and cruelty of war among brothers, and we recoil from the idea.

Those among us who have pursued experiments in disorder during the late sixties and early seventies have discovered how easy it is to paralyze a society based on consent. Such societies are not police states. They are organized on the assumption that citizens normally obey the law. It has been intoxicating for young militants to realize that, for a moment, they can paralyze cities and institutions, and provoke situations of riot and siege. But they discover too that even the most tolerant and permissive societies do not submit to their own destruction. We are slow to anger, but hardly meek. Every government and every society has an inherent right to insist on obedience to its laws, to restore order, and to assure its own survival.

Thus the idea of treating a right of civil disobedience as an aspect of personal liberty under the Constitution is at war with the moral principles on which this civilization, and any liberal civilization, rests; and it is equally at war with the possibility of social peace and of personal liberty.

Individual liberty can be respected and protected only in a society based on a shared understanding as to the broad aspirations of the law. Social concord in this sense requires a general acceptance of the citizen's moral obligation to obey valid law. Respect for the agreed limits of social conflict is essential if men are to live in liberty, and not, in Hobbes's phrase, as wolves.

The social contract of the United States is an unusual one. The power of the majority is checked and restrained in many ways, not least through the Supreme Court, enforcing a written Constitution. Our notion is that freedom is a corollary of agreed restraints on freedom; that man cannot be free, especially in a democratic society, unless the state, and the majority, are not free, unless they can be compelled to respect rights which are "subject to no vote," in Justice Jackson's vivid phrase—rights essential to the dignity of man in a free society and to the vitality of its public life.

These rules and customs, which are the glory of our Constitution and of our national life, could be destroyed, leaving not a rack behind, if we fail to insist that the citizen owes duties to the law equal to those the law owes to him. Without deference to valid law, individual liberty would always be in peril. Equality would find itself at war with freedom. And a revolt of the masses could lead, here as elsewhere, to majoritarian tyranny in one or another of its modern forms. By another path, the ideas of egalitarian anarchy could lead to the same result, by dissolving organized society into its individual atoms, and inducing a war of all against all which could end only in the restoration of order by force.

Chief Justice Stone once said that the doctrine that men had a right to destroy valid and constitutional laws by tactics of planned disobedience was contrary to the most fundamental principles of the Constitution. The rule against systematic resort to the violation of law as a political tactic, he wrote, ranks in importance with "the principle of constitutional protection of civil rights and of life, liberty and property, and the principle of representative government" among the quintessential features of our social contract. "It is," he declared, "a principle of our Constitution that change in the organization of our government is to be effected by the orderly procedures ordained by the Constitution and not by force or fraud."[34]

---

34. Schneiderman v. United States, 320 U.S. 118, 181 (dissenting opinion) (1943). See also Illinois v. Allen, 397 U.S. 337 (1970): "The social compact has room for tolerance, patience, and restraint, but not for sabotage and violence." (Concurring opinion of Douglas, J., p. 356.)

In a society of consent, where democratic procedures of political action are open and functioning, the use of illegal means to achieve political ends cannot be justified, whether the ends sought be deemed major or minor, moral or political.

A prolongation of the tactics of riot, however, would have tragic consequences if fear comes to dominate the political atmosphere, and if policy turns to a reliance on repression rather than on social progress as the primary method of order. Repudiating the principle of majority rule, as Jefferson said long ago, can lead only to military despotism. Violence and counterviolence, sooner or later, generate forces that demand social peace, even at the price of personal liberty.

It could happen here. We cannot expect to be immune from the experience of all mankind if we defy the principle of democratic consent, which thus far has been the essence of our destiny, and of our freedom.

Appendix

The Constitution and the War in Indochina

While it is natural for Americans to claim that whatever they dislike intensely is also unconstitutional, the constitutional base for the war in Indochina is impregnable—far stronger than the base President Truman had in Korea. The argument takes this course: (1) While it is sometimes difficult to draw the boundary between the inherent powers of the President and those of Congress in the field of foreign affairs, there are no such difficulties when the President and the Congress act together. Then the nation speaks with one voice; (2) in Indochina, Congress and the President have acted together (although some members of Congress may regret their votes): the Presidency through the successive military and diplomatic decisions of four Presidents, Congress through SEATO, the Tonkin Gulf Resolution, and many appropriation and other statutes; (3) SEATO provides that in the event of aggression by means of armed attack against any of the parties of the treaty, or against any state or territory which the parties designate as subject to the protection of the treaty —that is, Laos, Cambodia, and South Vietnam—each party "agrees that it *will* in that event act to meet the common danger in accordance with its constitutional processes [my italics]." Correlative provisions deal with a variety of other facts or situations that could threaten "the inviolability or the integrity of the territory or the sovereignty or the political independence" of parties to the treaty, or states or territories under its protection; (4) what are the "constitutional processes" for an American decision to act under the SEATO treaty? In Korea, President Truman proceeded under the United Nations Charter—a treaty ratified by the United States—without the support of a specific Congressional resolution, whether in the form of a declaration of war or otherwise. In Vietnam, the actions of three Presidents under the treaty were ratified and reaffirmed by Congress in the Tonkin Gulf Resolution, as well as by statutes.

Many contend that no military action can or should be taken by the United States except pursuant to a formal declaration of war, invoking all the consequences of a state of war in international law. This popular view is entirely erroneous. Armed force has been used by the United States more than 130 times since 1789, only five times pursuant to a declaration of war. No declaration of war has been issued by any nation since 1945.

Perhaps the most clear-cut answer to the popular view that war in Vietnam is illegal (because no "declaration" of war has been issued) arose from President John Adams's "undeclared war" with France between 1798 and 1800. In that subtle and delicate affair, Congress authorized maritime hostilities, but did not declare war against France. The constitutional validity of this procedure came before the Supreme Court several times in prize cases. The Court said Congress was wise, and entirely within its powers, in not making France "our general enemy," but in authorizing limited war to re-inforce the complex American diplomacy which ultimately led to the Louisiana Purchase. Bas v. Tingy, 4 U.S. (4 Dall.) 37 (1800). The Congress which made these decisions, and the Supreme Court which approved them, were filled with men who had been deeply engaged in making the Constitution a few years before. Their decision —that a declaration of war is not the only means through which the Constitution authorizes the use of armed force abroad—has never been questioned or challenged. It has dominated the pattern of constitutional usage since 1800.

Five

The Lawyer and His Client

I

My topic is not nearly so erudite as those of some of the papers which have been presented as Morrison Lectures in the past. My thoughts in preparing this talk turned to a more mundane feature of the landscape described by the terms of the lecture. Those terms, you may recall, are as follows: "It is desired that the lectures deal with subjects relating to the advancement and development of our law as a system for the administration of justice, or which will deal with the subject of the professional ideals of the lawyer and of his duties to the public, and of the duties of the public with respect to the administration of justice." In seeking to satisfy the command of the trust, I thought it might be useful to consider some aspects of the relationship between the American lawyer and his client, and the way in which that relationship affects the professional ideals of the lawyer. The view we take of our duties and responsibilities as lawyers determines the social performance of the law. And it measures the possibility that our profession fulfill its ideals of professional and civic morality.

I should like to approach this theme in its social setting. The lawyer is an integral part of a legal system, including the courts and legislatures, the police and the penal institutions, the law schools and the professional organizations. That legal system is in turn part of a larger society—the whole panorama of habits and ideas, of organizations and arrangements which constitute the United States of America. All legal systems have certain common characteristics.

With minor revisions, this chapter is adapted from the Alexander F. Morrison Foundation Lecture delivered on September 28, 1961, at the Annual Meeting of the State Bar Association of California and published in 48 A.B.A. JOURNAL 25–30, 146–51 (1962). © 1962 by the American Bar Association.

They perform certain common functions. And their literatures show the influence, in a pattern of endless debate, of common ideas about the nature of law and its goals. Yet any particular legal system is the product of the particular social, moral, and intellectual experience which determines its shape and structure and fixes the limits of its capacity for change. It is easy to fall into error about the rules of a given legal system by viewing it too abstractly, and without reference to the social context—the whole universe of forces—which brought it into being, and to the functions it actually performs, and those we think it should perform.

No professional group exists, as Durkheim has said, without its own moral discipline, its own ethics.[1] Every man is a citizen, a member of a family, and usually a member also of a variety of social organisms and bodies, private and public, depending on his interests. A lawyer, like members of other specialized professional groups, is subject to the special ethical rules of his guild, which often present problems of conflict and accommodation with the ethical rules applicable to individuals and to families, and to those of citizenship generally.

> As professors, we have duties which are not those of merchants. Those of the industrialist are quite different from those of the soldier, those of the soldier from those of the priest, and so on. ... We might say in this connection that there are as many forms of morals as there are different callings, and since, in theory, each individual carries on only one calling, the result is that these different forms of morals apply to entirely different groups of individuals.
>
> These differences may even go so far as to present a clear contrast ... a real opposition. The scientist has the duty of developing his critical sense, of submitting his judgment to no authority other than reason; he must school himself to have an open mind. The priest or the soldier, in some respects, have a wholly different duty. Passive obedience, within prescribed limits, may for them be obligatory. It is the doctor's duty on occasion to lie, or not to tell the truth he knows. A man of the other professions has a contrary duty. Here, then we find within every society a plurality of morals that operate on parallel lines.[2]

One of the main functions of codes of professional ethics, Durk-

1. ÉMILE DURKHEIM, PROFESSIONAL ETHICS AND CIVIC MORALS 14–15 (Leçons de sociologie physique des moeurs et du droit; Am. ed. 1958).
2. *Id.* at 4–5.

heim says at a later point, is to reconcile these contrasts and conflicts between individual and group interests, and those of the community at large. In order for groups within a society to persist, he remarks, "each part must behave in a way that enables the whole to survive."[3] The moral discipline of the professional group, he adds, "is a code of rules that lays down for the individual what he should do so as not to damage collective interests and so as not to disorganize the society of which he forms a part."[4] We might add to Durkheim's exposition the more affirmative thought that the function of professional ethics in the life of the group is not merely to avoid damaging conflicts between the code of the group and that of society, but actively to further, through the work of the group, the fulfillment of goals approved by the society to which the professional group belongs.

It is the interplay between such groups within society and society as a whole, and, equally, the interplay between the individual member of the group and the group itself, which do much to fix the character of a given society. Adjustments of this order help to determine whether a society allows much or little freedom to the individual, whether group interests prevail in a feudal way, or whether general interests keep group interests in check, and give the individual member of the group a larger field for his own discretion and creativeness.[5]

II

With these cautions in mind, I should like to contrast the English and, more generally, the British view of the lawyer's relation to his client with that which prevails among us.

In his novel *John Caldigate,* Trollope describes the dilemma of a great barrister, Sir John Joram, to whom newly discovered evidence is brought after his client has been convicted of bigamy at the Assizes. Sir John's client had gone to Australia and made a fortune in gold. On returning to England, he married a most respectable lady. While in Australia, however, Trollope's rather susceptible hero had lived with a woman who now sought to blackmail him on the strength of the .claim that he had married her there. The evidence discovered after the trial indicated that the testimony and the principal exhibit

3. *Id.* at 14.
4. *Ibid.*
5. *Id.* at xxxix (intro. by Georges Davy).

which established the Australian marriage were fraudulent. Reluctantly sacrificing part of his holiday to the task, Sir John composed a document for the Home Secretary, who was charged with recommending clemency to the Crown; and the Minister sent the papers to the judge who had presided at the trial—a stern and impeccable judicial figure named Bramber. The barrister concluded his presentation with the these words: "As it is quite manifest that a certain amount of false and fraudulent circumstantial evidence has been brought into court by the witnesses who proved the alleged marriage, and as direct evidence has now come to hand on the other side which is very clear, and as far as we know trustworthy, I feel myself justified in demanding her Majesty's pardon for my client."[6]

Trollope's account of Mr. Justice Bramber's ordeal is a brilliant elucidation of the ways in which evidence is weighed, and evaluated, by a first-rate lawyer who is also a human being. The judge started by reacting strongly against the barrister's submission. As a matter of principle, he hated the reconsideration of cases after trial. And he hated even more the tone of the lawyer's document.

> He first read Sir John Joram's letter and declared to himself that it was unfit to have come from anyone calling himself a lawyer. There was an enthusiasm about it altogether beneath a great advocate—certainly beneath any forensic advocate employed otherwise than in addressing a jury. He, Judge Bramber, had never himself talked of "demanding" a verdict even from a jury. He had only endeavored to win it. But that a man who had been Attorney-General,—who had been the head of the bar—should thus write to a Secretary of State, was to him disgusting. To his thinking, a great lawyer, even a good lawyer, would be incapable of enthusiasm as to any case in which he was employed. The ignorant childish world outside would indulge in zeal and hot feelings,—but for an advocate to do so was to show that he was no lawyer,—that he was no better than the outside world. . . . It had been the jury's duty to find out whether that crime had been committed, and his duty to see that all due facilities were given to the jury. It had been Sir John Joram's duty to make out what best case he could for his client,—and then to rest contented.[7]

By way of comparison, let me recall an episode which illustrates quite a different attitude towards a lawyer's identification with his client, and his client's position. In the early 1950s, I was a member

6. Anthony Trollope, John Caldigate 513 (Oxford World's Classics, 1952).
7. *Id.* at 522–23.

of the Attorney General's National Committee to Study the Antitrust Laws. At an early stage in the life of the committee, the issue
arose as to how divergent or dissenting views were to be presented,
and whether members should have the privilege of identifying themselves by name with minority opinions in which they happened to
believe. In the course of an entirely amicable discussion of the problem with Judges Barnes, who was co-chairman of the committee, it
became apparent that there was a difference of opinion on the question, which represented a considerable problem in reality. By and
large, the academic members of the committee, for whom ideas are
the principal business of life, took it for granted that each member
of the committee should assume full personal responsibility for each
position taken in the report. For the members who were in practice,
however, the issue was not nearly so simple. Many felt that a rule
of anonymity would give them more professional and intellectual
freedom to support views of the law which they believed to be sound,
as students of the subject, than the principle of personal responsibility. As counsel for their clients, or as habitual counsel for plaintiffs or defendants in antitrust cases, they were in fact so identified
with views of the law they advanced in practice that they would have
been embarrassed, or even compromised, in their relations with clients and prospective clients by espousing a contrary view in public
as members of the committee. At the time, I found this attitude a
disturbing indication that practitioners were not in fact as independent as I thought they should be. I could not imagine a physician,
for example, or an engineer, being inhibited in writing an article for
a scientific journal because his professional opinions might not be
congenial to those of his patients or clients.

It became clear that the problem we faced was a genuine one, reflecting fundamental aspects of the lawyer's role and status in our
society, and that it was far beyond the jurisdiction of our committee
to resolve or alter. It was therefore agreed that each member would
be free to identify himself with minority views as he saw fit. In the
main, only the academic members of the committee availed themselves of the privilege, which to some seemed a duty as well.[8]

The same point emerged in another way when the committee's

8. United States Congress, House of Representatives (84th Cong., 1st Sess.,
1955), Judiciary Committee, Subcommittee No. 5, Hearings on Current
Antitrust Problems, Part III, Serial No. 3, 1865–1919, 1946–1948, 1954–1965;
Rostow, Report of the Attorney-General's Committee in Perspective, ANTI-
TRUST LAW SYMPOSIUM 64 (1956).

report was published. Some members of Congress sought to discredit the report on the ground that it was the product of a group dominated by lawyers for very large companies, who were presumed to be interested in eviscerating the antitrust laws, if not in abolishing them. This seemed to me an unfair attack on the professional integrity of the Committee's members, and I protested against it.

In this debate, I think, we see in microcosm an aspect of the life of our profession which is worth examination. We are all familiar with the fact that most lawyers today, even in smaller communities, are no longer detached professional gladiators of the bar, whose services, in court or out of it, are available to any litigant. The inevitability of specialization, and the decline in the relative importance of litigation in lawyer's work, have had their impact. And I suspect that the romantic vision of the old-fashioned barrister as a knight in shining armor, ready to try any lance offered to him, was never quite so true in the United States as we like to think. Even in Lincoln's time, in the fellowship of circuit riders to which we look back with nostalgia, there were railroad lawyers and those who fought the railroads, men who habitually wrote the best wills and those who didn't.

Whatever the actual position was a century ago, today, in every community I know anything about, we have not lawyers only, as a single homogeneous group, but a complex hierarchy of lawyers: plaintiffs' lawyers and defendants' lawyers; men who represent insurance companies and refuse all plaintiffs' cases, and those who live to prosecute tort claims. In the corporate field, lawyers who habitually defend stockholders' suits or antitrust cases often decline to bring them as counsel for plaintiffs, on grounds of professional policy. The problem is the same in many other fields—labor law, for example, or the handling of malpractice cases. The men who represent publishers in libel cases are sometimes unavailable to those who wish to initiate such suits. In a few areas—taxation, admiralty, and criminal law, for example—the link between the lawyer and his client's position is somewhat weaker, although even in criminal law it is hard to imagine some lawyers with a reputation for the defense becoming district attorneys.

This feature of our professional life has given rise to grave concern throughout our history, when lawyers hesitated to accept clients who were violently unpopular, or were involved in controversies which aroused strong hostile feelings. John Adams defending the British soldiers in Boston, William H. Seward establishing the de-

fense of insanity against a charge of murder, Clarence Darrow and
Arthur Garfield Hays in some of their adventures at the bar, Whitney
North Seymour in the *Herndon* case, and many like episodes are
part of our professional memory, and of our professional pride. But
the problem symbolized by these great moments persists, in the
difficulty the Bar has faced in recent years in providing counsel of
the highest professional standing in many controversies over civil
rights—those stemming from the enforcement of the Smith Act, for
example; those arising out of the loyalty-security programs of the
national and state governments; and the cycle of cases asserting the
right of Negroes under the Fourteenth Amendment.[9] Cases of this
order, where the legal process confronts an inflamed public opinion
and challenges social habits with deep roots, provide the ultimate
moral test of our profession and of the law. The troublesome questions such controversies present go beyond the issue of providing an
adequate defense for the legal rights of unpopular defendants. They
raise queries about the genuineness of our professional independence
—questions which touch and color every aspect of our professional
performance. Without independent lawyers, capable of asserting the
claims of the law in the courtroom without fear of reprisal, our legal
system cannot be true to itself, and cannot hope in the long run
to meet its basic social duties. Equally, in the less dramatic affairs of
the everyday world, the lawyer is not really a lawyer in advising a
client about a contract, a will, or a merger, unless he can freely insist
on the professional position he regards as right, in the accommodation of his client's interests to the law, even if the client doesn't like
it. In the delicate equilibrium between the lawyer's duty to his
client and his duty to the law, every device for protecting the lawyer's
professional integrity is worth careful consideration, for much is at
stake. The real problem, as I see it, is whether lawyers represent
the law as officers of the court, or whether they are no more than
paid agents for the interests and preconceptions of their regular and
expected clients.

9. See Leon Jaworski, *The Unpopular Cause,* 47 A.B.A.J. 714 (1961);
Charles H. Tuttle, *The Ethics of Advocacy,* 18 A.B.A.J. 849 (1932); American
Bar Association, Report of the Standing Committee on the Bill of Rights,
August 1961, 86 A.B.A. Rep. 474–93; Report of the Special Committee on
Individual Rights as Affected by National Security, 1953, 78 A.B.A. Rep.
304–8; Supplemental Report of the Special Committee on Individual Rights as
Affected by National Security, 1956, 81 A.B.A. Rep. 335–37.

III

The prevailing view in Britain provides a useful starting point for analysis.

It is of course commonplace that the profession of law in the United States is organized quite differently from the dual system of solicitors and barristers which flourishes in England, and that our bar, by and large, is less unified, less controlled, and far more loosely organized than the profession in Britain. It is equally commonplace that the history, atmosphere, and tradition of the English, Scots, and Irish bars have greatly influenced not only our past, but our present sense of what our calling is, and should be. The pugnacious independence of Coke and Erskine, like other features of the struggle for constitutional liberty in Britain, is as much a part of our bone and blood as of theirs. The image of the lawyer's duty which dominates our minds is a mosaic in which the wigged figures are almost as conspicuous as those in homespun and broadcloth.

The comparative method in law can teach us much, but it must be employed with discretion. No rule or practice from one system can be transferred bodily to another, without a careful exploration of its origins, functions, and position in the network of rules and habits constituting the legal system of which it is a living part. Indeed, it is a reasonable presumption that no such wholesale transfer can ever be safely accomplished.

In order to compare the Britsh and American rules about the lawyer's duty, we must consider why the profession has developed so differently in the two countries, despite their common beginnings.

We and the British are alike in our general views of the law, in our methods of trial and adjudication, in our stubborn notion that the law protects the individual not only against other persons, but against the state as well. Unlike many other peoples, both we and the British take an incurably sporting view of litigation, which generations of procedural reformers have been unable entirely to destroy, and we both cherish rules which give the underdog a fighting chance. Our judges, like theirs, are encouraged to write opinions in the form of personal essays, in an ancient fashion which lawyers trained in other traditions can never quite accept or understand. And both we and the British believe that an independent bar is as vital to the rule of law as an independent judiciary. It is our common conviction that the legal process, conducted by independent judges, will be incapable of resisting public or private tyranny unless the judges are aided in the course of trials, and in all other aspects of the work of the profession, by equally independent lawyers, who have been schooled to provide a fearless and intransigent inquiry into every relevant circumstance of the problem being dealt with. We take it for granted, in our trials of Soviet spies or Japanese generals, that the lawyers for the defense should press every factual and legal issue to the limits of proper advocacy, as the British do—for example, in the trials of Roger Casement or Lord Haw-Haw. We can appreciate the fundamental importance of that practice to the reality of our constitutional safeguards for the individual if we recall the recent trial of Francis Powers, the American U-2 pilot, in the Soviet Union. In that case, Powers's Russian lawyer, evidently a competent technician, did not raise what would seem to have been the most important legal issue available to his client—whether flights over the Soviet Union at 60,000 feet were to be regarded as trespasses within the municipal air space, like flights at 10,000 feet, or legitimate voyages in outer space, like the trips of Sputniks and similar spaceships.[10]

Despite the basic similarities of the law and the legal profession in Britain and the United States, there are fundamental differences as well. The formal distinction between barristers and solicitors is no longer known among us. Our barristers are often members of large firms, providing a variety of specialized services to their clients, and most of them do solicitor's work as well as practice alone, aided only by a few young lawyers. In the realm of business and governmental affairs, our lawyers normally play a far more active role in the formation of policy than their British counterparts. The work of British lawyers, save in the case of comparatively few solicitors, is limited to the more narrowly technical aspects of the lawyer's work. Many of the business policy services provided for corporate clients in this country by lawyers are supplied in England by accountants. We regard it as sound and desirable professional practice for a corporate lawyer to be continuously familiar with his client's business prob-

---

10. See L. Lipson, *The Gagarin and Powers Flights,* 17 Bull. Atomic Scientists 274 (1961); *Poland Pressing Curb on Lawyers,* New York *Times,* September 17, 1961, 1st sec. at 15, col. 1 (Report of criminal proceedings against lawyers for excessive ardor in defense of their clients in cases with political implications.)

lems, and to participate in the shaping of his policies. It is common in the United States for lawyers to be directors of their corporate clients, although the professional wisdom of the practice has been questioned. In England, a barrister who is a director of a company cannot accept a brief for that company, or advise or settle documents professionally for it, although solicitors may represent companies of which they are directors.[11]

More generally, the role of lawyers in our public and private affairs is far larger than that of the profession in Britain. In proportion to population, we have many more lawyers than the British, and we need them. We live under a constitution which frequently requires lawyers to advise, and judges to decide, on the boundaries of governmental power. We live in a federal system which has in modern times developed formidable habits of regulation, and generates legal problems unknown in Britain, so that with us major business transactions are almost never undertaken, and should not be undertaken, save on advice of counsel. These features of our public life have given the law, the courts, and the bar a set of functions and a place in the political process quite different from those which prevail in Britain. This atmosphere of special importance for the law has carried over from the public realm to those generally deemed more private. While the duties of counsel in criminal and civil trials are similar in the two countries, the other labors of the profession are quite different. And even in criminal cases the similarities may be misleading, since in Britain much of the work of prosecution for crime, and other representation of governmental interests, is handled by barristers briefed in individual cases rather than by full-time civil servants.

For the British, the ultimate guarantee of the independence of the bar in all its functions—the accepted symbol of its professional detachment—is the rule that a barrister is bound to accept any brief in the courts in which he professes to practice. Normally, but not in cases of great public moment, the barrister can refuse a brief only if the fee offered is not properly professional, in view of the length and difficulty of the case. Otherwise, he can decline a brief only under

---

11. W. W. BOULTON, CONDUCT AND ETIQUETTE AT THE BAR 25 (2d ed. 1957). The rule for solicitors is stated in SIR THOMAS LUND, A GUIDE TO THE PROFESSIONAL CONDUCT AND ETIQUETTE OF SOLICITORS 13, 32–33 (1960).

special circumstances of conflict of interest, embarrassment, and the like.[12]

This ancient rule, acknowledged in England by the sixteenth century, was recently discussed by Sir Hartley Shawcross, Q.C., M.P., as Chairman of the General Council of the Bar, in the following terms:

> I have recently heard it said, although I believe incorrectly said, that certain members of the Bar in one of Her Majesty's Colonies refused to accept a brief to defend an African, accused of offense of a quasi-political nature against public order. The suggestion is that those barristers made excuses and declined to act, their true reason being that they thought their popularity or reputation might be detrimentally affected by appearing for the defense in such a case. For the prosecution they might appear, but not for the defense.
>
> I believe this report is incorrect. I profoundly hope it is, for if it were true it would disclose a wholly deplorable departure from the great traditions of our law and one which, if substantiated, both the Attorney-General and the Bar Council, of which I happen to be Chairman, would have to deal with in the severest possible way.
>
> It remained true that among laymen on both sides of politics there were some foolish and short-sighted enough to think that a barrister might, and should pick and choose the case in which he was prepared to appear. Socialist lawyers had been thus subjected to bitter attack in Communist organs and by fellow travellers who did not like the subject matter of cases in which those lawyers had been briefed to appear or the politics of the clients who might have retained them.
>
> It would be well if those gentry remembered how the present rule—that a barrister must accept a brief on behalf of any client who wished to retain him to appear before any court in which he held himself out to practise—was finally established. It arose in 1792 over the prosecution of Tom Paine for publishing the second part of his Rights of Man. The great advocate, Erskine, who accepted the retainer to defend Paine, and was deprived of his Office as Attorney-General to the Prince of Wales for doing so, said—and said truly—in a famous speech: "From the moment that any advocate can be permitted to say that he will or will not

12. Boulton, *supra* note 11, at 4, 17, 24–31.

stand between the crown and the subject arraigned in Court where he daily sits to practise, from that moment the liberties of England are at an end."[13]

The idea was pungently stated by Mr. Justice Neville in 1913: "As it once was put to me, always remember that you are in the position of a cabman on the rank, bound to answer to the first hail."[14] The principle is alive in British practice, and is regarded there as an indispensable bulwark of personal liberty, and a vital protection for the integrity of the profession. Ingrained in the public mind, accepted by public opinion as the order of nature, this doctrine more than any other keeps lawyers in Britain at one remove from their clients, as a group apart, and makes it impossible to imagine a situation in that country in which lawyers are long identified with their clients' views, or criticized or penalized for providing them with professional services. I don't mean to suggest that lawyers in England are more popular than they are elsewhere, or that they are greatly loved. In England, as in every other country, the old suspicion persists, in Swift's famous words, that lawyers are men bred in the art of proving "that white is black and black is white, according as they are paid." But what I do mean is that in England, under the protection of the "cab rank" rule, the bar can perform its basic task of representation or counsel on a stiffly professional and independent footing, without the restrictive influence of reprisal or penalty, and without becoming permanently identified with the views or status of any one client or class of clients. The barrister is much more closely linked to the law and to the courts than to his clients.

The code of ethics of the American bar has never accepted the British rule in its full majesty, even in criminal cases. Canon 31 of the Canons of Professional Ethics adopted by the American Bar Association declares that "no lawyer is obliged to act either as adviser or advocate for every person who may wish to become his client. He has the right to decline employment." The canon stresses the lawyer's individual responsibility for accepting or declining requests for professional services. And it makes no reference, directly or indirectly, to the principle of the English rule as a factor the lawyer is to take into account in exercising his responsibility. It should be added, however, that the lawyer's oath, recommended by the American Bar

13. The Times (London), February 19, 1953, at 4, col. 3.
14. The Times (London), June 16, 1913, at 3, col. 1.

Association, and widely used, contains these words: "I will never reject, from any consideration personal to myself, the cause of the defenseless or oppressed." At least one authority has said that "where the English rule is obligation to accept except under special circumstances, the American rule is obligation not to refuse where special circumstances exist."[15]

Many circumstances have led to this development within the American legal profession. Professor Simeon E. Baldwin thought the unity of the bar in America, as contrasted with the divided profession in England, was a fundamental factor. The English barrister has no direct contact with his client; he is briefed by a solicitor, who can if he wishes refuse to accept a client or a case. The barrister confronts a brief backed by the solicitor's professional opinion that the matter is worth pursuing, and therefore to decline a brief is a breach of professional etiquette as well as of principle.[16] Beyond this distinction, I should suggest that the sustained responsibilities of many American lawyers for the policy problems of their clients, especially in business, labor, and government, would make the British rule unworkable, and probably undesirable among us, for the larger part of the profession. Responsibilities of this order, implicit in the political system of the United States, and the extraordinary importance of the legal element in the process of making policy decisions throughout our society, can best be discharged by counsel who are thoroughly familiar with the factual realities of their client's position, without losing their professional detachment and freedom of maneuver.

On the other hand, the American bar has long felt uneasy about its departure from the British rule. Many of our greatest men, especially among our trial lawyers, have sought to live by it.[17] We have tried to preserve the essential idea behind the British rule, and to achieve

15. E. S. Cox-Sinclair, *The Right to Retain an Advocate*, 29 L. MAGAZINE AND REV. 406, 411 (1904). See, however, J. F. Sutton, Jr., *Guidelines to Professional Responsibility*, 39 TEXAS L. REV. 391, 406–7 (1961).

16. Simeon E. Baldwin, *The New American Code of Legal Ethics*, 8 COLUM. L. REV. 541, 544–46 (1908).

17. Felix Frankfurter, *A Lawyer's Duty as to a Retainer in an Unpopular Cause*, 34 A.B.A.J. 22 (1948) (views of Arthur Hill of the Boston Bar, on his duty to accept representation in the Sacco-Venzetti case); 1 S. G. BROWN, THE WORKS OF RUFUS CHOATE, WITH A MEMOIR OF HIS LIFE 274, 282, 283 (1862). See J. W. HURST, THE GROWTH OF AMERICAN LAW—THE LAW MAKERS 366–75 (1950); H. F. Stone, *The Public Influence of the Bar*, 48 HARV. L. REV. 1, 4–12 (1934).

its goals by other means. Thus the bar has acknowledged, as a part of its uncodified tradition, the obligation "to see that all defendants, however unpopular, have the benefit of counsel for their defense."[18] For the bar, this rule is clearly implicit in the Sixth Amendment. Courts and bar associations pay deference to the principle, but it is still too often honored in the breach. We have as yet developed no mechanism to vindicate it, comparable in effectiveness to the British "cab rank" rule.

IV

A comparison of the professional position of the lawyer in Britain and the United States illuminates several problems which we should face, and solve, within the pattern of our own history. In defining those problems, we should accept the present functions of the lawyer in our complex society, and particularly those of the specialist in business and corporate law, as necessary and desirable. They represent a creative response to the special circumstances of American life. At its best, as Mr. Justice Brandeis once said, the role of the American corporation lawyer is an influence in the direction of professionalizing business.[19] At its worst, to recall Chief Justice Stone's warning, it is a factor tending to commercialize the profession of law.[20] We should acknowledge that both these comments represent aspects of reality. Starting with that premise, we must recognize that we have much to do—both individually and collectively—in developing the ethical code of our profession, and its sense of discipline, before we can claim that we are in fact meeting and discharging our fundamental duties to society.

Our weakness as a professional body is a corollary of our strength. The bar in the United States has undertaken, and in the main it has carried out well, a share in the process of making policy decisions

18. American Bar Association, Report of the Special Committee on Individual Rights as Affected by National Security, 1953, 78 A.B.A. Rep. 304, 305 (1953).

19. L. D. Brandeis, *The Opportunity in the Law,* 39 AM. L. REV. 555, 558 (1905), reprinted in BUSINESS—A PROFESSION 329–43 (1933). See also *The Living Law,* 10 ILL. L. REV. 461 (1916), reprinted in THE CURSE OF BIGNESS 316–26 (ed. O. K. Fraenkel 1934), and in BUSINESS—A PROFESSION 344–63.

20. H. F. Stone, *The Public Influence of the Bar,* 48 HARV. L. REV. 1, 7 (1934).

which has no real counterpart in Britain. But the pendulum has swung too far. In many instances, we have become so identified with our clients, so much a part of their daily lives, that we have lost a large part of our professional freedom and our professional standing, both in our own minds and in public opinion. Too many lawyers find themselves in situations of conflict between their professional convictions and their continuing connections with their clients. We all know many occasions, in business, in labor, and in government, comparable to the moment when President Franklin Roosevelt turned on a distinguished lawyer who held a high post in his first Administration and had just given him some unpalatable advice. In a state of considerable irritation the President said, "When I want to do something, I expect my lawyers to tell me how it can be done, and not why it can't be done." And, beyond the implications of this anecdote, somber as they are, it is apparent that lawyers exclusively involved in the affairs of one client, or one limited class of clients, have lost a large part of their freedom to represent the Tom Paines of this world. Such occasions do not arise often, and not all of us can expect to face tests of this order even once in a professional lifetime. But they do arise, and in the United States they arise more frequently than they do in Britain. When they come, they measure the difference between life and death.

If we aspire to fulfill the professional ideals which are the essence of our history, a series of steps are indicated in the interest of strengthening the professional independence of the bar, and of dramatizing that position in the consciousness of the American people. I hasten to add that I am talking about acts and deeds, and not about programs of public relations. The public sees the bar, and reaches conclusions about its performance, in thousands of everyday transactions. Those events properly have more weight in shaping its judgments than all the releases all the bar associations have ever issued. I do not minimize the importance of explaining the law, and the duties of the bar, to the wider public for many reasons. But we should be sure first that our house is in order, so that our programs of public education rest on reality and do not defeat their larger purpose by revealing inconsistencies between what we say and what the public sees. Such conflicts can only encourage cynicism about the law and the lawyers, and weaken the respectful public acceptance of law on which a society of consent must rest. They can also discourage the flow of some of our ablest and most idealistic young people to the law, and thus irrevocably weaken the profession in the long run.

Let me give a few examples of the kind of acts and deeds I have in mind, to illustrate what might be done to carry out a policy of fortifying the independence of the bar.

First, I suggest that lawyers reconsider their established habit in many types of cases of accepting only clients on one side of the battle —only plaintiffs or only defendants, as the case may be, only trade unions or only management in labor controversies, only stockholders or only directors in situations of corporate conflict. Nothing could be more offensive to Trollope's Judge Bramber than the idea of a lawyer so suffused with enthusiasm for a single class of clients that he would refuse briefs in behalf of their rivals. By breaching this destructive custom, a few resolute lawyers in every community could do much to restore the concept of the lawyer as primarily an officer of the court and an agent of wide public interests.

I recognize, of course, the claims of specialization, although I rather think they are overdone in many instances. It is after all more comfortable for all of us, and more conducive to a pleasant life, to specialize more and more narrowly. The leading lawyer of Connecticut, general counsel to large corporate interests, some years ago took on a political libel case in behalf of an artist accused of sympathy with communism, and did a masterly job in the spirit of Erskine. And several members of the Yale law faculty, rebelling at specialization, have done some roaming in recent years and found it an exhilarating experience. Our distinguished professor of taxation, for example, has taught constitutional law, and has been designated as appellate counsel by the Court of Appeals for the Second Circuit in several criminal cases involving problems under the Fourteenth Amendment. His status as a tax expert has not suffered in the event, and he has enjoyed the work, and the warm commendation of the court for jobs well done. Still, I acknowledge that it takes a great deal of time and experience to master some of our more complex bodies of law, and I recognize that many good patent lawyers might well be at sea in a will contest. But the legitimate claims of specialization, sympathetically considered, hardly require a lawyer to appear for a single kind of litigant within his field of specialization.

In this connection, our governmental agencies, national, state, and municipal, could do much to develop the professional independence of the bar by enlarging the practice of retaining outside counsel to represent them in a certain number of cases and negotiations. The procedure is well known in our history, and once was more familiar than it is today. Many of the most important cases handled by

Charles Evans Hughes, Henry L. Stimson, John Lord O'Brian, and others of an earlier generation were cases in which they represented public bodies, while chiefly engaged in private practice. I don't suggest that we consider adopting the British practice, or weakening the fulltime legal staffs of government agencies. Nor do I criticize in any sense the way in which government lawyers discharge their duties. But, from my own observation, I think governmental legal staffs would be stimulated by the occasional participation of distinguished outside lawyers in their counsels. And the effect of such a trend on the bar, and on its capacity to fulfill its public functions, should be genuinely constructive. Many more lawyers would gain the inestimable advantage of viewing the world in the perspective of governmental interests, an experience which invariably contributes much to their professional outlook. The pattern of professional life would be altered, as lawyers habitually represented both public bodies and private clients. The consequence of such experience should be, in many cases, the formation of more detached and more professional lawyers, primarily identified with the law rather than with the interests of any single class of clients. In my experience, such lawyers always provide their clients with better and more valuable services than lawyers so deeply absorbed in their clients' viewpoints that they fail to see the strength of the opposing case, and to meet it in time. I know that the conscious fostering of this practice would present problems, particularly in connection with conflict-of-interest statutes. I submit that the public advantages to be gained over the long run by reviving and extending the custom are well worth the effort.

Third, we should reexamine the practice of lawyers serving as directors of corporations, or officers of trade unions. Both Paul D. Cravath, head of the great New York firm which still bears his name, and Mr. Justice Brandeis took the view that lawyers should not serve as directors of corporations they represented professionally. "Long ago it was recognized," Justice Brandeis wrote, "that 'a man who is his own lawyer has a fool for a client.' The essential reason for this is that soundness of judgment is easily obscured by self-interest."[21] A corporation needs and should have lawyers, bankers, and other pro-

---

21. BRANDEIS, OTHER PEOPLE'S MONEY AND HOW THE BANKERS USE IT 198 (Norman Hapgood ed. 1932). The view is widely though not universally held. See for example, 2 ROBERT T. SWAINE, THE CRAVATH FIRM AND ITS PREDE-CESSORS,1819–1948, at 9–10 (1948). (With rare exceptions, members of the Cravath firm have not owned securities of a client, nor served as directors.) See also J. W. HURST, THE GROWTH OF AMERICAN LAW 368 (1950).

fessional advisers who give advice based on full knowledge. But it should be *outside* advice; such professional counsel should never represent a judgment upon the wisdom of counsel's own acts as part of management.[22] Can the general counsel of a corporation give truly professional advice to his client, taking into account the interests of stockholders and bondholders, if he is also a director, whose interests may conflict with those of other participants in the corporate process? In a union situation, counsel may find himself in a position of conflict with the rights of members, if he also takes on the responsibilities of being an officer or a member of an executive committee. Does the lawyer gain a professional advantage by being a director as well as general counsel of the corporation, or an officer as well as general counsel of a union? Would it be more consistent with a strictly professional view of his duties as lawyer to maintain the boundaries of his position with care and emphasis, in order to preserve his full freedom as a lawyer, and to avoid even a remote risk of conflicting interests?

I have suggested several practical areas where we might well take steps, individually, and as members of the organized bar, to carry out a policy of guiding the evolution of the bar along lines which should more effectively protect its independence and integrity, and deepen its sense of professional responsibility. Other actions to the same end will suggest themselves, if we pursue the policy as a major goal.

Action of this order is needed if our performance at every level is to match our professions, and if the bar is to remain capable of providing society with the great services to human liberty which are the burden and the promise of our heritage.

I am one of those who have expressed concern, over the years, about the future of the profession: both about its capacity to attract a fair share of our best young people to the study and practice of law, and about its ability to prevent an undue attrition of outstanding lawyers from the independent bar to business, banking, and other pursuits.[23] In this connection, there is high promise in the decision of the American Bar Association, at its August 1961 meeting in St. Louis, to approve the thoughtful recommendations of its Special Committee to Study Current Needs in the Field of Legal Education, under the chairmanship of Bethuel M. Webster, of New York. The

22. Brandeis, *supra* note 21 at pp. 198–199.
23. Annual Report of the Dean, Yale Law School, December 15, 1956, at 3.

program proposed by that committee should do much to help the law schools of the nation and to attract to the law a larger number of students of high professional promise. The activities which will develop, following the adoption of the Webster report, will be in vain, however, if the existence of a truly independent bar is threatened both by an excessive rate of withdrawal from the bar to other pursuits, and by trends within the bar which compromise its autonomy and its capacity to take independent action in time of stress. It is for this reason that I put so much emphasis on the fundamental importance of an ethical code, and a sense of professional discipline, which could confirm in fact our belief that lawyers should be a free guild within society, serving their clients best by serving the law first. A bar which lives by this rule, a bar which serves a variety of clients and enjoys a variety of experiences, will not have trouble in protecting itself against the risks of excessive attrition. And such a bar, visibly independent, should be able to do much more than we have been able to do thus far in those situations which most urgently challenge the legal process —the provision of counsel for the poor, and for unpopular litigants.

The provision of legal services to the poor, both in civil and in criminal matters, is in most communities of the nation scandalously inadequate. And for that failure we of the bar are primarily responsible. There are outstanding Legal Aid bureaus here and there, and some effective Public Defender programs. But their strength only highlights our general failure to meet a real social need. The poor man cheated of a few hundred dollars by his landlord or his finance company, the boy swept up by mistake in a police raid, suffer losses and indignities quite as important to them and to society as those incident to lapses of the law which touch larger interests. Here, as in other fields of social welfare, we may be sure that if private and professional organizations fail to act, government will sooner or later take the initiative.[24]

My final illustration is that which presents the simplest and most searching test of our legal system—protecting the constitutional rights of persons involved in controversies which stir great passions. Aroused feelings have been, and always will be a normal incident of

24. United States Congress, Senate Committee on the Judiciary, Subcommittee on Constitutional Rights, Legal Counsel for Indigent Defendants in Federal Courts (87th Cong., 1st Sess. 1961); Emery A. Brownell, *A Decade of Progress: Legal Aid and Defender Services,* 47 A.B.A.J. 867 (1961).

the cases in which the great constitutional guarantees of personal freedom are vindicated. Such rights are rarely challenged save under the pressure of difficult circumstances which stir strong and hostile feelings. It was precisely for this reason that the makers of our Constitution entrusted a major part of the task of enforcing it to the courts. They thoroughly understood both the capacity of the American people for political turbulence and their overriding respect for law. As Jefferson said, writing to Madison, "In the arguments in favor of a declaration of rights, you omit one which has great weight with me; the legal check which it puts in the hands of the judiciary. This is a body, which, if rendered independent and kept strictly to their own department, merits great confidence for their learning and integrity. In fact, what degree of confidence would be too much, for a body composed of such men as Wythe, Blair and Pendleton? On characters like these, the "civium ardor prava pubentium" would make no impression."[25]

Our history has confirmed Jefferson's insight. The development of judicial review as a check on the legality of official action has been one of the great achievements of our political system and one of the basic guarantees of democratic procedure among us. In that process, as Professor Hurst points out, an independent bar was an indispensable auxiliary of the independent judges. "The availability of an independent bar, supported by private retainer, bulwarked the courage of individuals and groups to put officials upon their proof and justification, provided more skill and knowledge than private persons typically could muster otherwise to meet the maneuvers of official power."[26]

Under the goad of circumstance, our law of civil rights has been developing rapidly for about thirty years—and developing, in the main, along lines which should fortify our pride. In the nature of the Cold War and of the transformations occurring in American society, we can expect conflicts over civil rights to persist, and perhaps to become more acute, unless the mediating influence of the law is made more effective by the wise and vigorous action of the courts, the legislatures, and the bar. It is prudent to anticipate at least as much

25. JEFFERSON, LIFE AND SELECTED WRITINGS 462 (Modern Library ed. 1944).
26. J. W. HURST, LAW AND SOCIAL PROCESS IN UNITED STATES HISTORY 324–25 (1960).

growth in the law of personal liberty during the next thirty years as has occurred since *DeJonge v. Oregon*[27] and *Powell v. Alabama,*[28] a generation ago.

Nowadays, controversies of this kind involve not only the propriety of prison sentences, but the legality of private and public actions which touch men's reputations; their rights of privacy; their political privileges; and their opportunities to study, to travel, to live where they choose, or to pursue callings of their choice. The patient, sober exploration of these novel and difficult problems, invariably touching acute sensibilities, will require even greater efforts of the bar than have been made in the past.

I have two areas of action by the bar particularly in mind: the defense of the courts against misguided and unwarranted public attack, and the establishment of arrangements which could assure the leadership of the bar itself, and of its ablest members, in the preparation and presentation of cases involving civil liberties.

On other occasions I have criticized the organized bar for its posture of general silence during the controversy over the Supreme Court in recent years, and I do not propose to repeat those criticisms now.[29] Suffice it to say that, with a few notable exceptions, the organized bar has left the federal judges almost alone in their lonely efforts to uphold the law. I do not believe that we have begun to meet our obligations, recited in the first Canon of Professional Ethics, to help maintain the capacity of the courts to discharge their supremely important functions in these stormy times. The canon includes this sentence: "Judges, not being wholly free to defend themselves, are peculiarly entitled to receive the support of the Bar against unjust criticism and clamor." There has been a great deal of clamor against the Supreme Court lately, and not nearly enough support from our professional organizations.

With regard to the provision of counsel in civil liberties cases, much remains to be done before we can claim that we are living up to

---

27. 299 U.S. 353 (1937).
28. 287 U.S. 45 (1932).
29. *American Legal Realism and the Sense of the Profession,* 34 Rocky Mountain L. Rev. 123 (1962), and *Education for a Society of Law,* in Man and Learning in Modern Society 17, at 25–27 (1959). See also A. J. Goldberg, *New Frontiers for Lawyers and the Law,* 45 J. Am. Jud. Soc. 56 (August 1961); R. E. McGill, *A View from a Tight Small Compartment,* 12 Harv. L. Sch. Bull., No. 6, at 6 (June 1961).

our responsibilities. The American Bar Association adopted an important resolution in 1953, on the recommendation of its Special Committee on Individual Rights as affected by national security. The heart of that resolution, for present purposes, is its second article:

II. Resolved,

1. That the American Bar Association reaffirms the principle that the right of defendants to the benefit of assistance of counsel and the duty of the bar to provide such aid even to the most unpopular defendants involves public acceptance of the correlative right of a lawyer to represent and defend, in accordance with the standards of the legal profession, any client without being penalized by having imputed to him his client's reputation, views or character.

2. That the Association will support any lawyer against criticism or attack in connection with such representation, when, in its judgment, he has behaved in accordance with the standards of the bar.

3. That the Association will continue to educate the profession and the public on the rights and duties of a lawyer in representing any client, regardless of the unpopularity of either the client or his cause.

4. That the Association requires all state and local associations to cooperate fully in implementing these declarations of principles.[30]

Thus far, in many communities, the resolution remains an aspiration at best. In its 1961 report, the American Bar Association's Standing Committee on the Bill of Rights noted a number of situations in different parts of the country where the constitutional right to the assistance of counsel was "restricted or violated." The report commented in the following terms:

Complaints have come from different areas where accused persons have been deprived of right to counsel because of the refusal of members of the bar to represent discredited defendants or become involved in unpopular cases.

Throughout the year, and particularly in recent weeks, instances have been reported to the Committee of the fact that persons

30. American Bar Association, Proceedings of the House of Delegates, 1953, 78 A.B.A. REP. 133.

under criminal charges in certain sections of the South have been deprived of their right to effective counsel because of the refusal of lawyers of the Caucasian race to appear in the defense of colored defendants; and a late request has come to the Committee that it assist in providing counsel to represent so-called "freedom riders" when they are arrested in the South and cannot obtain the services of local white lawyers to defend them.[31]

We should acknowledge the fact that the kind of problem to which the committee's report calls attention is implicit in the relationship between the American lawyer and his client, as it has emerged over the years, and that it will not be cured by prayer and admonition.

If we consider the development of our law of civil rights, and the present and prospective pressure on the law in this area; if we face the social conflicts which that pressure involves, including its bearing on the integrity and independence of the courts, then I think we should agree that the time has come to contemplate more fundamental changes than those as yet recommended by the American Bar Association's useful Committee on the Bill of Rights. The various piece-meal devices we have employed to accomplish the accepted goal of Lord Erskine's principle have not worked as well as they should. Thus far, we have depended on the sense of duty of a small number of individual lawyers, who in these cases have rendered a service to the law beyond praise. And excellent work has been done over the years by the American Civil Liberties Union, the National Association for the Advancement of Colored People, the Association on American Indian Affairs, and certain other special groups, interested in the welfare of aliens, immigrants, and similarly disadvantaged people. In view of the nature and magnitude of the task, it is wrong to leave the burden of representation in civil liberties cases entirely to individuals, and to organizations of this kind. If we believe what we have always said on the subject, the organized bar itself, as the body primarily charged with the duty of articulating and enforcing our code of professional ethics, has an ultimate and nondelegable responsibility to see to it that no man's rights be lost for want of a qualified lawyer to present them. Any lesser rule for our profession could make due process of law a mockery. A visible and effective program for carrying out the principle, as it was expressed in the

---

31. American Bar Association, Report of the Standing Committee on Bill of Rights, 1961 (mimeographed text) at 7.

American Bar Association's 1953 resolution, could do more than any other single act to clarify public thought on the role of law and lawyers in society, and to strengthen the influence of law in the evolution of public opinion with respect to the controversies which now swirl about the heads of the justices of the Supreme Court of the United States.

What concrete steps are now indicated to make such a program a living part of the daily life of our society?

At the level of educating the bar to its obligations, it might prove useful if the principle of the American Bar Association's 1953 resolution, declaring the bar's continuing duty to provide counsel "even to the most unpopular defendants," were stated in the somewhat more solemn and readily available form of the Canons of Professional Ethics. The canons are hardly self-enforcing. Still, such a declaration could help keep the problem more firmly in the foreground, both for lawyers and for bar associations.

A formal step of this kind could hardly have a revolutionary impact on our habits. One possible approach to a practical answer may emerge from the development of the College of Trial Lawyers, that honorific organization of some of our most eminent specialists in trial practice. Over the long run, the rules of that distinguished society might well embrace a considerable part of the "cab rank" principle of the English bar, at least for civil liberties cases, where the need is most acute. It would have a most salutary effect on public opinion, and provide a most wholesome example to the bar as a whole, if the leaders of our trial bar regularly took some of the most difficult and controversial of our civil rights cases. No practice could more effectively demonstrate the independence of the bar, and the weight we attach to the importance of protecting the humblest and most despised persons against arbitrary action by the state or by private groups.

I do not believe that such steps would be sufficient to meet the weight of our obligation at this time. We have faced in our country, and we face today, a mood of resistance to law which denies the premise of our national existence. This denial of legality has not reached the point of open revolt which the Algerian conflict so tragically produced in France, or that which the Curragh mutiny represented in Great Britain sixty years ago. But the issues are the same, and the challenge is quite as real. In the national effort to overcome this menace to the rule of law, the organized bar should play a far more active and decisive role. In some areas of the South, conflicts over the Constitution have given rise for the moment to a state of opinion which even the most eminent lawyers hesitate to confront alone. We must avoid the easy course of being self-righteous about the difficult problems of the South. Comparable situations have developed, from time to time, in other parts of the country, and will doubtless do so again. I might recall, here in California, the wartime controversy about the deportation of Japanese aliens and of American citizens of Japanese descent, as an instance of the nature of the risks we all face. In confronting this phenomenon, I propose that we build on the successful experience developed by several state bar associations during the most heated period of Senator Joseph McCarthy's heyday: that of providing counsel by court assignment, through strong committees of the bar associations themselves. Action of this kind should suffice to meet the difficulties unpopular litigants sometimes encounter, under our legal system, in obtaining the aid of counsel.

What I have in mind, however, would go farther. The American Bar Association's Committee on the Bill of Rights is authorized, under certain circumstances, to appear in court as amicus curiae, or as counsel of record, where "vital issues of civil liberties are deemed to be involved." State and local bar associations have similar powers, exercised either through committees or through the governing bodies of those associations. We do not hesitate to go to court or before legislatures, in the name of the bar itself, to protest against what we regard as the unauthorized practice of law, or to seek tax privileges for our period of retirement. I do not criticize such programs, but they hardly exhaust our capacity for collective action. Why should we not be as vigorous in maintaining some of the more affirmative canons of our code of ethics as we are in protecting our economic interests? The troubled history of our law during the last twenty years, and the prospects of trouble ahead, require, I suggest, a more sustained effort not only by lawyers but by their professional organizations. I am sure that some of our public spirited foundations would support such programs of the bar, as they have supported and now support other worthy initiatives of our professional bodies. What I envision is the development of vigilance and the habit of action, on the part of our national, state, and local bar associations, in the interest of protecting and helping to develop those constitutional guarantees which distinguish free societies from tyrannies. Programs of this kind would include the making of studies and the publication of reports—a field in which the Association of the Bar of the City of New York has provided such notable leadership in recent years. It would also, and in my view indispensably, include court appearances and appearances before legislative committees, to put the weight and prestige of the bar itself into the process through which our law evolves. I do not suggest that the American Bar Association's Committee on the Bill of Rights acquire a monopoly of representation in civil liberties cases—heaven forbid. Nor do I have in mind that it replace the individual lawyers and civic associations who now carry so much of the load, and carry it, on the whole, so well. What I do propose is that such agencies of our national, state, and local bar associations emerge as forceful participants in this area of law, whose content is of such far-reaching significance to the character and quality of our legal system, and that they do so on a continuing basis. By such action, I think, we could match the performance of the British bar, in ways more appropriate to our customs than any attempt to take over the English rule for ourselves.

V

When we meet together to consider our profession as a profession —as a working part of society's quest for justice—we necessarily face large and difficult questions, easily passed over with platitudinous answers. Let me conclude by recalling the theme of Lord Radcliffe's recent Rosenthal Lectures at the Northwestern Law School, "The Law and Its Compass." Lord Radcliffe starts with the proposition that it is more important to decide what law is for than what it is.[32]

Let us apply his method to our problem—the lawyer and his client.

We are all taught to believe that the freedom of a lawyer to represent only the law and his client, without pressure from the government, from the judges, or from the thrust of public opinion, is an extremely important—indeed an indispensable—feature of the life of our profession. Why? What ends are served by independence in that sense?

---

32. RADCLIFFE, THE LAW AND ITS COMPASS 4 (1960).

Erskine gave one answer, which has never ceased to echo in our conscience:

> I will for ever, at all hazards, assert the dignity, independence, and integrity of the English Bar; without which, impartial justice, the most valuable part of the English constitution, can have no existence. . . . If the advocate refuses to defend, from what he may think of the charge or of the defense, he assumes the character of the Judge; nay, he assumes it before the hour of judgment; and in proportion to his rank and reputation puts the heavy influence of, perhaps, a mistaken opinion into the scale against the accused, in whose favour the benevolent principle of English law makes all presumptions, and which commands the very Judge to be his Counsel.[33]

The reason for the rule extends beyond the area of criminal law. It includes related fields, like libel, admission to licensed callings, and other proceedings where the liberty of an individual is in forfeit. In these instances, a person may lose his reputation, his privacy, or his capacity to pursue his chosen work; to travel, to live where he would, to exercise his privileges of freedom of speech, of thought, or of religion. We also believe the independence of the bar is important to the effective discharge of our professional obligations of counseling in chambers: of representing the law to our clients, and our clients to the law, in the vital work of guiding and shaping the mass of social conduct which is organized by lawyers but rarely tested in the courts.

We live in an age of crisis—a crisis compounded equally of external threats and of rapid changes in the structure of domestic society. The modern liberal state, to use Lord Radcliffe's phrase, is more complex, more highly organized, more regulated by government, than any of its predecessors since medieval times. At the same time, it has freed itself from the older view that positive law, for all its patent imperfections, was "one link" in a "majestic and harmonious sequence," drawing its sanction from the divine.[34] That link cannot be recreated in its original form. Unless we accomplish its equivalent, Lord Radcliffe urges, law loses its meaning, and loses also its hold upon the loyalties of men.[35] The citizen looks to law as

---

33. 2 The Speeches of the Hon. Thomas Erskine, When at the Bar, on Subjects Connected with the Liberty of the Press and Against Constructive Treasons, 90–91 (collected by James Ridgway 1810).
34. Radcliffe, *supra* note 32, at 5–6, 69.
35. *Id.* at 8–11.

more than the repository of his own views: "He feels in his bones that the law which the learned judge interprets to him from the bench is the voice of something more stable and more fundamental than the aspirations or convictions either of himself or of the judge."[36] In the adaptation law must make to the changed climate of ideas in which it functions, our most vital obligation is to understand the purposes, the goals, the values which animate our most routine duties and infuse them with meaning.

"Often I think," Lord Radcliffe remarks, "that the work of the lawyer has dwindled, in these smooth modern societies, to that of the traffic policeman. It is only redeemed, as so much of the institutions and activities of those societies can only be redeemed, if there burns the fire of belief in the value of what is guaranteed, which is the symbol of an unextinguished faith."[37] For us, that faith is the conviction "that the purpose of society and all its institutions is to nourish and enrich the growth of each individual human spirit. This is liberty in the sense in which we have chosen to understand it."[38] Our Constitution and its amendments help to remind us daily that these are indeed the goals of law, by drawing an "enduring outline of what it is to be a free man and so by implication declare the national faith and the purposes from which the law of the nation must never turn away."[39] The body of beliefs which these precepts represent is the compass of the law, in Lord Radcliffe's argument, the compass by which we must steer, at our peril, as we seek to apply the values of our heritage to the novel and difficult problems of an extremely difficult and dynamic society. The vastness of the task, under modern circumstances, is formidable. If we are to help build a legal order which fulfills the goal of individual liberty, in our law of corporations and contracts and restraint of trade, as well as in our criminal law; in our handling of trade unions, and licensed callings, as well as in our law governing the press, television, and the conduct of congressional committees, we shall require all the learning, all the courage, all the independence which our professional tradition commands.

That the work is hard, and the stakes high, is what makes the prospect exhilarating. Who enjoys climbing a little mountain?

36. *Id.* at 11.
37. *Id.* at 71–72.
38. *Id.* at 65.
39. *Id.* at 79.

Part Three

Ethical Problems of Economic Policy

For this section, I have selected three of my articles on economc themes which deal directly with the roots of law in policy, and with the way in which the law of a particular society kneads and reconciles the competing claims pressed upon it.

Six

British and American Experience with Legislation against Restraints of Competition

---
I

Comparing the legal experience of two countries in dealing with roughly similar problems is a popular sport and, on the whole, a useful one. Like skiing and many other exhilarating sports, however, it is also dangerous.

The charm of comparative law is as obvious as that of foreign travel. Who can resist a sense of pleasure as he leaves the familiar horizons of his own country and soars over the fence into the gay, exotic tourist's world of another? Familiar features are differently costumed and differently oriented. Policemen, judges, and lawyers appear in guises as alien as those of the taxis and the restaurants. Even parliaments, governments, political parties, and the process of election itself fall into new patterns. It is easy to get caught on the fence as you sail over it, and come a cropper. The temptation always is the song from *My Fair Lady* which might be rendered for present purposes as "Why can't the British be more like us?" From the point of view of legal theory, the sin is quite as bad if the song is given in the alternative form: "Why can't *we* be more like the British?"

For the essential point about any two legal systems is that they are and must be different, even when they seem to be most alike. A system of law, to recall Holmes's phrase, embodies the moral history of the people who made it. It is spun of their social and political experience; formed by their customs and their modes of thought; polarized by their past, and by their aspirations for the future. A given rule or practice in any legal system can be understood only in rela-

Originally given as a lecture at the London School of Economics and Political Science, University of London, on December 1, 1959, this paper was developed through several drafts, under the hospitable pressure of speaking engagements at Birmingham, Cambridge, Belfast, and Bristol during the spring of 1960. It was published in a slightly different form in 23 MODERN LAW REVIEW 477–506 (1960). © Modern Law Review Limited, London, 1960.

tion to the whole of which it is a living part. At a level of considerable generality, Britain and the United States, and indeed all the Western societies, are bound together by their common allegiance to certain social and moral ideas, and to certain ways of organizing society. At an even higher level of abstraction, one can discern uniformities, derived from the common literature of law, which Western legal systems share with those of the communist countries of Eastern and Central Europe. But when one descends to the region of work-a-day detail, the differences become as important as the similarities. The composition and design of each corpus of law are necessarily unique —as unique as a fingerprint, or a cathedral.

All the differences between systems of law, however, are not predetermined and immutable. Law is part of history, even as it helps to shape history. But history is hardly a clockwork mechanism which must reveal itself in unalterable patterns. In its catalogue of causes, purpose and accident have a place. The historic configuration of forces within a society offers the men of each of its generations a zone of choice, which they may use or fail to use, for good or for ill. We can hardly concede that reason must always yield in the growth of law to custom, tradition, and unreason.

I started by saying that comparative studies could be useful. If they are conducted with a strong sense for the sociological character of law, they can be very useful indeed. The comparative method in law study is of great value to students, in giving them perspective toward their own systems. Comparative studies often shed new light on how a given system of law came to be what it is, and help one to glimpse more clearly the direction in which it is moving. In a contracting world, the comparative method helps to break down the forces of inbreeding and isolation which so frequently narrow our outlooks. And, above all, comparative law can be, and should be, a fertile source of law reform. Many of the most creative periods in the history of law, like comparable moments in the history of other branches of thought and of art, were precipitated by the revelation of foreign practice. Institutions can almost never be transferred intact from one social system to another. But ideas can migrate, and often do. No American can forget the role played by Montesquieu's highly original view of the British Constitution in the formation of our own. It is sometimes easier to learn from the successes and failures of others than from our own.

These cautionary warnings apply with special force to the subject matter of this paper, for the social and economic problems of monopoly and restraints of competition arouse a wide public opinion, and have roots deep in the intractable history of every society.

II

An almost instinctive concern for the dangers of excessive power is the central theme of American public life. All our social arrangements derive from the same premise—the conviction that a person can be free, and that people can be equal, only in a society of pluralism, where power is dispersed and the boundaries of power are established and maintained by law. As Tocqueville observed nearly 140 years ago, the assurance of equal personal liberty is the first goal of public order in America, a goal tenaciously valued as an end in itself, not a means to an end.

One sees the pattern everywhere.

The national government is one of limited powers. And the division of authority between the states and the nation is still a reality, although the balance has shifted in favor of the national government in recent years. Each governmental unit is organized in accordance with the principle of the separation of powers. The purpose served by that principle, as Justice Louis D. Brandeis once remarked, is not efficiency in government, but a state of tension maintained by the inevitable friction of the parts, which is a safeguard against tyranny and the safest and most favorable setting for a system of individual liberty.

The same preoccupation with the problem of power is evident in our economic system. After our early experience with the Bank of the United States, the fear of the money power is so deep in the American political psyche that we had no central bank until 1913. Even now, the Federal Reserve System is a loose coalition of regional central banks, and its authority is qualified and limited. The great banks of New York can have branches in Tokyo, London, or Sydney, but not in Chicago, Houston, or Los Angeles—or, indeed, even in Albany or Buffalo. Our commitment to capitalism, as the basic rule for organizing economic activity through free and competitive markets, rests in the end on the same idea. The private ownership of property, and private initiative, are accepted not primarily on grounds of natural law, ideological commitment, or economic efficiency, but as an indispensable part of the strategy of freedom. Only an open capitalist economy can assure a wide diffusion of economic power, and equal opportunity for those who seek to climb the economic ladder.

After the middle of the nineteenth century, and more particularly in the last quarter of that century, the perennial problems of monopoly and restraint of trade began to present themselves in a new guise in all the industrialized countries. Such problems, raising basic issues of social justice and economic policy, have always been of concern to the law—occasionally, as in Tudor and Elizabethan times, of acute concern. About one hundred years ago, however, they changed in content and appearance. Both British and American courts began to face situations more difficult than price rings among local brewers, coopers, or salt merchants, and restrictive covenants in the sale of doctors' practices. Science was creating new industries, often on a large scale, and transforming the organization of old ones. To the familiar rhythm of the railway age, there was added the equally familiar rhythm of the modern factory system. Populations speeded up their movement from farm to city in the vast trek which everywhere defines the industrial revolution.

In the United States, the new industrial economy of the late nineteenth century took shape in a pattern which was somewhat different from that in Great Britain, France, and Germany. American corporation law—the law governing the powers of joint stock companies—was state law, and not national law, for reasons characteristic of our federal system. At the time, it was weak law. And Gresham's most famous principle tended to make it weaker. It offered great freedom to the business leaders of the period in devising and carrying out schemes of amalgamation. The vigorous and enterprising business leaders of the day, supremely confident in themselves and in their ideology, put empires together. In many fields, their companies achieved monopoly power, or something close to it. The barons of the railroad industry in particular seemed to threaten the country with combinations too vast and too ominous to be tolerated, holding the power of life and death over people, regions, and industries. Other industries were not far behind.

As Marshall remarked, the industrial temper in the United States was quite different from that in England.

> Here few of those who are very rich take a direct part in business, they generally seek safe investments for their capital; and, again, among those engaged in business the middle class predominates, and most of them are more careful to keep what they have than eager to increase it by risky courses. . . . In England . . . the dominant force is that of the average opinion of businessmen, and the dominant form of association is that of the joint-stock com-

pany. But in America the dominant force is the restless energy and the versatile enterprise of a comparatively few rich and able men who rejoice in that power of doing great things by great means that their wealth gives them, and who have but partial respect for those who always keep their violins under glass cases. The methods of a joint-stock company are not always much to their mind; they prefer combinations that are more mobile, more adventurous, and often more aggressive. For some purposes they have to put up with a joint-stock company; but then they strive to dominate it, not to be dominated by it.[1]

The American Titans hid neither their lights nor their violins. Advised by an imaginative bar, and financed by imaginative bankers, they established a series of giant holding companies which had few exact counterparts in Britain and were in turn different from the Continental cartels. While the trust device was rarely used as the legal form of such combinations, the word *trust* took on a new meaning, which has survived to this day. Whether the monopolies of the era were formed by merger, or holding company, or otherwise, they were known as the "Oil Trust," the "Steel Trust," the "Whiskey Trust," the "Powder Trust," and so on. Tactics of coercion were freely used in building up these companies. Discriminatory advantages were obtained in transport costs and other facilities. Indeed, in one famous case, competitors were forced to pay a tithe to the dominant company in their industry on every sale they made.

Toward the end of the century, companies of this kind, or somewhat looser groupings of a few great combinations, had acquired positions of monopoly or near-monopoly in many basic industries—in steel, oil, sugar refining, anthracite coal, explosives, tobacco, meat packing, the manufacture of farm machinery and shoe machinery, and certain other important trades. Local railways were put together into regional systems, and programs were developed to eliminate competition among them. One man of towering ambition, E. H. Harriman, even tried to combine all the railway networks of the country into one.

In the United States, as in other countries, protest against the burdens and injustices of industrialization and urban life gained in strength as the movement itself accelerated its momentum. Discontent was aggravated by the prolonged depression of the late nine-

---

1. *Some Aspects of Competition* (1890), in MEMORIALS OF ALFRED MARSHALL 266–67 (ed. A. C. PIGOU 1925).

teenth century, punctuated in the United States by occasional financial crises and panics and by endemic and damaging bank failures. It was also a period of falling wheat prices, intensifying the protest of the farming regions. The adjustment of the economy and of the society to the vagaries of the trade cycle and to the pace of its rapid secular growth was both facilitated and complicated by the immense flood of immigrants who poured into the country at this time, largely into the industrial cities and towns. Trade unions were formed, and farmers' organizations of real power emerged, to seek redress against the railroads which transported their products, and against the groups dominating the markets in which they sold and from which they bought. Vehement and effective popular books, newspapers, pamphlets, and cartoons strongly colored public opinion, in the mood of what was then called "muckraking." And in that pre-television age, itinerant lecturers traveled up and down the land, denouncing the "malefactors of great wealth," in President Theodore Roosevelt's phrase, and the abuses they were inflicting on the American people. The business heroes of the time—or robber barons, if you prefer—provided a dramatic focus for the sense of protest. The grandiose scale of their activities, and their manifest power, helped to revive ancient fears of exploitation and gave strength to the outcry against monopoly.

The atmosphere was starkly described by Mr. Justice Harlan of the Supreme Court of the United States in 1911:

> All who recall the condition of the country in 1890 will remember that there was everywhere, among the people generally, a deep feeling of unrest. The Nation had been rid of human slavery—fortunately, as all now feel—but the conviction was universal that the country was in real danger from another kind of slavery sought to be fastened on the American people, namely, the slavery that would result from aggregations of capital in the hands of a few individuals and corporations controlling . . . the entire business of the country, including the production and sale of the necessaries of life. Such a danger was thought to be then imminent, and all felt that it must be met firmly and by such statutory regulations as would adequately protect the people against oppression and wrong.[2]

2. Standard Oil Co. v. United States, 221 U.S. 1, 83–84 (1911) (concurring opinion).

It was a time of violent strikes, of occasional riots, and of widespread bitterness. Words like Haymarket and Homestead, Pullman, the Molly McGuires, and Pinkerton ring in American ears with a force akin to the echoes in Britain of Peterloo and Chartism. "Populism" was the battle cry of those who opposed the tide: the democratic control of power; small business against big; the country at large against "alien" New York. Organizations of farmers and laborers were heard for the first time in American politics. Along with other groups, and other leaders, they sought the protection of national legislation against what all perceived to be the threat of concentrated economic power, marshaled by great New York bankers and spreading its tentacles into every corner of the land. To control the new national economy, we had to invoke the national power over interstate and foreign commerce.

Many opposed the demand for legislative relief. True believers in the survival of the fittest, these people thought it unfair and unsporting to turn on the men who had won the race of competition. Justice Oliver Wendell Holmes, a stout Darwinian, was convinced that the Sherman Act was a humbug based on economic ignorance. Natural forces, he was sure, would soon erode temporary positions of monopoly.

The vast majority was unimpressed by the metaphor of sport. They thought that there should indeed be limits to victory in the economic race. What was at stake—the risk of oligarchy or tyranny—was too serious to be left to the market alone.

The political expression of these grievances was accomplished through the forms of American politics, which, in the examples of Jefferson, Jackson, and Lincoln, had already established effective modes for dealing with social discontent.

The American movement of social protest never became Marxist, although there were strong socialists among its early leaders. Nor did it result, as was the case in Great Britain and other countries, in the formation of a political party based on the trade unions and the farmers' societies, or, more broadly, on the organized support of the working classes. The historic pattern of the American party system proved to be too strong to be radically altered at this time by the thrust and counterthrust of industrialism and reform.

The party system in the United States takes its shape from the electoral provisions of the Constitution. They make it necessary to elect a President through cumulative majorities, state by state. That need requires our national parties to be coalitions of state and regional parties, not truly national parties at all. Party alignments were then, as they probably are still, too strongly influenced by the passions of the Civil War and the Reconstruction period after it to be fundamentally affected by the new wave of popular feeling. The great cities of the North, with their large immigrant populations, were becoming largely Democratic in their party allegiance, along with the whole of the South. At that time, the South was agrarian and often, though by no means always, quite conservative in economic and social policy, save on the special question of the tariff. While the Republican Party after the Civil War was closely linked to the emergent business class, it included great farm areas in the West, which had been staunchly Unionist during the Civil War. And business groups were not at all united in their views on big business and monopoly. The smaller independent businessman and banker, and many large businessmen as well, were quite as opposed, then and now, to economic dominance by a tiny group of Titans as were the leaders of farm groups and trade unions. The Republican Party was therefore a coalition too, and, even after its catastrophic split in 1912, it was rich in progressive and even radical leaders, who appealed in many areas to the spirit of reform.

The nature of the party system determined the way in which the movement of protest found its fulfillment. The pressure of the movement was diffuse, and both parties responded to it, in a long cycle of legislative action which has continued to this day.

The first major response of the law to these demands was the enactment of two federal statutes, the Interstate Commerce Act of 1887, and the Sherman Act of 1890. Neither was passed by a party vote, and both parties have vied since in claiming credit for their passage, and their subsequent development. These statutes have become centers of far-reaching legal systems, whose influence has been felt in many parts of the economy and the public law.

The Interstate Commerce Act accepted the railroads as natural monopolies, and established an administrative agency, the Interstate Commerce Commission, to undertake their regulation on a continuing basis. At first the powers of the commission were far from adequate. Gradually, however, as experience accumulated, the statutes were amended, and the commission's understanding of its problems grew. That the laws and practices through which our transportation industries are now controlled require radical reform, in the light of totally changed conditions, is no reproach to the legislators ninety years ago who established the mechanism and set it on its course.

In the Sherman Act, Congress chose the opposite approach. It did not view monopoly and restraint of trade as inevitable outside the field of public utilities. Nor did it choose the path, which has often seemed congenial to Marxists, of rather encouraging the growth of monopolies, as a stage in capitalist development which could hasten the day when their capitalist integuments would fall away, so that they could readily be nationalized as instruments of the public good. Rather, Congress looked to the competitive market as the principal regulator of price and output, and of wages, interest, and profits. The congressmen and Presidents of the day were confident that a competitive economy would assure a wide dispersal of power and of economic opportunity; they thought it would preserve the most appropriate economic foundation for a political and social order which has always considered equality the first of its social ambitions. The policy of competition was even to be applied, to a significant extent, in the railroad industry itself, and later in other industries partially supervised by administrative bodies organized according to the model of the Interstate Commerce Commission.

The Sherman Act contains only two brief substantive provisions, which have not been changed in substance since the Act was passed. It condemns as criminal every contract, combination in the form of trust or otherwise, or conspiracy in restraint of trade or commerce among the several states or with foreign nations. And, equally, it condemns monopolizations, or attempts or conspiracies to monopolize any part of that trade or commerce. It embraces the entire constitutional area of Congress's power to regulate commerce, and declares for that realm two simple, and seemingly absolute, rules of business behavior. There follow several novel procedural provisions, which give the act a potentiality for influence far greater than that of the common law. The federal government is empowered to enforce the act in criminal proceedings, or, what is more important, through suits in equity. And private persons, injured in their persons or property by violations of the act, are authorized to sue, and to recover three times their actual damages and costs, including a reasonable attorney's fee. This provision reincarnates an old English device, and multiplies the number of enforcement opportunities under the act. There was a fourth enforcement procedure provided in the act, that of libel, or condemnation of property held under any contract or other arrangement which violated the act. It was an ingenious idea but has not proved to be useful.

The words in the statute reach back to the Middle Ages and beyond. But the Sherman Act gave the old words a new thrust, drawn, the courts said, from the conditions Congress was trying to correct.

On the face of it, the immediate background of the act, and the policy choices made by Congress in drafting it, offer several striking contrasts to the background and structure of the British legislation of 1948 and 1956. Why did Congress place its principal reliance on the ordinary federal courts, and why did it pass such sweeping legislation, absolute in form, and more complete in its prohibitions than comparable legislation in Great Britain and other countries?

Congress might have used an administrative agency, like the Interstate Commerce Commission it had just established, or specialized courts, like the Restrictive Practices Court in Britain, or our own Tax Court and Court of Customs and Patent Appeals. Experiments of that kind were in fact tried from time to time in the United States. We had a specialized antitrust court, called the Commerce Court, for a few years, and we still have the Federal Trade Commission, established in 1914 as a reform measure to improve antitrust enforcement. But the main enforcement agency for the antitrust laws was and remains that of the ordinary federal courts. Their inherent strength in the American scheme of things has made them more satisfactory and more acceptable than any rival institution, over the long run.

The reason for this decision, I think, is the special authority of the judiciary within our public law and public life. The extraordinary importance of the American judiciary derives in large part from its power to declare statutes and acts of the executive unconstitutional. The power is a discreet one. It is exercised in a common-law matrix, and can only be asserted when a constitutional problem arises inescapably in the course of public or private litigation. Often resisted, it has thus far always prevailed. And it has become a valued, indeed an almost sacred, part of the political system. It is accepted by the public as a way of keeping political organs within the boundaries of their constitutional power, and of protecting minorities against the risk of majoritarian tyranny. The influence of this function colors the attitude of the American judges to their work, and of the public to the judges. In consequence, our judges approach their tasks with a good deal of the freedom and vigor which characterized the common law of an earlier day. It was thus entirely natural, in the American setting, to turn the policy problems implicit in the Sherman Act over to the judges, who already had quite comparable responsibilities on their desks.

If the task of enforcement was to be carried out primarily by judges, why wasn't the idea of a specialized and expert court accepted? Part of the reason for this choice, I think, was the magnitude of the problem presented. If the Sherman Act was enforceable at all, it would be beyond the reach of a single court, however expert. Then, too, it was felt that offenses which occurred in different parts of the country should be passed upon by local judges and local juries. And, finally, there was an almost instinctive preference for a course which would require large parts of the bar, the judiciary, and the public to confront these trying problems, and to be educated in their meaning by participating in their solution. *Per contra,* there is an advantage in having technical problems finally resolved not by experts alone, but by the common sense of the ordinary judicial outlook.

The answer to the second question—why so sweeping a delegation of powers?—should be made in terms both of the situation to which the law was addressed and of the political system which enacted it. Congress was seeking to take a bold and massive step, commensurate with the visible growth of monopolies in the country and the high state of public feeling on the subject. Legislative records in those days were not so revealing as they are today, with the modern development of congressional committees. But enough is available to confirm that Congress wanted to move energetically in altering the pattern of economic organization. It was not notably precise in defining its goals, nor did it see clearly how far it could succeed in busting the trusts. But it wanted radical action, and sought to take it, through a statute whose words sounded comfortingly familiar to a group of common-law lawyers but were in fact untried. The absolute declaration of illegality in the act was thought by some to be at least a respectable version of the common law, and in the United States perhaps the dominant one; the rule, that is, that all general restraints of competition, as distinguished from partial ancillary restraints, are void without regard to their extrinsic reasonableness.

There is another theme in the debates of the time. Congress wanted to give the courts discretion in interpreting the law, but not too much discretion. The congressmen were seeking to confine the power they gave the courts, as well as to define it. They intended to confer what is sometimes called a "judicial" rather than a "legislative" discretion, a narrower rather than a wider range of choice for deciding cases in terms of the judges' own ideas of social and economic policy. By the logic of American public life, the courts were their natural choice among possible agencies of enforcement. But Congressmen are men of affairs, and realists. They know that judges tend to be older men, naturally conservative in spirit, who often reflect the ideas of the previous generation. By giving them a firm rule to administer, the Congress hoped to keep them from straying too far from the policy it had rather vaguely in mind.

For the first thirty years or so after 1890, the Supreme Court decided almost all the important cases which reached it in favor of the government. These decisions began to constitute a noticeable economic influence, first in the railroad industry, and then in other industries, as judgments multiplied and were translated by counsel into the realm of advice and, later, of managerial policy.

Even more important than the immediate economic consequences of the act, in this formative period, was the debate the judges conducted as to its essential meaning. Did the statute do no more than declare the common law rules against monopoly and restraint of trade for the federal realm of interstate and foreign commerce, where common law rules were deemed in this instance not to exist without legislation? Or did it assert a policy as distinctive as its mode of enforcement? Did the word "every" in section 1 mean "every," though the heavens fall, or some term of less universal implications? The inquiry focused on the chameleon word "reasonable," which the common-law judges had used in several senses in defining public policy toward the enforceability of contracts in restraint of trade.

The controversy with the Supreme Court was resolved in 1911, in two decisions which have remained, for all their ambiguity, as the basic starting point of American antitrust law ever since.[3] Those cases, and most notably the *Standard Oil* case, announced what was called "the rule of reason" in construing the statute. The formula was bitterly contested at the time, as a retrograde step which weakened the law. But the "rule of reason," as it was announced, and as it has developed in the course of more than sixty active years, differs strik-

---

3. Standard Oil Co. v. United States, 221 U.S. 1 (1911); United States v. American Tobacco Co., 221 U.S. 106 (1911). See H. THORELLI, THE FEDERAL ANTITRUST POLICY (1955); Letwin, *Congress and the Sherman Antitrust Law,* 1887–1890 23 U. CHI. L. REV. 221 (1956); id., LAW AND ECONOMIC POLICY IN AMERICA: THE EVOLUTION OF THE SHERMAN ACT (1965).

ingly from the "rule of reason" which was applied as a matter of common-law doctrine by some American courts, and by the British courts, and which is embodied in effect in the 1948, and especially in the 1956 British statute.

The American rule of reason is presented in the first place as an independent legislative policy, not a codification of preexisting common law.[4] This was a distinction of importance, which freed the act of a stifling potential incubus. The early cases had revealed that there were almost as many versions of the common law as there were judges. Any alternative solution would have sent our judges back to the Year Books, and loaded the act with a burden of history which might well have sunk it without a trace. This risk was heightened by the presence on the Supreme Court of Mr. Justice Holmes, a considerable legal historian and an acknowledged authority on the common law, who despised the Sherman Act and in several early cases presented a theory of the older doctrine that would have proved inadequate to the work before the courts.

In the *Standard Oil* case, the Supreme Court acknowledged that the Sherman Act used words which took at least their "rudimentary meaning" from their common law background. It then presented a version of that common law meaning which few of the judges or professors would have recognized. The common law, and the statute, the court said, were concerned with one question, and one question only: does the restraint, viewed in its market setting, constitute a quantitatively significant limitation on competition? If it does, it is illegal as an "undue" and therefore an "unreasonable" restraint of trade. "Restraint of trade or commerce" means "restraint of competition" in an economically definable market, and monopolization is simply "restraint of competition" carried to its ultimate limit. If the practice before the court is price fixing, or market division, or boycott, or other conduct which could be considered clearly anticompetitive in purpose, in nature, or in actual or necessary effect, then it is "conclusively" presumed to be illegal—that is, it is illegal *per se,* even though the defendants lack monopoly power, or anything close to it, and sometimes even if they hold relatively weak positions in the markets where they do business. Once the court has found an undue limitation of competition in this sense, its discretion under the

4. *Cf.* Wilberforce, Campbell, and Elles, The Law of Restrictive Trade Practices and Monopolies (1957), sec. 8.

"rule of reason" is exhausted. It can go no further in considering whether the prices fixed are reasonable or not; whether special circumstances in the industry, such as high fixed costs, secular decline, excess capacity, or the like, justify even a limited degree of cooperation among sellers, as in the public interest. In short, the act did not forbid bad trusts, and condone good ones. It applied to all, by equating the public interest strictly with the elimination of substantial restraints on competition.

The statute seems to condemn "every" restraint of competition. Congress could not have meant this literally, since even the merger of two small grocers involves the elimination of some competition. Therefore the act applies only when the elimination of competition accomplished by the restraint is substantial—quantitatively significant in a market. This is the essence of the "rule of reason."

This way of interpreting the Sherman Act has far-reaching implications. It means, for example, that "bigness" does not violate the antitrust laws unless it carries with it a degree of monopoly power in a market. It means also that it is not a defense under the antitrust laws to contend that the defendant is a progressive, civic-minded, well-managed company supporting the Community Chest.

The focus of the antitrust laws is the state of competition in a market, and their principal goal—perhaps their only goal—is to prevent significant private interference with the competitive potential of that market. The premise Congress had in mind, the courts have said, is that if such private restraints are prevented or undone, society can rely on market forces to achieve an economically efficient level of prices and output, and a sound allocation of its scarce resources of capital, entrepreneurship, and labor. Equally, society can rely on the impersonal decisions of competitive markets to maintain a decentralized pattern of economic power, and an economy in which opportunity is open to talent and ambition.

In any event, the judges said, they cannot and will not try to decide whether a trust is behaving well. Such issues should be left to the arbitrament of competitive markets. The courts are not utility commissions. They cannot keep industries under continuous control.

This approach to the problem of interpreting the antitrust laws is largely, but not entirely, economic in character. There is still room in the law for the set of mind which prefers small business to big, and gives some weight to the notion that the law is directed against the abuse of monopoly power rather than monopolization itself; against competitive behavior that seems "unfair" or "unethical" to judge or jury; against furtive or coercive behavior, or behavior intended to drive a rival out of the field. Usually, however, evidence of this color is mentioned to confirm or supplement the economic determinations which are supposed to be fundamental in each antitrust case: (1) "What is the market affected by the defendant's behavior?" (2) "Is that behavior a restraint of competition?" (3) "If so, does the restraint affect competition in the market enough to constitute a violation of Sections 1 or 2 of the Sherman Act, or of the Clayton Act?"

The consequence of the *Standard Oil* case, over the long run, was an essentially economic definition of the offenses established by the Sherman Act, condemning all monopolizations, and those restraints of trade, or partial monopolies, which significantly affected competition in the markets where the defendants carried on business, or, under the more limited tests of the Clayton Act, those restraints which were found to be probable potential clogs on competition in such markets.

This gloss on the rule of reason was not to emerge clearly for thirty years or more, in the normal ebb and flow of the judicial process. I warn you that some of my respected colleagues would not accept the view I have presented, even now. Nonetheless, I believe that it corresponds to the reasoning and the language of the 1911 cases, and, even more important, that it fits the pattern and doctrine of the latter decisions which derive from them.

The American antitrust statutes went through several cycles of development and interpretation. And they were significantly amended by Congress, most notably in 1914, when the Clayton Act and the Federal Trade Commission Act were passed; during the Depression of the thirties, when they were virtually suspended in favor of compulsory cartelization under the NRA; and in 1950, when the provision of the Clayton Act against mergers was revived from a condition of judicial euthanasia.

This is not the occasion to attempt even a summary sketch of contemporary antitrust doctrine, or an appraisal of its impact on the economy of the United States. I should contend that we have at last achieved a coherent antitrust theory. In terms of that theory, the various offenses of the Sherman Act and the Clayton Act are distinguished largely as embodying different degrees or quantities of monopoly power; and many restrictive practices are treated summarily as illegal, without lengthy trials, on the ground that they are obviously anticompetitive in character or in necessary effect, or that they impose on rivals disadvantages not based on superior efficiency. The ideas of the antitrust laws have spread widely throughout our public law. They play a part in many of the statutes which establish administrative regulation for the transportation and communications industries and for banking. Their weight is strongly felt in our law of patents, trademarks, and copyrights, and in other branches of law as well—the policy adopted for disposing of surplus plant owned by the government at the end of the war, for example.[5]

The economic consequences of this effort, extending over eighty years now, are harder to evaluate and impossible to reduce to statistics. The monopolies of the turn of the century have all disappeared, often in response to direct action under the antitrust laws. Several studies of the degree of concentration in the American economy show a rough balance between the forces making for monopoly, and those making for more competition. Studies of specific industries permit one to see the antitrust influence in action, along with the influence of changing technology, the development of substitutes, and declining costs of transportation, as a factor making for more competition in markets.[6] It is apparent to any observer that the law has denied to American industry some of the easy and efficient forms of open collusion in price making, such as most of those which come before the Restrictive Practices Court in Great Britain, and that it has forced businessmen interested in collusion to retreat

5. I attempted a general conspectus of the antitrust law, in chapter 11 of PLANNING FOR FREEDOM: THE PUBLIC LAW OF AMERICAN CAPITALISM (1959). In addition to the works cited and discussed there, see three important books published later, DONALD DEWEY, MONOPOLY IN ECONOMICS AND LAW (1959); CARL KAYSEN & DONALD F. TURNER, ANTI-TRUST POLICY: AN ECONOMIC AND LEGAL ANALYSIS (1959); and A. D. NEALE, THE ANTITRUST LAWS OF THE UNITED STATES (2d ed. 1970). The law on the subject is reviewed in the REPORT OF THE ATTORNEY-GENERAL'S NATIONAL COMMITTEE TO STUDY THE ANTITRUST LAWS (1955).

See also J. S. McGEE, IN DEFENSE OF INDUSTRIAL CONCENTRATION (1971); ALMARIN PHILLIPS, PERSPECTIVES ON ANTITRUST POLICY (1965); YALE BROZEN, ed., THE COMPETITIVE ECONOMY (1975); ROBERT A. SOLO, THE POLITICAL AUTHORITY AND THE MARKET SYSTEM (1974); H. J. GOLDSMID et al., eds., INDUSTRIAL CONCENTRATION: THE NEW LEARNING (1974).

6. The successive editions of EDWARD H. CHAMBERLIN, THEORY OF MONOPOLISTIC COMPETITION, contain a most useful bibliography of literature in this field. A good deal of the economic impact of antitrust enforcement is perceptively reviewed in SIMON N. WHITNEY, ANTI-TRUST POLICIES, AMERICAN EXPERIENCE IN TWENTY INDUSTRIES (1958), and considered in larger perspective by Dewey, and by Kaysen and Turner, *supra* note 5.

to less obvious, and often less workable, procedures of cooperation. I believe that the laws have had a considerable effect, if not always a uniform one, on the evolution of the American economy—on its structure, its price behavior, and its atmosphere—and have helped especially to minimize barriers to entry that might otherwise have been insuperable.

The politics of American antitrust are also worth noticing. The antitrust laws are defended by sensitive and well-informed members of Congress. The state of public opinion, and the balance between our parties, are such as to require from a Republican administration an antitrust enforcement program quite as zealous and far-reaching as the antitrust program of its rival. Even if it wished to do so, the Republican Party could not safely relax or amend the law without risking the accusation of favoring big business against small—a rallying cry any sensible politician would much rather not have to confront.

III

The British legislation of 1948, 1953, and 1956 is the product of a political environment conspicuously different from the one I have sought to describe in section II of this paper. And it came out of an economic setting which reveals significant differences as well.

If we go back to the eighties and nineties of the last century, when the American antitrust tradition took shape, several formative differences between the relevant circumstances in the two countries appear.

In the first place, nothing like the exuberant and dramatic American merger movement occurred in the United Kingdom. A few big combines were formed, it is true, but there was no general explosion of monopoly or near-monopoly in railroads, banking, steel, coal, textiles, shipbuilding, engineering, or other key industries. Interestingly enough, where one such company was established—the Imperial Tobacco Company—it seems to have been created defensively, in response to a violent intrusion into the British market by the American Tobacco Company.[7] And several of the monopolies which

7. United States v. American Tobacco Co., 221 U.S. 106, 171–72 (1911). See REAVIS COX, COMPETITION IN THE AMERICAN TOBACCO INDUSTRY, 1911–1932 (1933); W. H. NICHOLLS, PRICE POLICIES IN THE CIGARETTE INDUSTRY (1951); WHITNEY, *supra* note 6, ch. 11.

emerged later functioned in new industries, such as the chemical industry, or in the older model of the great colonial trading companies. Practices of collusion probably existed, as did certain trade tactics generally regarded as coercive or unfair—blacklisting, harassment, the use of bogus independents, ordeal by patent litigation, and the like. Donald Dewey concludes that such tactics "were never so ruthlessly and blatantly employed in Britain" as in the United States, "although they may have been more widespread than was generally believed."[8] What documentation there is confirms that both industrial cooperation and local price fixing were far from rare in the British economy, in part by reason of the persistent survival of habits rooted in the customs of the eighteenth century and earlier times. But, as is so often the case, the facts in this instance may be of less importance than what people thought them to be. Public opinion in Britain was not agitated, as American opinion was, by the specter of an octopus of monopoly.

Secondly, British industry, evolving from its earlier forms of corporate organization without a dramatic break in continuity, was far more exposed to international competition, and far less protected by tariffs, than its American counterpart. The industrial sector of the American economy, conducted behind the protective wall of a high tariff, was then mainly oriented to a vast and growing domestic market. The importance of this factor in British thought about the monopoly problem is evident in the judgment of Lord Parker of Waddington in the *Adelaide Steamship Company* case. He was commenting on the concept of monopoly as a limiting factor always establishing unreasonableness at common law, and as an element in the Australian Industries Preservation Act. "[M]onopolies," he said, "in the popular sense of the word are more likely to arise and, if they do arise, are more likely to lead to prices being unreasonably enhanced in countries where a protective tariff prevails than in countries where there is no such tariff."[9]

---

8. MONOPOLY IN ECONOMICS AND LAW 285 (1959). Professor G. C. Allen concludes that in the decades before 1914 large combines were important in the soap, alkali, explosives, salt-mining, tobacco, whisky, and cement industries. "Monopoly and Competition in the United Kingdom," in EDWARD H. CHAMBERLIN, MONOPOLY AND COMPETITION AND THEIR REGULATION 88 (1954).

9. Attorney-General of Australia v. The Adelaide Steamship Co., Ltd., (1913) A.C. 781, 796.

Thirdly, the prolonged depression of the late nineteenth century was probably somewhat shorter and less acute in the United Kingdom than in the United States. Depression, obviously, is a great exacerbator of social tension. And in the United States much of the animus heightened by that experience was directed at the target of big business and big businessmen.

From the point of view of public opinion, the immediate context of political action, two differences between the countries seem worth special notice. The mood of social protest was of course quite as vehement in the United Kingdom as in the United States. But it was concerned with a somewhat different combination of issues and aims.

First of all, like most modern British political philosophy, British opinion was not nearly so preoccupied as American political thinking always is with the problem of power. Many elements of American experience, as I remarked earlier, make American politics extremely sensitive to the risks of concentrated power. It was historically natural that American opinion reacted strongly and emotionally to the threat of economic dominance by a small group of rich men, most of whom lived in New York. And it was equally natural that the threat of economic concentration seemed less real, and less ominous, in Britain. The British social order is historically different from the American, far more unified, and seemingly less egalitarian in all its symbols of prestige. The system of Cabinet government represents a unification of political power, in fact and in form. And it hardly seems shocking to British opinion that the reins of authority be held in large part by small groups, centered in London, trained in the same schools, and moving in the same society. The thought of what is now called an Establishment carries one set of connotations in Britain, a modern democracy which has used and preserved the forms of an older social system, is governed from one capital, and has an immense capacity to canalize new social forces into familiar channels; but it carries quite another in the United States, a larger country, with many scattered centers of influence, governed neither from New York nor from Washiington, and obsessed with dreams of equality and with fears of anything resembling the ancient oligarchy against which it once revolted.

In the second place, the British literature of social protest toward the end of the last century was different in positive content from that of the United States. Its dominant voices proposed notably different approaches to the miseries and injustices of the day. The Webbs and

Bernard Shaw, the other Fabians, the cooperators, and the Toynbees were never interested in busting trusts. Socialism, not competition, was the favored radical answer to concentrated economic power. There was therefore notably little political interest in the kind of reform undertaken in the United States. The new Labour Party was on another track. Its members tended to regard the Sherman Act as either a sham or as a superficial and foredoomed attempt to interfere with the laws of history. Indeed, the Labour Party has only recently come to the view that legislation to prevent restraints of competition is worth much effort, or has much promise. The Liberal Party was absorbed in a variety of other problems of great public interest. And the Conservative Party had not yet seen its advantage, in the spirit of Tory democracy, in seeking by legislation to encourage more competition, more enterprise, and freer entry into the markets of the economy.

The economists were as much against monopoly in Britain as in the United States. But for all their influence, they never considered the monopoly problem a major issue of policy for the United Kingdom, comparable in importance to monetary policy or free trade.

Thus it happened that in the great wave of progressive political action in Britain before the first war, legislation to curb monopoly played no significant part, even as a proposal which failed of adoption after a useful battle.

This temper of relative disinterest in the problem of monopoly is reflected in the occasional opinions of the British courts, in passing on restrictive practices in the law of contract, tort, conspiracy, and property. There are not many such cases—very few, compared with the volume of litigation on the subject in an active commercial state like New York. Several factors may account for the contrast. The costs of litigation are reputed to be higher in Britain than in the United States, and the British businessman may be a less litigious creature than his American cousin. There may be a greater reluctance on the part of British businessmen to spoil commercial relations by litigation. Sir David Cairns has suggested that agreements among competitors, while frequent, were generally assumed to be invalid, and were therefore enforced privately and not put to the test in court.[10]

---

10. *Monopolies and Restrictive Practices,* in MORRIS GINSBERG, ed., LAW AND OPINION IN ENGLAND IN THE TWENTIETH CENTURY 176 (1959).

The British judgments are fairly consistent in expressing a point of view toward the problem of restrictive trade practices which only a minority of American courts supported before 1890. I must confess, on reading over this line of cases, that I found the differences between their holdings and those of the American courts to be rather less conspicuous than the differences in language and reasoning. The differences in articulating the rules, however, are clear enough.

The key issue in the battle over the meaning of the common law tradition can be seen perhaps most clearly in Judge Taft's classic opinion in the *Addyston Pipe* case, decided in 1898. That judgment was one of the most influential documents in the American debate which culminated in the *Standard Oil* decision of 1911, although the Supreme Court's opinion did not fully accept Judge Taft's view.

Judge Taft faced a contract among manufacturers of cast-iron pipe, largely sold to municipalities and utilities on public bidding. The partners, providing two-thirds of the supply in a large area of the country, agreed to meet secretly in advance of the contracts being let, and to bid among themselves for the work. The highest bidder in the ring became the lowest bidder at the sale, the others some-times putting in higher bids for the sake of appearances. The winner then shared his profits with his collaborators. The plan was defended on the usual grounds of preventing price wars, cut-throat competition, economic suicide, and the like.

The first question the court faced was whether the Sherman Act went beyond the common law, or adopted common law tests. Judge Taft thought the act was independent of the common law, but prudently put his opinion on the ground that the defendant's conduct violated the common law in any event, and therefore came within the defendants' theory of the statute. He distinguished two lines of cases in the common law, defining the public policy limitations on freedom of contract. The first view, which he supported, would confine the power to make contracts in restraint of trade to those situations where the restraint was ancillary to some other trans-action—the sale of good will, for example, the dissolution of a part-nership, an employment contract involving knowledge of the em-ployer's trade secrets. Such restraints, he said, were permissible, but only to the minimum extent that they were "reasonably" necessary to permit the principal object of the transaction to be effectuated, and "reasonably" confined as to time and space by the nature of that trans-action. In his opinion, all nonancillary restraints of competition, such as agreements among competitors as to the prices they charged, the markets they served, the supply they could offer, were invalid at common law, without more. "It is true," he said, "that there are some cases in which the courts, mistaking, as we conceive, the proper limits of the relaxation of the rules for determining the unreasonableness of restraints of trade, have set sail on a sea of doubt, and have assumed the power to say, in respect to contracts which have no other purpose and no other consideration on either side than the mutual restraint of the parties, how much restraint of competition is in the public interest, and how much is not.

"The manifest danger in the administration of justice according to so shifting, vague, and indeterminate a standard would seem to be a strong reason against adopting it."[11]

Be that as it may, the prevailing rule in the British courts, it is often said, did give precisely this gloss to the element of "reasonableness" which the judges could take into account in determining the enforceability of contracts which had no purpose other than the limitation of competition. While most of the modern British cases actually deal with the reasonableness of partial, ancillary restraints, such as those involved in the sale of a business, the liquidation of partnerships, the termination of employments, and the like,[12] there were several dicta, and a few decisions, which support the view commonly asserted. The courts seemed to take this position, in partial contrast to that of Judge Taft. The question of the reasonableness of the restriction on grounds of public policy is one of law, not of fact. The judges have been historically jealous of such contracts. Although older views were modified during the nineteenth century, such contracts will not be approved unless the judges are convinced they are reasonable, in reference to the interests of both the contracting parties and the public. Without more, restraints are contrary to public policy, and void, although special circumstances may be proved to

11. United States v. Addyston Pipe and Steel Co., 85 Fed. 271, 283–84 (C.C.A. 6th, 1898). The opinion continued by finding against the defendants under their theory of the common law, on the ground that the arrangement was unreasonable because it gave the defendants power to fix their prices, within considerable limits, or alternatively, if it should be considered necessary to determine the question (which Judge Taft doubted), because the prices they fixed were unreasonably high.

12. Or, alternatively, with the tortiousness of group refusals to deal, reprisals, and other forms of "boycott" or near-"boycott."

justify them. "The onus of proving such special circumstances must, of course, rest on the party alleging them. When once they are proved, it is a question of law for the decision of the judge whether they do or do not justify the restraint. There is no question of onus one way or another."[13] Where a trade or an industry has passed or is likely to pass into the hands or under the control of a single individual or group of individuals, or where a restraint of trade is likely to produce this result, the restraint may on grounds of public policy be unenforceable, as a monopoly illegal at common law and under the Statute of Elizabeth, however reasonable in the interest of the parties. Whether an effective attempt to secure such a monopoly is really being made is almost always a question of fact; in cases of lesser restraint, where the risk of monopoly in this sense does not arise, the judges may approve as enforceable even a general restraint deemed reasonable in the interest of the parties, and not otherwise injurious to the public. In such cases, however, where the reasonableness of a restraint between the parties is in issue, the parties must be seeking to protect some interest other than their advantage in avoiding competition: "the covenantee is not entitled to be protected against competition *per se*,"[14] and, finally, the concept of criminal conspiracy is not coterminous with that of the unenforceability of contracts. "[N]o contract was ever an offence at common law merely because it was in restraint of trade. The parties to such

13. Herbert Morris, Ltd. v. Saxelby (1916) 1 A.C. 688, 707 (judgment of Lord Parker of Waddington). See also, Mason v. Provident Clothing and Supply Co., Ltd. (1913) A.C. 724, 733. ("The respondents have to show that the restriction they have sought to impose goes no further than was reasonable for the protection of their business.") These views, derived from Lord Macnaghten's judgment in Nordenfelt v. The Maxim Nordenfelt Guns and Ammunition Co. Ltd. (1894) A.C. 535, 565, seem to provide a basis, or at least a background, for the presumption of illegality in the Restrictive Practices Act, and for the distribution of burdens of proof it establishes. For a discussion of presumptive illegality, see Appendix 1 to this chapter, p. 208.

14. McEllistrim v. Ballymacelligot Co-operative Agricultural and Dairy Society, Ltd. (1919) A.C. 548, 564, and see also 574, 579, 582. (Rule of dairy co-operative held invalid on suit of farmer member, as an illegal restraint of trade, *ultra vires* the society, for requiring members to sell all their milk to a creamery of the society, it being impossible for a member to withdraw from the society without the consent of its governing committee. The rule is unreasonable between the parties, without regard to larger questions of the public interest, as going beyond what is reasonably necessary for the protection of the covenantee, especially in view of the rules about withdrawal, which

a contract, even if unenforceable, were always at liberty to act on it in the manner agreed."[15]

From these cases there emerges, although not sharply in terms of holdings, the position that, in the absence of monopoly, the British courts could and should consider whether general, nonancillary contracts in restraint of competition among competitors should be upheld as reasonable, or condemned as unreasonable, in the light of the prices charged, the circumstances of the trade, and other factors of private and of public interest.[16] In the *North Western Salt Co. Ltd.* case, for example, which turned in the end on a question of pleading, Lord Parker of Waddington remarked, "The competition between salt producers within the area covered by the agreement . . . either *inter se* or with salt producers outside this area may have been so drastic that some combination limiting output and regulating competition within the area so as to secure reasonable prices may have been necessary, not only in the interests of the salt producers themselves, but in the interest of the public generally, for it cannot be to the public advantage that the trade of a large area should be ruined by a cut-throat competition."[17]

This line of thought does define a difference between the common law in Britain and in the United States, and between the British law and the law of the Sherman Act. The approach of the British courts helps to fix the approach taken in the British statutes of 1948 and 1956.

What would seem more important than this difference in the content of the word "reasonable" was the difference between the two systems in modes of enforcement. After 1890, the American courts faced a wide range of cases, largely selected by the government for

virtually enslave members.) See Horwood v. Millar's Timber and Trading Co. Ltd. (1917) 1 K.B. 305; Joseph Evans & Co., Ltd. v. Heathcote (1918) 1 K.B. 418 (Court of Appeal), especially at 434. Compare however, English Hop Growers, Ltd. v. Dering (1928) 2 K.B. 174 (Court of Appeal).

15. Attorney-General of the Commonwealth of Australia v. Adelaide Steamship Co. Ltd. (1913) A.C. 781, 797 (words of Lord Parker of Waddington). See, however, the judgment of Lord Dunedin in Sorrell v. Smith (1925) A.C. 700, 716–29, especially at 725.

The summary in the preceding text paragraph draws on language used in several of the leading cases, particularly *Adelaide Steamship Co., Mason, Morris, North Western Salt,* and *McEllistrim.*

16. For a discussion of cases pertaining to nonancillary agreements, see Appendix 2 to this chapter, p. 210.

17. (1914) A.C. 461, 479–80.

their public importance and exploring every aspect of the economic problem of monopoly. The British courts dealt with only a trickle of cases, brought by the happenstance of private litigation and largely concentrated on the fringes of the problem. They were hardly cases which might have led the British judges to consider whether they really meant what they occasionally said about the possible reasonableness of nonancillary restrictive arrangements among competititors.

The first of the committee reports which led to the 1948 legislation was filed in 1919. It proceeded from the investigation of profit levels during the First World War. The Committee on Trusts commented that trade associations and combines "are rapidly increasing in this country, and may within no distant period exercise a paramount control over all branches of British trade." Academic study of the problem, following Marshall's lead, developed slowly but steadily with the work of Sargent Florence, Macgregor, Plant, Macrosty, Allen, and the Robinsons. They prepared the way for the present wealth of monographic investigations, which now constitute a considerable part of the literature of British economics. And a series of committees and commissions continued to examine various aspects of the problem, especially the vexed matter of resale price maintenance. Neither the twenties nor the thirties proved to be times for action on this front. Britain's painful and depressing ordeal of the twenties was dominated by other issues, and by the attitudes which had crystallized earlier. During the thirties, the setting of the problem of industrial organization in Britain changed. Free trade was abandoned; cooperation among domestic competitors continued to increase, unrestrained by countervailing effort; and there was more and more British participation in European cartels. And what might be called the Keynesian period in the orientation of economic policy began, with far-reaching consequences in this as in other areas. The British White Paper on Employment Policy in 1944 suggested two aspects of the monopoly problem which have played a considerable role, I should guess, in the development of Britain's vigorous and confident postwar economic policy: the potentialities of more competition in keeping prices down during periods of near-inflation; and the advantages of competition over monopoly in permitting the economy to adjust quickly to programs of stabilization and growth based on the use of fiscal and monetary policy.

Confronting the prospect of postwar inflation, the 1944 White

Paper urged caution and moderation in wage and price policy. One could hardly admonish trade unions not to press for higher wages without contemplating the forces which may lead to rises in the price of goods. Beyond its precatory words to labor and to business, the White Paper commented on the apparently cumulative growth of monopolistic arrangements and influences in the British economy, and promised that the government would look into the question further, and consider the possibility of public action against monopoly and restraints on competition.

The second theme of the White Paper—the superior cyclical resilience of a more competitive economy—was barely hinted at in the document, and was certainly not developed. The relationships between market structure and the course of the trade cycle have been a neglected problem in economic theory. But the suggestion of the White Paper is certainly not implausible, both from the point of view of the flexibility of the economy in responding to moves of fiscal and monetary action, and, perhaps more important, as a factor in the complex sociological process of innovation and productivity.[18]

The inflationary bias of postwar full employment, the increasing urgency of British concern with productivity in the struggle for export markets, and, more recently, the articles, books, and discussion stirred up by the reports of the Monopolies' Commission and judgments of the Restrictive Practices Court, have tended to bring the monopoly question for the first time into the forefront of consciousness in British thinking about economic policy. Developments in political thought about economic problems served to reinforce this professional and governmental interest, and to give it a wider popular base. As the Labour Party's program of nationalization began to meet increasing political and intellectual resistance, it was natural for some members of that party to become more and more attracted to antimonopoly legislation as an alternative. This swing of the pendulum in public opinion was heightened by the unpopularity of direct controls as a means for dealing with the price consequences of excess purchasing power. Although the theory was wrong— under the pressure of excess purchasing power, prices seem to rise more in competitive than in monopolistic markets—it was widely believed that competitive market freedom, reinforced by the influence

18. I have tried to review this web of issues in chapter 10 of the book referred to *supra* note 5.

of legislation, could help to limit the price impact of excessive spending. Both in Britain and on the Continent, one of the recurring themes in discussing programs for broader trading areas is the importance of international competition in keeping prices down. Then again, other countries, and the European Economic Community, were experimenting with antimonopoly legislation, and visiting Americans never fail to preach its virtues. This trend in postwar thought, and law, was emphasized by the prolonged and, thus far, ineffective efforts to secure an international treaty against restrictive business practices, first through the Havana Charter and later through a special United Nations committee.

Against this background, the British Monopolies and Restrictive Practices (Inquiry and Control) Act of 1948 was passed, to be amended slightly in 1953, and substantially changed in content and procedure by the Restrictive Trade Practices Act of 1956, following on the important report of the Monopolies' Commission on Collective Discrimination in 1955. The 1948 act, in retrospect, seems to have been primarily an attempt to explore the realities of the problem in depth—a research effort, intended to accumulate information on the basis of which policy might later and more rationally design a suitable law. In that perspective, the 1956 act appears as a first, but probably not the final, response of the British Parliament to a problem whose contours are only beginning to be revealed.

There is no need here for a detailed description of the plan of these two statutes, and of the ideas they embody.[19] Suffice it to recall for present purposes that the British law now establishes four distinct procedures and standards in this field.

19. In addition to the several useful legal treatises on the statute and its interpretation, reference should be made at least to R. B. STEVENS & B. S. YAMEY, THE RESTRICTIVE PRACTICES COURT (1965); A. HUNTER, ed., MONOPOLY AND COMPETITION (1969); C. Grunfeld and B. S. Yamey, *United Kingdom,* in W. FRIEDMANN, ed., ANTI-TRUST LAWS: A COMPARATIVE SYMPOSIUM 340 (1956); Grunfeld & Yamey, *Restrictive Trade Practices Act, 1956* PUBLIC LAW, 1956, at 313; G. C. Allen, *Monopoly and Competition in the United Kingdom,* in EDWARD H. CHAMBERLIN, ed., MONOPOLY AND COMPETITION AND THEIR REGULATION 88 (1954) (also contains a useful bibliography at 108–9); John Jewkes, *British Monopoly Policy, 1944–1956,* 1 J. LAW & ECON. 1 (1958); S. R. Dennison, *The British Restrictive Trade Practices Act of 1956,* 2 J. LAW & ECON. 64 (1959); D. Cairns, *Monopolies and Restrictive Practices,* in M. GINSBERG, ed., LAW AND OPINION IN ENGLAND IN THE TWENTIETH CENTURY (1956), p. 173. C. Grunfeld, *Antitrust Law in Britain since the Act of 1956,* 6 AM. J. COMP. L. 439 (1957); A. Sutherland *The Restrictive Practices Court and Cotton Spinning,* 8 J. IND. ECON. 58

First, certain classes of agreements or arrangements among competitors in the production and supply of goods in the United Kingdom must be registered under the 1956 act, when they contain "restrictions"[20] as to prices, terms of sale, the kinds or quantities of goods to be produced, the use of processes, customers, or areas where sales or purchases can be made. Once agreements are registered, the Registrar, whose important office is established by the act, must bring proceedings to test their validity before the Restrictive Practices Court, consisting of lay and legal members. While the act does not so specify, the Registrar acts in these proceedings as something like a Public Prosecutor, in most instances thus far opposing a declaration of legality. The court must then determine whether the proponents of the agreement have met their burden of proof in establishing that it is in the public interest. Under the act, it is presumed that a registered agreement is contrary to the public interest unless the court is satisfied under section 21 on any one or more of seven defined grounds of possible reasonableness which might justify the restriction,[21] and is further satisfied that the restriction is not unreasonable, having regard to the balance between these seven considerations and the interests of the consuming public, or those of actual or potential competitors of the respondents, not parties to the agreement. Under this act, as of August 7, 1959, 2,180 agreements were registered, of which 600 were abandoned, canceled, or allowed to expire. One hundred and thirty more agreements had by then been

---

(1959); A. Hunter, *Competition and the Law,* 27 MANCHESTER SCHOOL 52 (1959); J. B. Heath, *The 1956 Restrictive Practices Act: Price Agreements and the Public Interest,* 27 MANCHESTER SCHOOL 72 (1959); J. T. Craig, *A Survey of Recent Case Law,* 13 NORTH IRELAND LEGAL Q. 225 (1959). I have also had the advantage of reading unpublished papers by A. Beacham and T. Wilson.

20. *I.e.,* "any negative obligation, whether express or implied, and whether absolute or not": s. 6(3).

21. The famous "gateways" of s. 21 (1). They are (a) that the restriction is reasonably necessary, in view of the character of the goods, to protect the public against injury in connection with the consumption, installation or use of the goods; (b) that the removal of the restriction would deny the public "other specific and substantial benefits or advantages enjoyed or likely to be enjoyed" by them; (c) that the restriction is reasonably necessary to counteract measures taken by a person not party to the agreement, with a view to preventing or restricting competition in the parties' business; (d) that the restriction is reasonably necessary to enable the parties to deal fairly with

presented to the court, or were being prepared for presentation, and it was thought that their fate would govern that of 1,050 other agreements on the register. The remaining group of 400 agreements were being studied, according to the Registrar.[22]

Secondly, the act of 1956 authorizes individual enforcement of resale price maintenance agreements and prohibits their collective enforcement, authorizing the Crown, apparently in the High Court, to enforce this provision by proceedings for injunction.

Thirdly, the Monopolies' Commission retains jurisdiction in cases under the 1948 act that are not covered by the 1956 Act. More concretely, this means that in the absence of a registrable agreement, the commission has the power to make investigations, and to report back to the Board of Trade, when the board asks it to determine whether the public interest is being served by an industry where one company, or any interconnected group of companies, produces more than one-third of the goods supplied to any British market, home or export. When such reports are made, they may be laid before Parliament by a competent authority, and such recommendations by way of remedy as Parliament may approve can be carried out by the Executive. Beyond this power to act on reference in the case of particular industries, the commission may under section 15 make general studies, at the request of the Board of Trade, such as its important study of collective discrimination.

And fourthly, considerable common law jurisdiction remains after the passage of these statutes—perhaps unimpaired common law jurisdiction, at least in theory, as some commentators have suggested.[23]

"preponderant" suppliers or purchasers; (e) that the removal of the restriction would be likely to have a serious and persistent adverse effect on the average level of unemployment in the areas affected by the agreement or (f) to cause a reduction in the volume or earnings of a significant export business; or (g) that the restriction is reasonably required in connection with the maintenance of another restrictive agreement approved by the court. See B. S. Yamey, *Restrictive Agreements and the Public Interest: a Critique of the Legislation* (1960) PUBLIC LAW 152.

22. These figures come from a paper *Progress under the Restrictive Trade Practices Act, 1956* delivered by the Registrar, Mr. R. L. Sich, before Section F of the British Association, September 1959, and kindly made available by him in manuscript.

23. See, *e.g.,* WILBERFORCE, CAMPBELL AND ELLES, THE LAW OF RESTRICTIVE TRADE PRACTICES AND MONOPOLIES (1957), §§ 4, 201.

On the face of it, the system for investigation and enforcement established by these two statutes is not complete. It does not purport to deal with all, nor even with almost all, aspects of the economic problem of monopolization and restraints on competition. Earlier studies, and the useful reports of the Monopolies' Commission, document significant tendencies toward monopoly and concentration of power, and widespread habits of restriction in the British economy.[24] Many of the most significant questions raised by this panorama are either exempt from both statutes, or are remitted to the commission under the 1948 Act. Mergers, monopolizations, tying clauses, the abuse of patent rights, discriminations, arrangements in the export trade, for example, seem to be left entirely or partially in limbo, or most doubtfully to be squeezed into one or the other of the statutes, by heroic construction.

Further, both the enforcement procedure of the Monopolies' Commission and that of the Restrictive Practices Court give rise to serious doubts on grounds of efficacy in the light of American experience.

The complex procedure of the Monopolies Commission, as Mr. Yamey has pointed out,[25] raises difficult and embarrassing questions for the Executive, by making every attempt at action under the 1948 act a political event. The problem of political pressure would be even more acute for members of Parliament, should the procedure be much used, for the parties in interest would naturally turn for help in many instances to members of Parliament, either as constituents or as friends. Yet a political appeal is the only possible appeal under the act from a report of the commission. I cannot imagine this enforcement procedure to be a practical or satisfactory way for dealing with large numbers of problems over the long run, from the point of view either of the government or of the individuals concerned. After all, private business affairs may be transformed or reorganized in the end by executive order under the 1948 act, without an oppor-

24. See D. BURN, ed., THE STRUCTURE OF BRITISH INDUSTRY (1958);
R. EVELY & I. M. D. LITTLE, CONCENTRATION IN BRITISH INDUSTRY (1960);
P. E. Hart, *Business Concentration in the United Kingdom,* 123 J. ROYAL STATISTICAL SOC'Y 50 (1960); P. L. COOK & R. COHEN, EFFECTS OF MERGERS (1958).
25. B. S. Yamey, in "United Kingdom," *supra* note 19, at 384–90. See also S. R. Dennison, *supra* note 19, at 65.

tunity to have the evidence of the responsibility of the individuals concerned reviewed by ordinary appeal.

The judicial procedure of the Restrictive Practices Court seems more promising to an American eye.[26] Here the question in my mind is whether the standard of judgment in section 21, codifying in considerable part Lord Macnaghten's philosophy in the *Nordenfelt* case, does not require too much of the judges. Their task is not the difficult but finite one of determining whether competition has been substantially restrained, but the almost boundless question whether such restraints, when established, are in the public interest. It is already clear under section 21 that the court will consider whether prices are "too" high or "too" low during the period being studied.[27] The American courts have consistently said that they would not and

26. Much of the objection to action by the Monopolies' Commission under the vague formulas of the 1948 act is cured by the more specific definition of legislative policy in the 1956 act. A good deal of the debate as to whether it is constitutionally appropriate or politically wise to delegate "policy-making" functions to the Judiciary, or to an administrative tribunal, derive from the fact that the 1948 act was essentially one to authorize investigation, not a statement of policy, such as that through which the Congress delegated enforcement responsibility to the judges under the Sherman and Clayton Acts, and the comparable delegation by Parliament in the 1956 act. The debate is also featured, however, by traces of the ancient popular myth that judges do not "make" but only "find" the law, and that they should not be concerned with issues of "policy," as distinguished from "law." The naïveté of such views does not require comment. Experience in this as in other fields of legislation confirms that direct action by government departments is an almost unworkable procedure for carrying out policies of this kind, and that either administrative or judicial methods are almost indispensable if a legislative program is to be consistently and fairly applied to a wide range of complex factual situations.

27. Re Yarn Spinners' Agreement (1959) 1 All E.R. 299; L.R. 1 R.P. 118, for example, does not finally clarify whether the agreement was held illegal because all minimum price-fixing is a statutory detriment; because the minimum prices actually set in this case were actual prices, higher than they would otherwise have been; because the minimum prices were calculated in accordance with a formula which the court regarded as yielding an "artificial figure calculated on a hypothetical average cost" (p. 312), and not a genuine stop-loss scheme which might have been acceptable (p. 313); or because the prices fixed were in some sense "too" high, or at least higher than they would have been in a free market (p. 314). See also Re Water-Tube Boilermakers' Associations' Agreement (1959) 3 All E.R. 257; L.R. 1 R.P. 285, 335, 341, Re Blanket Manufacturers' Agreement (1959) 2 All E.R. 1; L.R. 1 R.P. 208; Re Wholesale and Retail Bakers of Scotland Association's Agreement (1960) L.R. 1 R. P. 347.

could not make such determinations, since prices which seemed reasonable today might become unreasonable tomorrow, so long as the power to fix them survived.[28] How the competing values of section 21 are to be balanced by the court is not yet clear. Several observers have commented that the range of choices open to the court under section 21, and the comparable range of choices open to the commission under section 6 of the 1948 act, are so much a matter of discretion that no case can become a precedent for any other case under either statute, and that no rational coordination of the enforcement policy of the law could be achieved by appellate review.

Risks of this kind may not materialize if the lead of some of the early cases decided by the Restrictive Practices Court is pursued. These crisp and vivid judgments, especially that in the *Yarn Spinners* case, are in the finest style of British statutory interpretation, and represent the common law instinct for policy at its vigorous best. But the *Boilermakers'* case has somewhat fudged the line marked out by the *Chemists' Federation* and *Yarn Spinners*.[29] And there is no *a priori* ground to suppose, until the higher courts have spoken, that the presumption of illegality under section 21, the weight to be given by its last paragraph to the public interest in price competition, and the extent of the respondent's burden of proof, will have the all but conclusive force given them in *Yarn Spinners*.

Suppose, however, that this should turn out to be the case. What then? Let us suppose, that is to say, that most registrable agreements are found on inquiry to be against the public interest. Suppose that the custom of making open agreements for the self-regulation of competition is substantially weakened in British business practice. Would that result solve the problem to which the statute is addressed and substantially increase the degree of competition in the British economy?

Economic studies indicate that in many British industries the degree of concentration is quite as high as in the American economy, and that in important sectors a large part of market supply is offered

28. United States v. Trenton Potteries Co., 273 U.S. 392 (1927); United States v. Socony-Vacuum Oil Co., 310 U.S. 150 (1940); Kiefer-Stewart Co. v. Joseph E. Seagran & Sons, 340 U.S. 211 (1951).
29. Re Chemists' Federation Agreement (No. 2) (1958) 3 All E.R. 488 L.R. 1 R.P. 75, and cases cited *supra* note 27. See B. S. Yamey, *Water-Tube Boilers: Contradictions and a Paradox,* 23 M.L.R. 79 (1960).

by not more than three, four, five, or six firms.[30] By reason of their small number, these firms have a considerable capacity to avoid price competition, by finding forms of cooperation without open collusion which could permit each competitior to guess with some assurance as to the policy of his rivals and as to his rivals' response to a move of his own. The British people have earned, and deserve, an enviable reputation for respecting the law. But would a group of oligopolists violate the law, in such circumstances, if they gave up their older agreement and fell back on one or another of the familiar patterns of loose but effective oligopoly cooperation? They might use direct price leadership, announced lists, basing-point practices, statistical exchanges, customary discounts, or other common means for minimizing uncertainty.[31] Or equally, would they be violating the present law if mergers brought the number of companies in a market down to the level which would make cooperation of this kind irresistibly tempting, without the formality of agreement?

Before such a development, the law could take two lines. By interpreting section 6 of the 1956 act broadly, it could move to find registrable as "arrangements," or as "trade association recommendations," "express or implied," a wide variety of intangible but effective techniques for organizing or disciplining the modes of competition in markets "of the few." Alternatively, the courts could refuse jurisdiction under the 1956 act for a considerable class of such problems, on the ground that they involve arrangements too impalpable to be registered, and remit them either to the Monopolies' Commission, if they could be reached under the 1948 statute, or to effective immunity if they cannot be so reached.

But can the British law as now framed undo mergers, or break up monopolies or near monopolies, if found to be against the public interest? Section 14 of the 1948 act seems to include in its definition of the public interest "all matters which appear in the particular circumstances to be relevant" to the following issues, among others: the most efficient and economical possible production at prices which best meet requirements; the organization of industry and trade in such ways as best encourage progressive increases in efficiency and new enterprise; the fullest use and best distribution of

---

30. See studies referred to *supra* note 24.
31. See, for example, *Restrictions Off the Register,* 195 ECONOMIST 267 (April 16, 1960), reporting on the development of "open-price" plans.

resources, the development of technical improvements, expansion, and the opening of new markets. Section 7 gives the commission an apparently comprehensive power to make recommendations for action to be taken "to remedy or prevent any mischiefs which result or may be expected to result" from conditions or acts found to be against the public interest, "whether under this act or otherwise," by public authority or by the parties. But section 10, enabling a competent authority to make orders "for the purpose of remedying or preventing any mischiefs which in their opinion result or may be expected to result" from conditions found to be against the public interest, appears to be much more limited. The five operative subsections of section 10 (2) deal with the enforceability of agreements or arrangements, withholding goods, preferences, and tying clauses, and there is no catch-all clause that might give section 10 the same scope as section 14. It would appear that "orders" under the 1948 act are more narrowly confined than the "recommendations" made possible by section 7.

The distinction has not so far been of importance in the circumstances of particular investigations. And in any event, such recommendations, whether for action under section 10 or otherwise, would require special legislation before they could be made effective, situation by situation.

Whether the present statutes provide even a theoretical remedy against mergers, monopolies, or near-monopolies, it is difficult to see how they would permit either the court or the commission to deal with some of the most pressing problems of oligopoly, which are among the most important economic aspects of the monopoly problem in all modern economies.

A large part of the litigation under the Sherman Act has been concerned with problems of this kind—that is, with determining whether a given plan or pattern of action in a market of the few was in fact a collective program which significantly interfered with the price mechanism. These cases were often difficult to decide, for the programs in question frequently had other purposes or effects, and they were defended by the same anthology of bad but plausible economic arguments which have bombarded the Monopolies' Commission, the Restrictive Practices Court, and the High Court. But the task of the American courts under the Sherman Act is finished when they find a concert of action which can be brought within reach of section 1 of the Sherman Act as a combination, and found to constitute a significant limitation on competitive conditions. With these questions in mind, the American courts have studied plans for disseminating statistics, joint buying and selling arrangements, programs requiring the public announcement of prices or adherence to announced prices, basing point price plans, and other devices and arrangements which may reduce the effective number of sellers or the independence of their price policies.

Even if such situations could be brought within reach of either British statute in the absence of fairly clear-cut agreements, would the statutory criteria of the public interest suffice? Patterns of market behavior of this kind affect not only the short-run implications of the monopoly problem—whether prices and output are higher or lower than they would be under competition—but the infinitely more important long-run consequences of monopoly, in its generic sense: the entry of new firms, and the rate of growth of old ones; the pace of innovation; and the strength of economic incentives to adopt cost-reducing changes in technique and in management. I am inclined to guess, for example, that the greatest sin of cooperative oligopolies, in America at least, during the postwar period, has been a tendency to keep prices too low rather than too high. Economic "statesmanship," the pressure of public opinion and of labor relations, the admonitions of ministers, and a strong long-run economic interest in discouraging the entry of rivals have all combined to lead such groups to price "moderation," as it is called. Such policies might well meet with the approval of the Monopolies' Commission and the Restrictive Practices Court, if they could be brought before it. But in the long run they would distort the flow of capital, and affect the rate of growth of the economy in ways which might do very great damage indeed.

IV

To what conclusions does this comparison lead? Both legal systems now face the same series of problems—difficult, interesting, and important problems of economic and of social policy. They include issues of efficiency in the short-run and long-run use of resources, issues of fairness in opportunity, issues of political principle in the dispersal of power. Each system has approached these problems differently, despite the fact that we shared the common law of the subject and all that went into it. Differences in experience, differences in opinion, differences in intellectual climate have affected the course of events. The contrast offers an intriguing subject to the historian and theorist of law, and to those interested in observing the many-sided interaction between law and the society it serves and helps to govern.

I doubt whether comparative studies of this kind should be considered a final stage in the quest for law reform. They can be of value, rather, in helping to formulate the issues, in distinguishing the relevant from the irrelevant, and in achieving a clearer definition of ends and of means. And they should help to identify the problems on which more knowledge is needed before change within each system according to its own genius can and should be undertaken.

This, I take it, is one of the justifications for the academic study of social policy.

Appendix 1

Presumptive Illegality before the 1956 Act

The matter of presumptive illegality, and of the onus of proof in demonstrating it, was not without difficulty before the passage of the 1956 act, despite the famous passage in Mitchel v. Reynolds (1911) 1 P. Wms. 181, 192. The most extended modern consideration of the problem appears in North Western Salt Company, Ltd. v. Electrolytic Alkali Company, Ltd. (1914) A.C. 461. That case was an action for damages, arising from conceded breaches of a 1907 contract under which the plaintiff-appellant, a combination alleged to include substantially all the salt manufacturers of northwest England, agreed to purchase respondent company's entire commercial output of salt (subject to a minor exception) for a four-year period, amounts and prices being specified. The respondents agreed in return not to sell salt, save as distributors for the combination, on the same terms as other distributors. Respondents exercised a repurchase option under this contract, and controversy arose as to its interpretation, and also whether respondents were required to sign a distributor's agreement. Respondents secretly sold salt to the trade, in breach of the contract. In their pleadings, after full consideration of the point, the respondent company did not allege the invalidity of the 1907 contract, but the question arose in the course of cross-examining one of appellants' witnesses. Leave to amend was denied, the trial judge taking the view that if he was satisfied after trial that the contract was on its face illegal and unenforceable as a matter of law, he would take judicial notice of this and disallow the claim. The legality of the 1907 contract, on its face a four-year output contract between a manufacturer and a distributive group, was deemed to turn on its connections with the distribution agreement, and with another agreement (dated 1906), between the plaintiffs and certain other salt manufacturers. Before the court could conclude that the 1907 contract was illegal, it should have had the distribution contract and the 1906 contract fully presented to it, and, further, it should have had evidence as to the competition faced by the plaintiffs from foreign or nonmember domestic rivals and advantages and disadvantages to the public of the arrangements made, in the light of economic circumstances and the like. While the court agreed that there were instances where it should refuse to enforce a contract illegal on its face, even though that fact was not pleaded, here it might easily lead to "a miscarriage of justice" (p. 469) to reach such a result, since plaintiff might have been able to produce evidence, had he been warned by the pleadings to do so, "rebutting any presumption of illegality which might be based on some isolated fact" (*ibid.*) The court lacked evidence on questions of fact material to the legality of the contract, and the pleadings "had thrown on the appellants no duty to bring forward such evidence" (p. 470). The case not being completely presented, it was the court's duty not to decide it on this ground.

Viscount Haldane's judgment says that "to be valid a clause imposing a restraint must be reasonable, and he who says that a restraint is so must make it out" (*ibid.*). But evidently this burden is soon discharged, in many instances it would seem as a matter of construing the text of the contract rather than of producing evidence to explain it. Then there is an onus on the party alleging the *illegality* of the contract as unreasonable with respect to the public interest to show that it "is calculated to produce a monopoly or enhance prices to an unreasonable extent; . . . once the court is satisfied that the restraint is reasonable as between the parties the onus will be no light one" (p. 473).

This distinction—that the onus of proof of reasonableness as between the parties is upon the proponent of the contract, while its opponent bears the risk of not persuading the court that the contract is void as contrary to the public interest, notwithstanding its reasonableness as between the parties—is frequently met: Morris v. Saxelby (1916) 1 A.C. 688, 706, 707 (enforceability of covenant restricting employment of former servant). However, the distinction between the two kinds of reasonableness is difficult to sustain. The rules confining ancillary restraints to the minimum compatible with the performance of the principal object of the contract derive from strong rules of public policy—the public interest in allowing a man to pursue his own calling, and in competition as well; these are the same considerations which emerge when the reasonableness of nonancillary restraints is independently examined.

Appendix 2

Nonancillary Contracts in Restraint of
Competition

Among the few cases which may be read to uphold nonancillary agreements restraining competition are Wickens v. Evans, 3 Y and J. 318 (Exch. Pleas, 1892) (general demurrer denied to counts of declaration in assumpsit alleging breach of agreement among three trunk and box makers not to compete with each other in designated parts of England, there being no risk of monopoly or clearly defined collective restraint on the entry of rivals; agreement good against demurrer as a "partial" restraint, on the consideration of the mutual advantage of the parties, in the absence of a showing of disadvantage to the public); and perhaps Shrewsbury and Birmingham Ry. v. London and Northwestern Ry. (1951) 21 (3) L.J.Q.B. (N.S.) 89, a brief opinion overruling a demurrer in a suit on an agreement between two railroads not to compete on a particular line, there being no risk of monopoly or of depriving the public of the benefits of competition generally; the agreement "is no more illegal than it would be for two persons engaged in trade to agree that one shall not exercise his trade nor compete with the other in a particular district," (p. 93); English Hop Growers, Ltd. v. Dering (1928) 2 K.K. 174 (Court of Appeal) (hop growers' cooperative, established as exclusive agency for the sale of the members' crops, sues for liquidated damages under the contract, defendant having sold his hops independently. There was no argument to the reasonableness of the contract in the public interest; it was held not to be unreasonable between the parties).

Mogul Steamship Co., v. McGregor, Gow & Co. (1892) A.C.25, may possibly be classed in this group, although it is by no means apparent that a person injured as a result of others making a contract unenforceable among themselves as in unreasonable restraint of trade is *ipso facto* entitled to sue for damages or an injunction, in the absence of a statute (see Lord Field's remarks at p. 57), or a showing of something that could be identified as "malice" rather than commercial rivalry. Unless the element of combination made a difference, absent monopoly or near-monopoly, the legality of a clause in a contract of carriage offering a lower rate for exclusive dealing would seem a problem in interpreting "ancillary" contracts, in Judge Taft's sense of the term. The facts in the *Mogul* case should be recalled in this connection. The case denied both damages and an injunction to a plaintiff shipping company against the program of the defendants, a "conference" comprising a large number of the independent, regular shipping lines providing year-round service to Hankow and Shanghai. The conference members offered a 5 percent discount to shippers who dealt exclusively with them, to the disadvantage of plaintiffs and other "tramp" operators who sought to share the China tea traffic during its annual six-weeks peak season. There was no showing of malice, beyond defendants' desire to secure for themselves as much of the tea shipped from Hankow as their ships could carry, nor of monopoly, since the court assumed that entry into the business was easy, and (p. 50) that competition would naturally increase if rates rose.

Attorney-General of Australia v. Adelaide Steamship Co. (1913) A.C. 781, rests on the Australian Industries Preservation Act, whose criteria, the Judicial Committee on the Privy Council held, were different from those of the common law and of the Sherman Act.

See, denying the claim, Master, Wardens, and Society of the Mystery of Gunmakers v. Fell (1742) Willes 384 (by-law of Gunmaker's Company goes beyond the reasonable regulation of the trade in protecting the public against defective gun-barrels by forbidding any members to sell barrels to nonmembers in London or within four miles, there being no reason to suppose that nonmembers cannot fit gun-barrels to stocks as well as members); Kores Mfg. Co., Ltd. v. Kolok Mfg. Co., Ltd. (1958) 2 All E.R. 65 (Court of Appeal) (agreement among two important competitors in an industry of twenty firms not to employ each other's former employees for a period of five years from the termination of employment held to go beyond reasonable protection of permissible interests); McEllistrim v. Ballymacelligott Co-operative Agricultural and Dairy Society, Ltd. (1919) A.C. 548, summarized in note 14 *supra*; Joseph Evans & Co., Ltd. v. Heathcote (1918) 1 K.B. 418 (Court of Appeal).

Nor is Sorrell v. Smith (1925) A.C. 700 a clear instance, since it involved a contest between rival boycott policies in the same trade, and may have held no more than that plaintiff, having unclean hands, could not obtain injunctive relief. Plaintiff was one of a group of retail newsagents in London. They sought to control the number of newspaper shops by collectively refusing to buy from wholesale newsagents who dealt with retailers opening new shops without their permission. Plaintiff, for the group, ceased buying from R., because R. had sold to an unauthorized shop, and began to buy from W. Defendants, a committee of the newspaper publishers, countered by threatening to cut off W.'s supply unless W. refused to sell to plaintiff, for the purpose of restoring plaintiff's custom to R., and frustrating the retail newsagents' boycott policy. Plaintiff's attempt to restrain defendant publishers from putting economic pressure on W., so that the retailing group could freely put economic pressure on R., failed.

Seven

The Ethics of Competition Revisited

The theme of this distinguished lecture series, the morals of trade, directs thought to an unresolved conflict in our view of ourselves and of our society and culture.

With one lobe of our brains, we know that business, commerce, and industry, when well conducted, are socially useful activities, worthy of man's best efforts and of his pride. We know that they offer some men the opportunity to express and fulfill their creative instincts, and that they have greatly advanced the well-being of the human race.

Yet we never stop recalling another feature of the inner terrain —the memory that moralists whose words echo in our minds have frowned on moneymaking and driven money changers from the temple, considered money the root of all evil and poverty as morally superior to affluence. Indeed, some have found poverty a necessary condition of spiritual grace. Societies we respect have regarded trade as an occupation unworthy of gentlemen.

Some of our noblest men have preached against self-seeking, the key virtue of our economic order, as a sin. They have identified business with greed, rapacity, and other moral offenses, although pride, envy, and the more naked forms of selfishness are quite as evident in the noncommercial realms of life and power as they are in trade. Rules against usury are imbedded in our law, and in our thoughts. And many of the greatest spirits in our tradition have advocated organizing the economic activities of man in ways which they con-

This chapter was given as the Barbara Weinstock Lecture on the Morals of Trade at the University of California, Berkeley, in 1962, and published in a slightly different version in 5 (3) CALIFORNIA MANAGEMENT REVIEW 13 (1963). © 1963 by the Regents of the University of California.

sidered morally superior to the quest of individuals for personal gain: cooperation rather than competition; service rather than profit; craft rather than mass production; guild socialism or some other variant of ancient communal ideas, which they have thought would fulfill better than capitalism the command that all worldly goods be given to the poor, and that treasures upon earth not be laid up for oneself.

Responding to this underlying current of anxiety about the moral foundation of business, we have sought in recent years to call business a profession, and to give it the dignity and status our culture has reserved in the past for the ministry, the profession of arms, medicine, law, and the public service.

Common forms of speech reflect the duality of our views about economic affairs. People often distinguish "productive" from "unproductive" work. They view the social contributions of farmers, laborers, and scientists as "productive," while middlemen, bankers, and advertising experts are classified as social parasites. This usage recalls the wry observation of A. P. Lerner that after the 1917 revolution in Russia, during the period of disorganization and famine, bold men scoured the countryside for horses and wagons and brought wheat from the farms, where it was rotting, to the starving cities, where they sold it at a profit. When caught, these enterprising organizers of an essential social service were shot as speculators.

I shall try to deal with one aspect of this paradoxical problem: our attitudes toward competition and monopoly in economic life, and their place in our ethical universe. Here, as in so many areas, our law expresses not merely the economic and social policies of society, but its strong moral feeling as well.

Let me begin, after the fashion of lawyers, with a concrete problem.

In 1960, high officials of some of the great electrical companies pleaded guilty to charges of conspiring to fix prices in the sale of certain electrical products, and later a few actually served jail terms for their offenses. The episode was a shock to public and to business opinion, and it was much debated. The prevailing conclusion, I should guess, supported the view of the trial court that what these men did was a crime, repugnant not merely to the Sherman Act but to deeply established feelings of right conduct. To meet in secret, to use false names and a code to prevent detection, to arrange in advance for the low bid on contracts seemingly awarded after the public submission of competitive, sealed bids—these features of the case were considered to be convincing evidence of conscious wrongdoing.

And, quite apart from such melodramatic details, the act of fixing prices by agreement among competitors was in itself a violation of rules society had established and proclaimed as right for at least seventy years.

The view of monopoly as a moral and a legal wrong goes back, in fact, much more than seventy years in our customs and in our law. Some of the earliest English law books report the treatment of monopolies and conspiracies to limit competition as a crime. Medieval statutes confirm the view. And, from the eighteenth century on, both English and American cases reflect a strong public policy against all sorts of arrangements to restrict competition. It appears in our criminal law, and in our law of property, torts, and contract. This tradition in the law was given new dimensions, and new momentum, when Congress passed and the President signed the Sherman Act in 1890.

That statute translated the ancient public policy of the law into a far more effective pressure on the organization of business than had ever been the case before. It provided new procedures for affirmative action by the state, through which it could vindicate the statutory policy against monopolies and other restraints of competition. And, by using the old device of private litigation for three times the amount of damages sustained from a violation of the law, it made the reach of the law far greater, potentially at least, than the range of possible cases which the government could bring itself.

The statute was passed, the Supreme Court said, in response to the economic conditions of the times and the concern about concentrated economic and social power engendered by the merger movement of the period. There was a fear, Justice Harlan remarked, of "a new form of slavery," quite as odious as that which had been abolished on the battlefield only twenty-seven years before. Thus the law embodied not merely an economic policy toward economic organization—a rather neutral technical matter of calculating efficiencies and inefficiencies in the use of resources—but an old protest against what was universally felt to be an injustice—paying toll to a monopolist, or a near-monopolist, considered to be no better than a modern robber baron.

The reaction of opinion to the electrical industry cases of 1960 and 1961 attests the surviving power of the element of moral feeling in our antitrust law. The indignation expressed by the trial judge in charge of the case, and by many newspaper editorials, was heightened, I should guess, by an extrinsic factor: the extent to which opinion had come to accept the popular thesis, advanced on a wide front during the last few years, that business had entered a new era of maturity and social responsibility, and that it has acquired what some have described as a social conscience. The so-called managerial revolution, we are frequently told, assures us that our economic affairs are being benignly conducted by a new breed of business executive, who carries on the economic activities of society in a spirit of sweet reasonableness, if not benevolent despotism. Abandoning the callous rule of maximizing profits, the managers of industry are now said to conduct our economic affairs in the interest of workers, suppliers, and the community at large, and not merely to enrich the selfish stockholders. Against the background of these views, the behavior condemned in the electrical industry cases had distinct and unpleasant overtones of hypocrisy.

The early common law policy against monopolies and restraints of competition had always been regarded with special enthusiasm in America. Jefferson wanted a prohibition against monopoly included in the Bill of Rights. The suspicion of concentrated power so characteristic of all our political arrangements had its counterpart in the sphere of economic affairs. Equality, as Tocqueville rightly noted, is the first idea of American society. We are naturally as hostile to a closed oligarchy of business and finance as to political rule by hereditary dukes, earls, and lords. The most conservative business leaders of Houston and San Francisco do not react kindly to the thought of being ruled from Wall Street.

The social instincts favoring competition, and opposing monopoly, gained special strength in the United States from two sources.

The first of these is the Protestant tradition, with its stress on the individual's personal responsibility for his salvation, and the revolution in political thought which corresponds to it. The American culture was formed in the image of one of the most extreme of the nonconformist versions of Protestantism—that of Congregational Puritanism. The powerful creed of the New England Puritans, the true ancestors of the nation, molded an intense American ethic which taught generations of men and women to accept individual responsibility both for their own actions and for those of the community in which they lived.

The second general stream of ideas supporting competition and opposing monopoly came to the American mind from the literature of economics. Drawn from older French and English pamphlets and treatises, that literature was given modern scientific form in the books which stretch from Adam Smith and Ricardo past the Mills, Senior, and Jevons, to General Walker, Taussig, the Clarks, and Marshall. The inherent strength in our culture of ideas stressing the autonomous responsibility of the individual both for his salvation and for his government is reflected in our thought about economic affairs.

The individual, rather than the social group, was the center of attention and policy. His liberation was the beginning and end of religious and political thought. In this dialogue about man the atom, and man as a participant in the social order, we see a true kernel of distinction between ideas we often call liberal and those we like to identify as conservative. Those delightful words, around which such strong loyalties cluster, are often abused. They take on genuine meaning as a difference between those who favor the one at the expense of the many, and those who would sacrifice the freedom of the one to the greater good of the greater number; between those who see man and his soul as the be-all and end-all of social arrangements, and those whose first concern is the stable functioning of an assured religious and social order. In a stable order of that traditional kind, each person has an assigned task, and salvation for all is provided through the communion of the group in its common tasks, its common pleasures, its common loyalties and sources of pride, its common rituals and sacraments.

If the Declaration of Independence had been written by a Puritan from Connecticut, our society would no doubt have defined its great ambition as each man's "duty of life, liberty, and the pursuit of good." But the difference of view between Puritanism and the felicific calculus is a minor variation, a nuance on the liberal theme. Both the accepted Virginia version, and the alternate one I have suggested, gloss the same individualist and even existential idea: that man's freedom is the important thing, and society a necessary evil, to be kept to an indispensable minimum. Even at some risk of social disorder, man the individual should be assured the largest possible realm of privacy and discretion as a positive good in itself. Within that realm, like Jeremiah and Thoreau, man was to seek his own answers to fundamental problems of personal and social morality: "Wherefore doth the way of the wicked prosper? Wherefore are all they happy that deal very treacherously?"

These were not questions to which the liberated man, conscious of

his inescapable responsibility, could accept an official answer, even
from the Most High. If the principle of individual responsibility led
to a variety of views, and a diversity of sects, so much the better.
Religious orthodoxy was fragmented, and the old unified society
with it. The followers of Jeremiah were not concerned. Indeed, they
rejoiced at the weakening of orthodox dogma, although they grieved
because so many willfully refused to acknowledge the manifest
truth of the Puritan code.

The same premise led to the same corollary in the world of politics. The governors, we are authoritatively told, derive their just
powers from the consent of the governed. Man could no more escape
his responsibility for the acts of his state than for the morality of his
own behavior. Hence Thoreau wrote his famous tract on civil disobedience, raising again the issue of man's duty with regard to bad
laws which has been so notable and so difficult a feature of thought
and experience in this tragic century.

In political theory, Locke reconciled the claims of freedom and
those of society in the form which we in this country have found
most satisfactory and acceptable. The men of the Philadelphia Convention, following Locke and Montesquieu, put the free atoms into
workable social molecules, without unduly qualifying their freedom
of motion or of thought. They confined diversity a little, but within
ample limits—limits, nonetheless, and limits well short of chaos.

The classical economists accomplished a comparable feat for our
economic affairs. They developed the theory, so firmly imbedded in
our minds, that if each man pursued his own economic interests in
ways which seemed most profitable to him, a harmonious economic
structure would emerge, serving the best interests of society as a
whole. Economic freedom, freedom of contract, and the free market
were not alone enough, even in the eyes of the most devout believers
in laissez-faire, to assure this happy and automatic reconciliation
of the interests of the one with those of the many. Not even the classical economists were anarchists. They knew that society exists, and
must exist, and that the many have rights as well as the one. They
were radicals determined, in the name of liberal freedom, to sweep
away many of the laws and customs which still shaped society in
feudal and mercantilist patterns.

At the same time, however, they believed in strong traditions of
charity, and favored action by the state, as well, to lay down the
rules of the game for the market and to establish the essential facilities

and preconditions which made even its theoretical functioning possible: the institutions of order; a monetary system; laws against fraud and monopoly; arrangements to assure access to markets and to information; poor laws; laws protecting the weak; and so on. Given these qualifications, they thought a free competitive ordering of economic affairs would be the economic analogue of individual freedom in politics: "the obvious and simple system of natural liberty," in the famous phrase.

Experience, and the development of theory, provided both a more systematic justification for this approach and a fuller realization of its shortcomings. If markets were free and competitive, and resources could be shifted from one use to another, the theory of competition provided the only norm economics has ever developed for measuring efficiency in the use of resources, and for measuring equity in the distribution of the income arising from their use. The pressure of competing demands from consumers played upon the market for goods and services, establishing prices at any moment of time. Producers responded to those prices, continuing to offer supplies so long as it paid them to do so. Relatively high profits in one sector attracted entrepreneurs, capital, and labor from other sectors, increasing the volume of their offerings, and driving down prices and profits.

Thus, in "the long run" so dear both to the classical and to the contemporary tradition in economics, profits tended everywhere to be the same; prices reflected the relative intensity of consumers' demands for different goods and services, and of their competing desire to assure the future through savings; wages measured the productivity of labor at the margin of the employer's indecision, where he compared the extra revenue he would receive from selling one more unit with the extra cost he would incur in producing it; and interest rates were linked to profits, and called forth the savings people were willing to offer, when they compared the pleasures of the future with those of the present.

A unified view of the whole economic system emerged, easy to translate into mathematical terms as general equilibrium theory. It was that of an economy constantly moving toward an equilibrium never expected to be reached. Unusually high rewards had the function of directing the flow of resources to those areas where demand was relatively intense.

In the absence of monopoly, and especially of monopolistic restraints on the entry of rival firms, the economists could reassure the public that such high rewards would be short-lived, as resources moved from less to more profitable uses. Wages were justified by productivity; the moral basis for prices was found both in the votes of the sovereign consumer and in the principle of marginal cost— Marshall's celebrated analogy of the two blades of the scissors; interest was linked to the expectation of normative profits, which tended to equality, with variations for risk. There were some anomalies—special rents for absolute scarcities, or for superior efficiencies, or advantageous locations, but they too drew an acceptable sanction from the ultimate source of power—the consumers' daily electoral decisions about spending his income for alternative goods or services, or holding it as cash, securities, bank deposits, or capital goods. Besides, no one was especially resentful at the high prices paid for old masters, or the high incomes of opera singers, novelists, and popular actors.

In "The Ethics of Competition," first published in 1923,[1] Professor Frank H. Knight summed up the traditional economic argument for individualism as follows: "A freely competitive organization of society tends to place every productive resource in that position in the productive system where it can make the greatest possible addition to the total social dividend as measured in price terms, and tends to reward every participant in production by giving it the increase in the social dividend which its co-operation makes possible."[2] But, Knight adds, while the proposition is in his opinion entirely sound, "it is not a statement of a sound ethical social ideal, the specification for a utopia." It is worth returning to Knight's classical paper, more than fifty years after its publication, for the intervening literature has not matched his contribution in insight and strength.

He approaches the subject under four headings: "Economic activity is at the same time a means of want-satisfaction, an agency for want- and character-formation, a field of creative self-expression, and a competitive sport. While men are 'playing the game' of business, they are also moulding their own and other personalities, and creating a civilization whose worthiness to endure cannot be a matter of indifference."[3]

1. 37 Q. J. ECON. 579, reprinted in THE ETHICS OF COMPETITION AND OTHER ESSAYS (1951). References to the paper will be to the 1951 reprint.
2. *Id.* at 48.
3. *Id.* at 47.

He addresses twelve criticisms to the efficiency of a competitive system—its efficiency, that is, as a mechanism for satisfying economic wants. We may put one of his most fundamental points to one side—that of instability of employment—not because it is incorrect, but because progress in thought and in social policy since he wrote has improved the capacity of society to control the trade cycle, and to regulate financial institutions in the interest of continuity. We have hardly reached an ideal state either of knowledge or of technique in this regard, and much remains to be done—particularly in the international sphere—before we can be confident of success. But at least we no longer imagine that we are relying on competitive individualism to regulate the monetary system and the trade cycle.

We are agreed now, as we were not agreed in 1923, that assuring a level of demand capable of eliciting full employment from the economy at stable prices is a fundamental duty of the central banking system and of the state, not of the markets of the economy, however competitive. The other questions he poses with regard to individualism as a want-satisfying mechanism fall into three groups: those concerned with problems of distribution; those which concern the side of demand; and, finally, issues on the side of supply.

With regard to demand, Knight points to several facts which qualify the efficacy of the price mechanism as a reliable measure of people's true choices. Individuals, he says, do not in fact constitute equal individual economic units, equally capable of knowing the quality of what is offered to them. Large parts of the population are dependent—children, old people, many women. Through inheritance and otherwise, some have received differential advantages which perpetuate inequality. Many find their decisions about wants made not with reference to their own desires, but to desires imposed upon them by society, by the desire to emulate others, by ignorance, impulse, the influence of advertising, and so on.

The result is that while the differential pressure of consumers' wants is indeed translated into prices by the market system, the prices that emerge cannot be regarded as an acceptable measure of comparative values in any more general sense. The ethical study of competition, Knight insists, cannot blindly accept price as the only standard of value, even in the limited task of judging the effectiveness of the economy as a means for using resources most efficiently in the satisfaction of wants.

If price were the only criterion of value, we should really have

to accept the phrase *de gustibus non est disputandum,* and concede
that the desire for heroin was to be regarded by society as equal in
every regard to the desire for education. This Knight refuses to do.
Instead, he preaches a gospel largely ignored since he issued his call:
the thesis that economics should not only make room for a rigorous
analysis of its problems, taking price as a datum, but equally that
it should encourage the independent ethical criticism of market results. Such criticism can never be mathematically precise, but that
is not an objection in Knight's view. In "Ethics and the Economic
Interpretation," published in 1922, he wrote:

> [W]e must learn to think in terms of "value standards" which have
> validity of a more subtle kind. It is the higher goal of conduct to
> test and try these values, to define and improve them, rather than
> to accept and "satisfy" them. There are no rules for judging
> values . . . it is the worst of errors to attempt to make rules—
> beyond the rule of to "use good judgment." . . . Professor Tufts
> has put the question in a neatly epigrammatic way which empha-
> sizes its unsatisfactoriness from a rational, scientific standpoint:
> "The only test for goodness is that good persons on reflection
> approve and choose it—just as the test for good persons is that
> they choose and do the good."
>
> If the suggestions above thrown out are sound, there is room
> in the field of conduct for three different kinds of treatment: first,
> a scientific view, or economics and technology; second, a genetic
> view, or culture history; and third, for a Criticism of Values. The
> discussion of the latter will, like literary and artistic criticism, run
> in terms of suggestion rather than logical statement, in figurative
> rather than literal language, and its principles will be available
> through sympathetic interpretation rather than intellectual
> cognition.[4]

This feature of the value problem justifies collective social decisions through governments, committees, foundations, or groups about
the superiority of some wants over others, and a limitation on the
range of decisions we leave to the individual and the markets serving
him. Standing in this university, surrounded by the overpowering
tentacles of California's formidable throughways and freeways, it is
not a startling thought to suggest that if all wants are equal in one
sense, some are more equal than others. Even a most individualistic

4. *Id.* at 40.

society rightly feels free to qualify its principles by deciding that in some cases it knows better than the individual what is good for him. To avoid inflamed controversy, I might cite only such collective decisions as those to establish communal water supplies and to put chlorine, if not fluorine, into them.

Viewing the value problem from the side of supply, Knight raises issues of comparable importance. The premise of laissez-faire, he says, rests on the model of perfect competition—a useful mathematical construct which necessarily deviates from reality at many points. It posits, for example, the divisibility and mobility of economic resources, whereas some of our most difficult and chronic problems are those which arise from the immobility of resources and from the fact that a carpenter, a business administrator, a cook—and, may I add, even a professor—are not perfect substitutes either for others in the same field of work, or for each other.

Knowledge of market conditions among sellers is quite as important to the workings of competition as knowledge among buyers. Many deviations from the competitive norm of efficiency occur because of the absence of knowledge. Where conditions of monopoly or near monopoly exist, or are sought, other deviations from the norm occur, and may well persist, for the factor of monopoly affects the long-run relation of costs to prices, the relation of wages to productivity, and the flow of capital among alternative possible uses in accordance with the relative intensity of demand for different products.

Sometimes I am inclined to think that the worst economic feature of monopoly positions is not that they permit the exploitation of labor in the older sense—the transfer of part of the social dividend from wages to profits—but the obverse phenomenon: the making of unduly high wages, not justified by the norms of productivity, in a bargaining setting where both sides believe that the employer has the power to increase his prices enough to validate any wage bargain made. Here the dynamics of bilateral monopoly, and the desire for peace, may well lead to the exploitation of capital by labor, unduly low profit rates, and the gradual euthanasia not of rentiers but of entrepreneurs. Does such a process explain the present plight of our railroad industry?

Knight stresses one point which time has confirmed as of crucial importance: the weakness of the competitive system in allocating resources to savings, to research, and to progress. There is a curious paradox in this cogent criticism, for the very possibility of economic progress depends on the rate of capital accumulation, and on the flow of new technology. Yet we have allowed our tax system to develop in ways which make a smaller share of income available as savings than is the case in most other capitalist societies, and in the socialist ones to boot. And for generations we have relied on charity as the main source of funds for research, although now we supplement charity a little by government financing in one or two areas of special interest to the Department of Defense.

Many of the factors which limit the utility of competition as a device for translating demands into prices which are also values, and for organizing flows of supplies which correspond to the pattern of demands in a matrix of indifference curves, apply also to the distribution of income under competition among the factors of production. In one sense, distribution theory is an alternative vantage point from which to view the way in which production is organized and carried on. But ethical criteria about the distribution of income raise distinct considerations, Knight says. The classical ethical defense of individualism and competition as a way of bringing about an ideal utilization of social resources is the idea of rewards justified by productivity. Part of Knight's objections to the distributive effects of the competitive order derive from his doubts about price as a measure of ethical or social value, and about the capacity in fact of the market to move resources to their most appropriate uses.

> A social system which sets artists to shining shoes and pays them what they are worth in that occupation is no less open to condemnation than one that sets them to work at their art and pays them what they would be worth as boot-blacks. . . . No one contends that a bottle of old wine is ethically worth as much as a barrel of flour, or a fantastic evening wrap for some potentate's mistress as much as a substantial dwelling-house, though such relative prices are not unusual. Ethically, the whole process of valuation is literally a "vicious" circle since prices flow from demand and demand from prices.[5]

Another part of his doubt arises because some rewards are based on ownership, rather than effort, which he finds ethically more attractive than ownership, especially where the reward to ownership is affected by factors of monopoly or its equivalent, the accident of

5. *Id.* at 55–56.

scarcity. However, the pattern of distributing income in accordance with productivity is so heavily qualified nowadays by the impact of the income tax, and of other taxes, that it is scarcely worth talking about, at least in terms of productivity alone.

Knight views the economic order not merely as a mechanism for producing and distributing the goods people want most—that is, not merely as a means to the end of consumption, but as an end in itself, the activity which takes up the larger part of people's lives, and the main sphere within which they succeed or fail in finding outlets for their creative impulses. Regarded in this perspective, as an activity rather than as a device for producing products, business, he says, is a game—a game with special rules; a game which some people enjoy and others hate, but which all must play; a game which can be won by special talents, by luck, and above all by competitive energy; and a game in which the players play very unequal parts. It is infinitely more fun for top managers—at least where they are successful—than for the mass of factory workers, whose role is often pure drudgery. One gets the flavor of Knight's pungent argument in these passages:

> We must bear in mind too, that the system is a want-satisfying agency at the same time that it is a competitive game, and that the two functions are inseparable, while the two sets of ideals are different. For efficiency in the production of goods a large concentration of authority is necessary. But this concentration violates the principle of equality of opportunity in the game; and when power of control carries with it the right to consume products accordingly, as it actually does, the result is flagrant inequality in this respect also. There appears to be a deep-seated conflict between liberty and equality on the one hand and efficiency on the other. In a system which is at the same time a want-satisfying mechanism and a competitive game we seem to find three ethical ideals in conflict. The first is the principle already mentioned, of distribution according to effort. The second is the principle of "tools to those who can use them." This is a necessary condition of efficiency, but involves giving the best player the best hand, the fastest runner the benefit of the handicap, and thus flagrantly violates the third ideal, which is to maintain the conditions of fairness in the game. . . .
>
> Admitting that business success tends in the large to go with business ability, we must face the question of the abstract merit of such capacity as a human trait, and hence of business as a game. It can hardly be denied that there is a preponderance of cultivated

opinion against it. Successful businessmen have not become proverbial for the qualities that the best minds and most sensitive spirits of the race agree in calling noble. Business as it is and has been does not commonly display a very high order of sportsmanship, not to mention the question which will be raised presently as to whether sportsmanship itself is the highest human ideal. As to the human qualities developed by business activity and requisite to enjoyment of and successful participation in it, there is no objective measure and no opinion will be accepted as free from "prejudice" by those who disagree with it. . . .

However favourable an opinion one may hold of the business game, he must be very illiberal not to concede that others have a right to a different view and that large numbers of admirable people do not like the game at all. It is then justifiable at least to regard as unfortunate the dominance of the business game over life, the virtual identification of social living with it, to the extent that has come to pass in the modern world. In a social order where all values are reduced to the money measure in the degree that this is true of modern industrial nations, a considerable fraction of the most noble and sensitive characters will lead unhappy and even futile lives. Everyone is compelled to play the economic game and be judged by his success in playing it, whatever his field of activity or type of interest, and has to squeeze in as a side line any other competition, or non-competitive activity, which may have for him a greater intrinsic appeal.[6]

These considerations lead Knight to his third category of questions: those about the ethics of competition as such. In this phase of his paper, Knight's questions center about the ethical quality of emulation as a motive for life, and of success in a contest as an ethical value. He can find no ethical justification, beyond the claims of economic efficiency, for competition as an ideal in human relations, or as a motive for action. "It fails to harmonize either with the Pagan ideal of society as a community of friends or the Christian ideal of spiritual fellowship. Its only justification is that it is effective in getting things done; but any candid answer to the question, 'what things,' compels the admission that they leave much to be desired."[7]

Against the background of the difficult and probing questions raised by Knight's paper, let me now return to the problem I posed

6. *Id.* at 61, 62, 65, 66.
7. *Id.* at 74.

at the outset: the reaction of opinion to the electrical antitrust cases, and to the policy they represent. Clearly, many people thought —or, more accurately, felt—that the defendants were not playing the competitive game according to the accepted rules; that their conduct was not sporting, to say the least, and that it merited severe social reprobation. In one sense, the defendants were viewed as modern analogues to Shoeless Joe Jackson and his fellow baseball players, who conspired to throw a World Series game some fifty years ago, and horrified the nation.

But let us look a little more closely at the defendants' situation. And here let us get away from the specific facts about the electric industry, and consider a generalized model of such large industries. Typically, in the basic industries of the country, there are no longer single firm monopolies, as there were seventy years ago, but patterns of organization in which a small number of large firms provide the dominant fraction of supply in the market or markets where they sell. Understanding the economics of imperfect competition and oligopoly quite as well as Cournot and Chamberlin, the businessmen in these situations know that no one of their rivals can change his share of the market by announced price cuts, and, equally, that no one of their rivals can increase prices unless others follow suit. Competitive rivalry is often active and intense. But it tends to avoid price competition, save through secret discriminations, and to concentrate on product variation, advertising, packaging, and other devices to explore the plasticity of consumer demand—that is, the response of demand not to variations in price, but to variations in selling costs.

In markets of this order, which constitute one of our most important problems in public policy toward industrial organization, the chief economic distinction to be made is that between what might be called cooperative and noncooperative oligopolies.

In the first class, the rivals play the game in effect as cooperative partners, avoiding price competition according to well-understood rules of price leadership—basing point plans, posted prices, cross-references in the price terms of requirements contracts, and so on. In the second, the modes of price formation are more ragged, discriminatory, and disorganized. Price wars are frequent, and sometimes chronic. Ignorance prevails, and it is difficult to develop effective devices for reducing each seller's uncertainty about the price and output policy of his rivals.

Noncooperative oligopoly may exist for a number of reasons. The number of sellers may be too large for easy and automatic coordination among the rivals. Perhaps the industry has never had a period of effective cartelization, under the NRA or otherwise, which might have taught all concerned the advantages of "live and let live," and established habits for making cartelization effective. One or more sellers may be incurable mavericks, who refuse to play according to the rules, and think, often rightly, that they can gain at the expense of market leaders by discriminating, aggressive selling, and otherwise behaving as "unethical," that is to say, as competitive competitors. In situations of this kind, the maximization of group interests, and the realization of monopoly profit, may well be impossible without resort to devices of overt collusion, sometimes enforced by reprisals.

The legal and moral problems raised by this phenomenon are exemplified by the dilemma in the electrical cases: what is the difference between a pattern of pricing and a division of markets achieved by cooperative oligopoly functioning smoothly, but without overt or express agreement, and the same economic result achieved by agreement, secret or otherwise? One of the mysteries of situations like that of the electrical cases is why the participants find such elaborate schemes necessary to achieve the result they desire. From the point of view of social and legal policy, we are left with the question whether the law opposes or should oppose the economic result, or only the particular means used to achieve it: that is to say, whether the Sherman Act and the other antitrust laws express an economic policy, or only a code of ethical business practices?

If we view modern oligopoly in the larger setting of Knight's questions about the ethics of competition, we see, I think, some of the fundamental problems it presents from the point of view both of efficiency and of ethical atmosphere. As Knight's paper makes clear, there are shortcomings in the idea of competition as a device for organizing the economic work of society, and as the dominant and pervasive social model for human behavior. When we move from the atmosphere of active competition to that of oligopoly or true monopoly, however, the disadvantages bulk larger, and the countervailing advantages are less manifest. The stability of cooperative oligopoly, its sticky prices and high advertising expenditures, its slowness to innovate, its comfortable and assured salaries and fringe benefits, and its stress on salesmanship—these among its features hardly correspond to the stern competitive ideal of economic efficiency.

And the rules of the friendly, back-scratching, clubbable game it suggests as desirable are even less attractive than those of perfect competition, with its premium on self-reliance, independence, energy, innovation, and all-out struggle.

In a thoughtful article about the implications of the electrical cases, Leland Hazard asks what society expects of men in the situation of the defendants in the electrical industry cases.[8] We tell them not to conspire with their competitors. Can society go further, and instruct them how to behave so that they will not be found to have acted as if they had conspired? How can they avoid pricing which is monopolistic in effect, and costs which may be greater than those of perfect monopoly, and much greater than those of perfect competition? How can they avoid falling into attractive grooves of cooperation —the famous situations of "conscious parallelism"—from which judges and juries may permissibly infer that they have in fact reached illegal agreements?

The men of big business function in economic settings which make agreements to limit competition extremely tempting, and easy to arrange. They are often in the grip of business ideas which make "playing along with the group" the sporting thing to do; for many, the alternative approach to price policy appears not only churlish but unethical. The go-it-alone member of an oligopoly group who cuts prices, grants discounts, and refuses to behave like the others is generally called a chiseler, or worse, by his confreres, and treated as an antisocial person. Under these circumstances, indulgence in illegal behavior may be as irresistible as illicit sex. And it is hard to be much more outraged in the one case than in the other.

The most reasonable inference of policy to be drawn from this fact, I should suggest, is a conscious program for reducing the degree of monopoly in markets "of the few." Popular and even professional opinion tends, quite wrongly, to think that the existing degree of monopoly in most markets is the consequence of technological imperatives. It is rare to find a market in which the size of existing units is the inevitable result of economies of scale in manufacturing or distribution. On the contrary, their size is often—almost normally— the by-product of mergers undertaken for quite different reasons, or of imperfections in the market for capital.

8. Leland Hazard, *Are Big Businessmen Crooks?* ATLANTIC MONTHLY, November 1961, at 57–61.

Many industries could be reorganized in the interest of competition without the slightest risk to efficiency. Indeed, such reorganizations would often increase efficiency, by reducing the high costs of bureaucratic oversight, by creating new incentives for managerial initiative, and by releasing the potential of competitive research. In some, the removal of existing barriers to entry should suffice to bring about the result. In others, it may be desirable to increase the number of sellers, by reducing the size of dominant firms, where their position is such as to constitute a significant restraint on the competitive potential of the market.

In an important recent book, Turner and Kaysen of Harvard propose a statute to this end, which would require the reorganization of industries in the interest of making them more competitive, where a given number of leading firms supply a given fraction of output in the market.[9] I should think much could be accomplished along these lines without a new statute, by a more selective program of antitrust action, both under section 1 and section 2 of the Sherman Act. The necessary doctrines exist.[10] They should be used.

Public authority has not yet systematically adopted such an approach to the problems of large-scale business, although important considerations of economic policy should lead in this direction—considerations with regard to trade cycle policy and labor, efficiency in the use and allocation of resources, and incentives for innovation. But the perspective of private interests is not greatly different. Freedom of price policy, and freedom to experiment, should be an economic advantage to a large firm now confined within the boundaries of a "market of the few." Market mastodons are not always and uniformly the most profitable participants in those markets. Structural and corporate change to increase the number of sellers in markets may well be accomplished by private as well as public action.

Public or private action to make the economy more competitive would not of course make our society a utopia, nor would it answer all the questions raised in Knight's essay. To those questions, I should suggest two further comments, which somewhat overlap.

The first is that the case for competition as a social force and a cultural influence is a good deal like the case for democracy in the

---

9. CARL KAYSEN & DONALD F. TURNER, ANTITRUST POLICY: AN ECONOMIC AND LEGAL ANALYSIS (1959).

10. See ROSTOW, PLANNING FOR FREEDOM 293–302 (1959).

sphere of politics—its theoretical footing is not altogether convincing, but all its alternatives are even worse. Success in a game may be, as Knight says, a childish standard of value: but what if the game is organized to recognize and reward superiority, or even excellence, in personal achievement? And what of a society where rewards are hierarchical, or inherited, or, even worse, distributed in accordance with the favor of friendship, political opinion, or blood?

The second general observation I should offer by way of conclusion is that the organization of society, like the conduct of life, never represents merely the logical application of a single rule taken as premise in all the spheres where it might be considered to apply. If we accept the essentially plural quality of our lives, and our faiths, we need feel no discomfort and no guilt in supporting competition here, in the name of efficiency and freedom, and restraint or even monopoly there, in the name of other values. A society is never a monistic construct, but a network of habits and ideas, simultaneously satisfying many desires. It can be altogether consistent, although it supports atomistic competition in some industries, and social action in health, education, and welfare. The United States can remain a relatively free and open society, true to its goal of individual liberty, although it is a mixed society of individual and collective effort, containing strong state institutions, like the University of California, as well as strong centers of direction and influence, like the university to which I belong, almost beyond the reach of the state.

In such a perspective, we can acknowledge the dualism and inconsistency of our prevailing views about the morals of trade as a normal and healthy paradox, and not as a symptom of schizophrenia. Shaped in a Puritan mold, we realize the utility and efficiency of business, when indeed it is efficient. But we also aspire to values we regard as more important than those of efficiency and private wealth. Sometimes we seem to value men only by their commercial success. But we celebrate the birthday of Robert Frost, and applaud those who resign as presidents of motor companies to become secretaries of defense.

We encourage men to become rich. Then we encourage them to follow the philanthropic examples of Carnegie, Rockefeller, and Ford, who responded to the deeper rule, that treasures upon earth not be laid up for oneself. We are creatures of a complex creed, which provides both a large measure of freedom for the individual, and standards for judging the ways in which he exercises his freedom.

We believe, in short, that trade is an occupation worthy of a gentleman only if the tradesman behaves like one. Our Puritanical, individualist, and socially responsible culture forms men in its image. We believe—we hope—that they will approach or at least acknowledge its values in all their daily tasks, as businessmen and as bureaucrats, as lawyers and as philanthropists, as citizens and as human beings.

Eight

**To Whom and for What Ends
Is Corporate Management
Responsible?**

I

The very words "corporate raider" imply a volume of values, all
unfavorable.

Who is a raider, and what is so bad about what he does? In normal financial usage, a raider is a man who tries to seize or capture[1]
control of a corporation, against the will of its management, by buying up or otherwise mobilizing a working majority of its common
stock. The raider may use his own money or credit for the purpose,
often in large quantities. Or he may proceed by organizing a raiding
party of like-minded stockholders, employing all the techniques of
political persuasion to attain his goal. He may be a long-time stockholder, restless under the rule of weak management. More often, he
is an outsider, eager to gain the privileges and perquisites of management for himself and his friends—the salaries, expense accounts,
chauffeur-driven Cadillacs, stock options, and pension rights; and
the attractive patronage, too, which goes with corporate power even
more dramatically than with high office of the political variety. The
raider may be a corporation in the same field, seeking an advantage
in competition, a hedge against tariff change, a foothold in another
market. Or the marauder may be a stranger to the line of business,
seeking to build up a fashionable conglomerate empire, on the un-
likely but popular assumption that skill in one kind of work is readily
transferable to another. His interest may be in power or in pelf. He

This chapter was published in a slightly different form by Harvard University
Press in THE CORPORATION IN MODERN SOCIETY (ed. Edward J. Mason, 1960).
© 1959 by the President and Fellows of Harvard College.
  1. The word "purchase" is never used in this context. "Take-over" and
"Take-over bid" have crept into the language from British usage.

may be a freebooter of the most noxious kind, or a serious-minded businessman, bent on canny, prudent, and well-calculated gain.

Whatever the raider's motives may be—and they are diverse in practice—the raider depends upon the ordinary legal machinery of corporate decision in order to displace the management. Where control of a publicly-held corporation of the familiar kind is at stake, the raider persuades the stockholders for once to act as if they really were stockholders, in the black-letter sense of the term, each with the voice of partial ownership and a partial owner's responsibility for the election of directors. This is the essence of the raider's offense: to attack the established management and to treat the fictional legal structure of the publicly held endocratic corporation[2] as if it represented reality.

In such circumstances, it is reluctantly conceded that the raider is exercising his historic legal rights as a stockholder in voting for one slate of directors rather than another. It would be agreed with equal reluctance that an investor who seeks out undervalued stock is helping the financial market to fulfill its classic function in guiding the allocation of capital. And it might be acknowledged, too, that the raider who replaces poor management with good is advancing the social cause of efficiency in the use of resources.

When all these concessions are made, however, the verdict remains clearly adverse: the act of raiding breaches a standard of business propriety with an even stronger claim to the loyalty of respectable opinion. Incumbent management, especially in the great endocratic enterprises, seems to have a half-acknowledged "right" to continue in power until it decides to change itself. This implicit power of managerial self-perpetuation is accepted the more readily when the challenge comes from men who buy stock in a corporation in order to participate in its control.

Raiding is regarded as something more than uncouth: increas-

---

2. Our language contains no word to identify the large, publicly-held corporation, whose stock is scattered in small fractions among thousands of stockholders. Following a suggestion of Herman W. Liebert, I shall refer to such corporations here as "endocratic" corporations or enterprises, to distinguish them from small or large corporations controlled by substantial stock ownership—"exocratic" corporations. The problems presented by these aggregates are the same, of course, when the enterprise is carried on in non-corporate forms: for example, some real-estate syndicates which mobilize the funds of the investing public.

ingly, it is treated as almost illegal. Is it an accident, for example, that three of the most severe cases holding mergers illegal under the antitrust laws concern attempted raids?[3] Statutes and judicial decisions frown on the purchase of stock for the purpose of exercising what the textbooks treat as one of its most fundamental privileges —that of voting.[4] Even Professor Bayless Manning, Jr., in his brilliant review of the problem,[5] seemingly approves an expansion of the doctrine "that shares improperly[6] acquired for fighting purposes only may not be voted."[7]

The development of this view measures an extraordinary paradox. Many of the men who adhere to it most strongly are also and almost equally incensed about the apathy of the average stockholder in endocratic corporations. Many studies confirm the impression that the common stockholder in such companies tends to ignore and subordinate his voting rights, whether he is an individual, an investment trust, a pension fund, or a university.[8] The typical modern shareholder is often a well-informed and well-advised investor, who carefully studies his stocks in the interest of prospective dividends or capital appreciation. But, increasingly, he regards the selection of directors as beyond his proper ken. It is difficult to persuade him even to return his proxy favoring the existing management.

3. Northern Securities v. United States, 193 U.S. 197 (1904); Hamilton Watch Co. v. Benrus Watch Co., 114 F.Supp. 307 (D. Conn., 1953), aff'd 206 F.2d 738 (2d Cir., 1953); American Crystal Sugar Co. v. Cuban American Sugar Co., 152 F.Supp. 387 (S.D.N.Y., 1957), affirmed 259 F.2d 524 (2d Circ., 1958). For a vivid account of the background of the *Northern Securities* case, see A. R. BURR, TRUE PORTRAIT OF A BANKER: JAMES STILLMAN 163–79 (1927).

4. See, *e.g.,* N.Y. GEN. CORP. LAW § 61; CALIF. § 834 (1); Del. § 327; FEDERAL RULES OF CIVIL PROCEDURE, Rule 23 (b). See Duncan v. National Tea Co., 14 Ill. App. 2d 280, 144 N.E. 2d 771 (1957).

5. Manning, Review of Joseph Livingston, *The American Stockholder* (1958), 67 YALE L. J. 1477 (1958).

6. If Professor Manning means that the purely buccaneering raid can be, and often is, an unsavory affair, involving no more than a contest over which band is to milk the corporation, I quite agree. Similarly, if his comment is meant to reinforce the conclusion that proxy battles "cannot be relied upon as an effective device for regularized supervision of management's stewardship." *Id.* at 1489. Aliter, however, if his sentence means what it seems to say, in one inflection—that is, that shares acquired for the purpose of gaining or seeking corporate control are improperly acquired.

7. *Id.* at 1494, n. 32.

8. JOSEPH LIVINGSTON, THE AMERICAN STOCKHOLDER (1958); A. A. BERLE, JR., THE TWENTIETH CENTURY CAPITALIST REVOLUTION (1954).

It is hard to imagine what canon of the capitalist ethic could be considered violated by the decision of the investor to buy corporate stock in order to vote it. But a powerful current of opinion, representing views widely and deeply held, regards raiding as wrong. Naturally, this view is coloring the older law. The prevailing business code goes well beyond the conventional image of the corporation as an entity "owned" and controlled by its stockholders. That code is having an increasing impact on our corporate mores, and on the law of corporations.

These comments are not meant to imply that corporate raiding is on the whole a Good (or a Bad) Thing. We know that under the indefensible New York decisions it is a procedure absurdly expensive to the enterprise;[9] we know, too, that it is often neutral, or negative, in its effect on the enterprise's business policy. All I do mean to say is that so long as the incumbent management acquires its office by a stockholders' vote, it is in no position to object in principle if others seek to do likewise.

The common attitude of repugnance toward the ethics of corporate raiding is mild, however, when compared with the general distaste for the stockholders' suit. "Strike suit" and "blackmail" are among the kindest words heard in higher business circles to describe the most important procedure the law has yet developed to police the internal affairs of corporations. The stockholders' suit is an imaginative creation, particularly in its American forms, intended to protect the corporation against fraud, overreaching, and other breaches of fiduciary duty on the part of officers and directors. It is true that in this area, as in some others, the law still relies on the seventeenth-century device of the private attorney general, who expects to be paid for his work in exposing and undoing the misdeeds of management. And it is true, also, that the law has always had a strong prejudice against those who stir up litigation, or engage in fights which are not, strictly speaking, "their" business. For these reasons, many rules have developed, some embodied in statutes, denying the right

9. Rosenfeld v. Fairchild Engine & Airplane Corp., 284 App. Div. 201, 132 N.Y. Supp. 2d 273 (1954), aff'd, 309 N.Y. 168, 128 N.E. 2d 291 (1955). See also Steinberg v. Adams, 90 F.Supp. 604 (S.D.N.Y., 1950); F. D. Emerson & F. C. Latcham, *Proxy Contest Expenses and Corporate Democracy*, 4 WESTERN RESERVE L. REV. 5 (1952); ARANOW & EINHORN, PROXY CONTESTS FOR CORPORATE CONTROL (1957). See also H. G. MANNE, INSIDER TRADING AND THE STOCK MARKET (1966).

to sue against corporate wrongs to stockholders who acquired that status only for the sake of starting or joining the fray.[10]

The stockholders' suit is not a uniformly effective remedy for the misdeeds of directors—indeed, it is not often an effective remedy for such misdeeds at all. Sporadic in its incidence, costly in its procedures, it has been, from time to time, a vehicle for extortion as well as for purification.

Nonetheless, one would expect those concerned for the integrity and future of private business institutions to applaud the intrepid souls who ferret out corporate wrongdoing, and risk their own time and money against a contingency of being rewarded, if, in the end, sin is found to have flourished. Not at all. Such men are not treated as honored members of the system of private enterprise, but as its scavengers and pariahs. Their lawyers rarely become presidents of bar associations, or trustees of charitable bodies. They receive no honorary degrees. At best they are viewed as necessary evils, the Robin Hoods of the business world for whom a patronizing word may sometimes be said, when they succeed in revealing some particularly horrendous act. Even courts and legislatures are unfriendly to stockholders' suits. Many judges dismiss them on any plausible technical ground. Procedural obstacles bristle, and are relentlessly enforced. The substantive doctrines of law, and especially the wide scope given to the directors' "business judgment," make liability infrequent. Both statutes and judge-made law treat as dubious, or worse, the professional stockholders' suit against those who misuse other peoples' money.

II

But are corporate funds "other peoples' " money, so far as the directors are concerned? Or, in the emerging ethos of the second half of the twentieth century, is corporate property really that of the

---

10. See *supra* note 4, and George D. Hornstein, *The Death Knell of Stockholders' Derivative Suits in New York*, 32 CALIF. L. REV. 123 (1944); *The Future of Corporate Control*, 36 HARV. L. REV. 476 (1950); *New Aspects of Stockholders' Derivative Suits*, 47 COLO. L. REV. 1 (1947). S. Solomont & Sons Trust, Inc. v. New England Theatres Operating Corp., 326 Mass. 99, 93 N.E. 2d 241 (1951); Pomerantz v. Clark, 101 F.Supp. 341 (D. Mass., 1951); Note, 36 BOSTON U. L. REV. 78 (1956).

directors and the management, to dispose of, as many suggest, in accordance with their own standards of business foresight, social statesmanship, and generalized good citizenship? The modern endocratic corporation embraces immense pools of capital and skill. Whatever its past, has it become a free collectivity, divorced in its business life from significant public or private control, save the will of the small group which happens to have inherited its management?

It is a pool of property, it is true, held in a vaguely defined trust for vaguely defined economic purposes. In terms of the accepted rules of the game, we should expect society to react, through its courts or legislatures, if the board of directors of General Motors began openly to spend corporate funds on a large-scale effort to propagate the doctrines of Social Credit or Buchmanism, to build dog-and-cat hospitals, to send Peace Ships to Archangel, or to restore Williamsburg. So long, however, as corporate property is employed in ways which the directors think will advance the long-term economic interests of the enterprise, broadly defined, does society wish to raise any questions, or allow any questions to be raised by private litigants, about the judgment of the management?

In the twentieth century, the modern corporation has been transformed beyond all recognition. Its ancestors included giants like the East India Company, devices of business and government which gave rise to deep-seated fears. The earlier private companies of the eighteenth and nineteenth centuries were puny institutions by comparison. Until recent times, corporations received restricted powers from the state. And they were generally viewed by the law and by public opinion with the suspicion which Anglo-American law has always reserved for potentially dangerous accumulations of private power. Their business activities were narrowly confined to certain designated lines of business, firmly written into their legislative charters or, later, into corporate charters granted by public officials. In some states, the absolute amount of property corporations could own was limited by law, well into the twentieth century.[11] A few such limitations survive as curiosities, even today.

All that has been changed, in a series of developments which began around 1880 and have continued without basic modification. Corpo-

11. See, for example, E. MERRICK DODD, JR., AMERICAN BUSINESS CORPORATIONS UNTIL 1860 (1954); Brandeis, J., in Liggett v. Lee, 288 U.S. 517, 548 ff. (1933) (dissent); JOSEPH S. DAVIS, ESSAYS IN THE EARLIER HISTORY OF AMERICAN CORPORATIONS (1917). See also B. C. HUNT, THE DEVELOPMENT OF THE BUSINESS CORPORATION IN ENGLAND 1800–1867 (1936).

rate charters are granted routinely, without substantial supervision. They normally confer, or can readily be amended to confer, almost unlimited freedom to engage in any kind of business. The problem of a company acting *ultra vires,* that is, beyond its authorized powers, has almost disappeared as a practical issue in business or law.

The corporation in its familiar form has become an accepted instrument of social policy—indeed, the chosen instrument of the law for carrying on a large part of the economic life of society.

Corporate directors are endowed with immense discretion. In endocratic corporations, where no stockholders own more than a few percent of the stock, the directors normally control, or come close to controlling, the electoral process from which their powers nominally derive. Where the board of directors consists largely or wholly of corporate employees, dependent upon the president for every step of their future careers, the board is simply a fictional projection of the president himself, whose power is diluted only by the possible presence on his board of bankers representing creditors' interests, or directors representing important customers, or an occasional so-called "public" director.

The directors must, of course, comply with national and state legislation and the rules of securities exchanges, requiring the disclosure of their financial affairs. The antitrust laws, labor legislation, and other laws impose certain patterns of conduct and define boundaries of power. Consciousness of fiduciary duty, and fear of the stockholders' suit, have genuine influence. And, occasionally, the dread figure of the raider may appear.

With these qualifications, the endocratic corporation is an autonomous body politic in a legal order of decentralized power. Its directors do not have quite the degree of freedom from public oversight which the law has afforded to clubs, churches, charitable foundations, universities, and, until recently, trade unions. And, given our philosophy of property, corporate directors have decidedly less freedom in disposing of corporate property than individuals who happen to possess "private" fortunes. One who has inherited or accumulated even a very large and potentially important estate is considered to have an unchallengeable option about its use, unless he is committed as insane—a risk against which great wealth affords a measure of protection. But it is not a distortion of perspective to view the modern corporation against the background of such institutions, as part of a spectrum of arrangements which the law has developed regarding the ownership and control of property. That spectrum ranges from the relative freedom of individual owners of property, at one extreme, past charities, clubs, ecclesiastical bodies, universities, philanthropic foundations, trade unions, and then business corporations, to the strictly supervised affairs of governmental and semigovernmental corporations, at its other end. Governmental bodies, of course, when duly authorized, can spend funds for any purposes deemed by legislatures to be for "the general welfare."

Viewing the corporation from this vantage point, it is immediately apparent that endocratic business enterprises and huge endocratic trade unions, too, present a problem in genealogy which does not arise in the other cases. The individual may acquire his wealth by economic success, or by devolution—legal procedures of ancient lineage, acknowledged as unquestionably right in the moral universe of the society. The property of churches, universities, clubs, and foundations is accumulated under protective custom, common-law doctrine, or legislation, as the gifts of persons interested in their declared and defined purposes. These bodies corporate are managed with great freedom; but they are managed as trusts, by men selected through established procedures of choice. While it is rare to have the courts review the decisions of such trustees in order to determine whether they have used trust property for an unauthorized purpose, suits of this kind are not unknown. And finally, of course, the mayors and aldermen, the governors and legislators, and the President and Congress, who handle the funds of governmental corporations and other public bodies, acquire their powers by political election, a source of authority which the society accepts as fully legitimate. But those who control trade-union funds, or the funds of endocratic corporations, often have much cloudier title deeds to their offices. So far, however, they too have enjoyed wide and undisturbed latitude in the exercise of discretion vested in them by elections which may or may not have been convincingly authentic. And there is a formidable resistance to any proposals for bringing such institutions under closer and more sustained supervision by the state.

Many decry this state of affairs; others rejoice in it, as an imaginative expression of our genius for pluralism.

III

The critics of managerial autonomy have long preached democracy as the manifest remedy for feudalism: if only stockholders could be more fully informed, protected by better proxy rules, and given cumulative voting and easier access to stockholders' lists, they urge, the stockholders' annual meeting would become a meaningful source of authority for the directors, and a meaningful procedure for reviewing their stewardship.[12]

It is becoming clear that such hopes for corporate "democracy" are bound to be disappointed, in the case of many—perhaps most —of the endocratic enterprises which have become so important a feature of the economic scene. They are not addressed to prevailing reality. In comparatively few large, publicly held corporations, managerial control is in fact exercised by or for considerable stockholding interests—as in the familiar instances of corporations where Ford, Rockefeller, Mellon, or Du Pont investments are dominant. In such companies, practice corresponds to the legal forms, as it does, by and large, in the case of smaller closely held companies: responsible ownership, using the voting powers of the common stock, provides a classically legitimate base for the power of the directorate. But cases of this kind are growing rarer every year. The estate tax, the antitrust laws, the process of dilution through growth—these and other forces tend to disperse large stockholdings formerly held by individuals, groups, or families who were willing to participate in management, or take responsibility for selecting it, in order to protect their investment. The current prototype, increasingly, is that of a corporation with stock widely scattered among individuals, investment trusts, or institutional investors, who faithfully vote for the incumbent management and resolutely refuse to participate in its concerns. In such companies, the stockholders obey the management, not the management the stockholders. Most stockholders of this class are interested in their stock only as investments. The prevalence of this view makes it almost hopeless to expect that the electoral

12. F. D. EMERSON & F. C. LATCHAM, SHAREHOLDER DEMOCRACY (1954); Wilber G. Katz, *The Philosophy of Midcentury Corporation Statutes,* 23 LAW & CONTEMP. PROB. 177, 188–92 (1958); F. D. Emerson, *The Roles of Management and Shareholders in Corporate Government, id.* at 231; Sheldon E. Bernstein & Henry G. Fischer, *The Regulation of the Solicitation of Proxies: Some Reflections on Corporate Democracy,* 7 U. CHI. L. REV. 226 (1940); Mortimer M. Caplin, *Proxies, Annual Meetings of Corporate Democracy,* 37 VA. L. REV. 653 (1951); Lewis D. Gilbert, *Wanted: A Program for Fair Corporate Suffrage,* INVESTOR, June 1953 at 28; *Stockholder Participation in Corporate Affairs,* 38 VA. L. REV. 595 (1951). See also JOHN SIMON, THE ETHICAL INVESTOR (1972); E. M. EPSTEIN, THE CORPORATION IN AMERICAN POLITICS (1969).

process can ever become anything more significant than an empty ritual. The reforms of the Roosevelt era accomplished much, in requiring financial and corporate disclosure and in establishing procedures for enforcing these requirements. But no amount of disclosure can make corporate democracy effective where the corporate vote belongs to weak, scattered individual investors or to institutional investors who cannot or will not take an effective part in the corporate electoral process.

Many believe that the prevailing state of gloom about corporate democracy may have gone too far. After all, they point out, political elections often fall far short of the ideal, both in the motivation of voters and in the level of discourse at which their franchise is solicited. Shortcomings of this order, if not too widespread, do not gravely impair the usefulness of the institution.[13]

But for the endocratic corporations the corporate election is frequently not a partial but a total farce. Well-informed investors, analyzing the company's documents, often prefer to sell their stock, despite the tax and other costs of such sales, rather than to engage in lengthy and dubious battles for remedying managerial shortcomings. It is better business for them, they conclude, to shift capital to a profitable company than to conduct a quixotic struggle against the inherently powerful and entrenched position of management. Thus far, investment trusts, welfare funds, and institutional stockholders have by and large refused to cross the line which in their view divides investment from management.[14] The few exceptions, like the Atlas Corporation, underscore the generality of the rule.

Various proposals have been put forward, intended to make corporate democracy more effective.

Mr. Justice Douglas, while he was a member and later chairman of the Securities and Exchange Commission, urged the development of a new profession—that of full-time directors. Vigorous and well-paid directors, he thought, purged of all conflicting interests, would provide sustained supervision over the work of management,

13. The proxy provisions of the Securities Exchange Act, and the rules of the Securities and Exchange Commission adopted under them, impose a far more severe standard of propriety in the corporate electoral process than prevails in political elections. Correspondingly, these regulations raise delicate problems under the First Amendment.

14. Most recently reported in LIVINGSTON, *supra* note 8, ch. 4 at 12. See also SIMON, *supra* note 12.

and protect the interests of those orphans of the business system, the scattered small stockholders, now doomed to impotence in most corporate environments. "The paid director," he wrote, "would revive and strengthen the tradition of trusteeship. His job would not be to represent the management or to represent himself. It would be primarily to represent the stockholder—to return to the stockholder the protection which today's stockholder has too frequently lost."[15] Unfortunately, the commissioner did not indicate how most corporation presidents could be persuaded to elect, and then to reelect, directors who would make their lives more difficult, perhaps even dangerous, or how paid directors could avoid becoming identified with the management which paid them.

Other critics have urged the formation of small stockholders' protective committees or councils, to pool their voting strength and to obtain representation on boards in behalf of their members.[16] The analogy of the Foreign Bondholders' Protective Council is sometimes invoked as a private device for encouraging or accomplishing this end.

Some reformers look to salvation through the development of new attitudes by investment trusts and other large fiduciary investors. The astronomic growth of welfare funds, they point out, will soon compel the managers of such portfolios to assume a responsibility for corporate management which they have so far largely shunned.[17] Then we should face a situation to arouse Professor Mills's ire—one group of professional managers supervising another, in an atmosphere, as he would view it, of tacit conspiracy among the members of the Establishment against the rest of us.

Writers like Scott Buchanan go even further.[18] They would accept the *de facto* autonomy which economic and legal history has conferred upon the management of the endocratic corporations, but they would seek to make its internal procedure more democratic. Solutions of this type, like those espoused in earlier periods by syndicalists, cooperators, and Guild Socialists, would seemingly enfranchise not only stockholders, but also workers and perhaps bondholders, who would then determine corporate policy through "re-

15. W. O. Douglas, Democracy and Finance 53 (1940).
16. Lewis D. Gilbert, Dividends and Democracy (1956).
17. A. A. Berle, Jr., Economic Power and the Free Society 12–13 (1958).
18. Scott Buchanan, The Corporation and the Republic (1958).

publican" forms of government. While Mr. Buchanan's prescriptions are vague, and difficult to isolate, he would apparently hope to cure the present shortcomings of corporate democracy in endocratic corporations by adding new groups of apathetic and disinterested voters to the masses of stockholders who now fail to exercise their franchise intelligently.

Such approaches would deny the possibility of public oversight for endocracies. After all, the endocratic corporation is an institution which deeply affects the public interest in many ways—not only as a potential monopolist or collaborator in monopoly arrangements, but as a reservoir of savings and a combination of men and skills, which for many purposes should be subject to publicly established rules governing the use of money, the modalities of finance, and even the pattern of business policy. General Electric and General Motors are private companies in form. They are also indispensable parts of the national defense establishment. Accepting the autonomy of the endocratic corporation would remit its government more and more completely to groups which have strong financial interests in certain lines of policy. These policies may, or may not, also serve the public interest.

IV

There is, on the other hand, a considerable opinion about modern corporations which welcomes the idea of self-perpetuating management, not genuinely based on the will of substantial stockholders' votes. Men of this persuasion question the relevance of the democratic model to the problem of organizing and conducting a business corporation or, for that matter, a trade union. And they find much to applaud in what they regard as a more civilized concept of corporate responsibility, which they detect emerging as the professional manager supplants the old style owner-manager in one business situation after another.[19] Dean Mason has recently characterized this literature as the "apologetics of managerialism."[20] While there is

19. BERLE, *supra* note 8; D. E. LILIENTHAL, BIG BUSINESS: A NEW ERA (1953); P. F. DRUCKER, CONCEPT OF THE CORPORATION (1946); H. R. BOWEN, SOCIAL RESPONSIBILITIES OF THE BUSINESSMAN (1953).

20. See, however, Theodore Levitt, *The Dangers of Social Responsibility,"* HARV. BUS. REV., September-October 1958, at 41; Edward S. Mason, *The Apologetics of Managerialism,* 31 J. BUS. 1 (1958).

variety in detail among the prescriptions of those who have contributed to this general view, they share certain attitudes.

First, they believe that something should be done to provide a substitute for or, more often, a supplement to the fading dream of corporate democracy in the large, publicly held endocracy. As Professor Berle has said,

> Whenever there is a question of power there is a question of legitimacy. As things stand now, these instrumentalities of tremendous power have the slenderest claim of legitimacy. This is probably a transitory period. They must find some claim of legitimacy, which also means finding a field of responsibility and a field of accountability. Legitimacy, responsibility and accountability are essential to any power system if it is to endure. They correspond to a deep human instinct. A man desires beyond anything else to have someone give him the accolade of "Well done, thou good and faithful servant," thereby risking the condemnation of "You have been no good—get out." If he has to say it to himself, or hear it from a string of people whom he himself has hired or controls, he is apt to die a cynical and embittered man.[21]

But no member of this school of thought would accept the proposals of the British Labour Party, that the government purchase shares of such companies, to achieve both legitimacy and accountability through socialism. Nor would many of them view with favor the postwar German practice of having workers' representatives on boards of directors, which Mr. Scott Buchanan seems to have had in mind in his recent pamphlet on the subject.[22] Most such reformers seem to be groping for a private device, or a device of state law rather than federal law, which could give the managers a more tangible source of authority than the accident of their own possession of the seats of power, and a more serious and official procedure of accountability than the empty histrionics of the usual annual meeting.

Professor Manning has sketched the outlines of an idea which has intriguing implications and merits further exploration.[23] His suggestion is addressed primarily to the issue of accountability, rather than to the problem of providing corporate boards with a more tangible mandate. His article proposes to consider the large, publicly held corporation as if it were in law what it often is in fact, a kind of

---

21. ECONOMIC POWER AND THE FREE SOCIETY 16 (1958).
22. *Supra* note 18.
23. *Supra* note 5, at 1478.

voting trust, where the stockholder delegates all his rights, save that of collecting his dividend, to the directors—that is, to the management. Viewing the corporation in the light of this theory of itself, Manning points out, immediately brings certain problems into the foreground, and indicates certain possibilities for remedial action. In order to establish more effective procedures for visitation and control, Manning has in mind the development of a new device, public or private, which could carry out certain functions presently neglected, or relatively neglected. He seems to visualize this device as preferably private, and as a kind of "second chamber," distinct from the board of directors, and with more limited powers. This "extrinsic" body would presumably review decisions of the board where conflicts of interest arise, particularly with regard to the compensation of officers; it could also pass on other board and managerial decisions, notably where corporate funds are spent for charitable contributions not directly related to the company's business. It might well have broader powers, in enforcing a full disclosure of the corporation's financial and business affairs, for example. In a corporate world organized in this way, the stockholder would hold in effect certificates in a voting trust. He would "own" his stock, and not the equity of the corporation, save for such problems as the determination of creditors' rights, where Professor Manning would not alter the existing law of contractual priority.

Professor Manning's proposal is in its preliminary stages, and it is not now without ambiguities. He seems, for example, to contemplate the continuance of the present stockholder voting machinery, and even the occasional catharsis of a good proxy fight.[24]

This original line of thought might well offer much to protect the corporation, in that important group of cases where stockholders as a class are unable to function in accordance with the expectations of legal theory. The development of the idea might be most fruitful if it clearly separated the directors' function from that of monitoring their work, and provided a device which excluded management from any role in the selection of the "Second Chamber"—perhaps by delegation to a trustee under an indenture.

Professor Manning's proposal does not solve the problem of managerial legitimacy in large endocratic enterprises, as he frankly recognizes. "Although the proxy system of electing directors is

24. *Id.* at 1494.

largely an engine of, rather than for, management control, someone has to select directors, and there would be no advantage in permitting them overtly to choose their own successors."[25]

Perhaps we can do no better, in a system of private property, where the claimants to the residual equity insist on delegating their interests to the managers. One can, however, visualize more constructive solutions. Building on a long if checkered experience with corporate trustees under bondholders' indentures, could we not consider requiring the issuance of stock in endocratic corporations in a form which gave small stockholders the option of delegating their voting rights to a trustee, who would act for them more effectively than they can ever hope to act for themselves?

V

In reviewing the literature about the current development of endocratic corporations, and about possible programs for their reform, one is struck by the atmosphere of relative peace. There seems to be no general conviction abroad that reform is needed. The vehement feelings of the early thirties, expressing a sense of betrayal and frustration at a depression blamed on twelve years of business leadership, are almost entirely absent. Ideas for reforming endocracy are not supported by anything like the sense of purpose which sustains the antitrust laws and the income tax.

I suspect that enlightened lay opinion could be summarized in these terms: "Yes, there are paradoxes and anomalies in the way boards of directors are elected in some large, publicly held companies. But what of it? There are irrational moments in most of our legal arrangements, some more illogical than this one. The disclosure requirements of the Securities Act and the Securities Exchange Act do a lot of good. And most boards of directors are not so bad. Business seems energetic. There's a good deal of competition—not enough, but still a good deal. Corporate executives are overpaid, but the income tax must take quite a lot of their excessive salaries. All in all, the system may be illogical, but it works. And besides, any serious reform would have to bring government agencies more directly into the internal affairs of corporations, and that would be worse."

25. *Id.*

So long as the problem of corporate responsibility is viewed in this pragmatic light, change will come only from within the system, in response to moves which corporate management may consider prudential and protective in the long run. Many such moves have characterized the development of the corporation during the post-war period, most notably the spread of the idea of "public directors,"[26] and the flowering of the view that the primary duty of the corporation is not to make as much money as possible for its stockholders, but to advance the public interest in some alternative sense.[27]

Many have proclaimed this doctrine as the dawn of a better day, in which the outworn maxims of Adam Smith have yielded at last to the higher virtue of responsible citizenship. Corporations have "souls" and "consciences," we are told. They no longer take a "narrow," "selfish" view of policy, but what passes for a more statesman-like attitude toward their problems.

It is difficult to give any palpable meaning to these ideas. Mr. Frank Abrams, chairman of the board of the Standard Oil Company of New Jersey, has said that the managers of his company conduct its affairs "in such a way as to maintain an equitable and working balance among the claims of the various directly interested groups—stockholders, employees, customers, and the public at large."[28] In urging his proposal for paid directors, Mr. Justice Douglas said, while chairman of the Securities and Exchange Commission,

> Today it is generally recognized that all corporations possess an element of public interest. A corporation director must think not only of the stockholder but also of the laborer, the supplier, the purchaser, and the ultimate consumer. Our economy is but a chain which can be no stronger than any one of its links. We all stand together or fall together in our highly industrialized society

26. See Wilbur T. Blair, *Appraising the Board of Directors,* HARV. BUS. REV., January 1950, at 101 ("the principle is unworkable").

27. Carl Kaysen, *The Social Significance of the Modern Corporation,* 47 AM. ECON. REV. (Supp. 1) 311, 313 (1957), "No longer the agent of proprietorship seeking to maximize return on investment, management sees itself as responsible to stockholders, employees, customers, the general public, and, perhaps most important, the firm itself as an institution. . . . Its responsibilities to the general public are widespread: leadership in local charitable enterprises, concern with factory architecture and landscaping, provision of support for higher education, and even research in pure science, to name a few."

28. Quoted by Mason, *supra* note 20, at 3.

of today. One function of the paid director would be to harmonize those various elements so far as possible. For although those elements may superficially appear to conflict, the fundamental interests of all social groups are identical over the long term. The corporate officer frequently recognizes these principles; but he is so close to his work that it is hard for him to look beyond its immediate necessities. But the paid director need not be afflicted with such nearsightedness. It would indeed be one of the defects which he would be paid not to have.[29]

Others, welcoming statements of this kind in the speeches of corporate presidents, have cheered the birth of a more benign stage in the evolution of capitalism. The observe great companies making gifts for scholarships,[30] establishing welfare procedures, and participating in community affairs. The "image" of the corporation has changed. It is no longer symbolized by a grim and energetic tyrant, single-mindedly driving his staff on to new feats of money making. Today the presidents of endocratic corporations wear buttoned-down striped shirts, not stiff collars; tweed jackets and flannels, rather than formal three-piece suits; wrist watches, not great gold repeaters at the end of heavy gold chains. In the public mind and in fact, the great corporation is more often than not a friendly committee of smiling bureaucrats, cheerfully sharing the burdens of the world around them.

Responding to these changes in atmosphere, public opinion has become far more tolerant of big business. In England, socialists say that the managers have already socialized capitalism, so that it is no longer necessary to invoke the cumbersome formality of public ownership of the means of production.[31] Besides, they note, the Russians are having lots of trouble conducting a system of unified control, and are moving to decentralize the direction of their business—that is, to give their managers something like the degree of free-floating autonomy the managers of great American and British endocracies already enjoy. The diseconomies of excessive scale are quite apparent, both in business and government. All over the world,

---

29. DOUGLAS, *supra* note 15, at 53.
30. RICHARD EELLS, CORPORATE GIVING IN A FREE SOCIETY (1956), reviewed by Manne, 24 U. CHI. L. REV. 194 (1956); *id., Corporate Giving: Theory and Policy,* 1 CALIF. MANAGEMENT REV. 37 (1958).
31. *Mouse with a Leer,* THE ECONOMIST, July 20, 1957, at 191.

the movement to decentralize is gaining momentum, as men seek to avoid being strangled by Parkinson's famous Law. The political consequences of the new model capitalism-with-a-social conscience begin to emerge very sharply.

A classic debate on the question was conducted by Professor Berle and Professor Dodd more than forty years ago, and Berle has now concluded that Dodd was right in the first place.[32] As is the case in many debates, the theses of the protagonists turn out on inspection to be quite compatible. Professor Berle starts with the proposition that all corporate powers are powers in trust, "necessarily and at all times exercisable only for the ratable benefit of all the stockholders as their interest appears."[33] In the light of this premise, he makes illuminating comments on a number of controversial issues of corporate law and practice. Professor Dodd agrees that corporate powers are powers in trust, to be sure. But the use of private property, he urges, is deeply affected with a public interest, and the development of public opinion is more and more acutely conscious of that fact. Recognition of the public interest in the use of corporate property, Dodd contends, requires that directors be viewed as trustees for the enterprise as a whole—for the corporation viewed as an institution—and not merely as "attorneys for the stockholders."[34] To this Berle replies by agreeing that the use of private property, notably in the case of large corporations, is indeed a matter of the highest public importance. But, he says, "I submit that you cannot abandon emphasis on the view that business corporations exist for the sole purpose of making profits for their stockholders until such time as you are prepared to offer a clear and reasonably enforceable scheme of responsibilities to someone else."[35] We have no such directing rule. In its absence, the consequence of Professor Dodd's argument would be to remit the control of corporations, and the orientation of their policies, entirely to the management. The older rule, Professor Berle contended, offers the

---

32. A. A. Berle, Jr., *Corporate Powers as Powers in Trust,* 44 HARV. L. REV. 1049 (1931); E. Merrick Dodd, Jr., *For Whom Are Corporate Managers Trustees?* 45 HARV. L. REV. 1145 (1932); Berle, *For Whom Corporate Managers Are Trustees, id.* at 1365; Dodd, *Is Effective Enforcement of the Fiduciary Duties of Corporate Managers Practicable?* 2 U. CHI. L. REV. 194 (1935); Berle, *supra* note 8.
33. Berle, *Corporate Powers . . . , supra* note 32, at 1049.
34. Dodd, *For Whom . . . ? supra* note 32, at 1145, 1161.
35. Berle, *For Whom . . . , supra* note 32, at 1365, 1367.

only chance of ordering business affairs in ways which would minimize managerial overreaching and self-seeking. With this position
Professor Dodd then agreed, although he felt that the rule had lost
all contact with reality, and with public aspiration.

> Profit-making for absentee owners must be the legal standard
> by which we measure their conduct until some other legal standard
> has been evolved. Granted—with some reservations—that this is
> all that the law can do at present, the question remains as to
> how effectively it can do that. If trusteeship for absentee invest-
> ors, in addition to being an ideal having little emotional appeal to
> managers, is an ideal that is losing ground in the community gen-
> erally and if the signs are multiplying that our economic order is
> evolving away from it, the prospect of its effective enforcement
> as an interim legal rule of conduct is not encouraging. Abandon it,
> as yet, we dare not—enforce it with more than moderate suc-
> cess, it is to be feared we cannot.[36]

In 1954, Professor Berle accepted Professor Dodd's initial position, apparently because he concluded that the directors of endocratic corporations, as keepers of the public conscience, can now be
safely trusted to exercise their vast powers in the public interest,
without the safeguard of either stockholder control or effective public
supervision.[37]

What content, if any, is there in the notion of directors' obligation
first propounded by Professor Dodd, and now accepted by Professor
Berle?

From the point of view of legal and economic orthodoxy, the
New Capitalism is all bewildering balderdash. The law books have
always said that the board of directors owes a single-minded duty of
unswerving loyalty to the stockholders, and only to the stockholders.
The economist has demonstrated with all the apparent precision of
plane geometry and the calculus that the quest for maximum revenue
in a competitive market leads to a system of prices, and an allocation
of resources and rewards, superior to any alternative in its contributions to the economic welfare of the community as a whole. To the
orthodox mind, it is therefore unsettling, to say the least, to have
the respected head of the Standard Oil Company of New Jersey

---

36. Dodd, *Is Effective Enforcement . . . ? supra* note 32, at 194, 206–7.
37. Berle, *supra* note 8, at 169.

equating the management's duty to stockholders with its obligation to employees, customers, suppliers, and the public at large.

The stubborn relics of an analytical tradition have difficulty translating the soothing formulas of managerialism into terms they can understand. And perhaps the task is impossible. In sectors of the economy more or less effectively insulated from market pressures, as the economists have long known, the negotiated solutions of multilateral oligopoly, or even of bilateral monopoly, are neither so uniform nor so predictable as those of the straightforward competitive model. In such situations, it has been customary to conclude, there is no equilibrium position toward which the market tends to move, but rather a zone of possible solutions within which ignorance, accident, or other bargaining factors yield an oscillating and unstable result, explicable only in the tenuous terms of game theory.

Accepting this reservation, however, what does the "new" concept of corporate responsibility imply? Does it mean that the management of a great corporation should not bargain very hard in negotiations over wages or the prices paid to suppliers? Does it mean that a statesmanlike and well-run company should charge less for its product than the market would bear, less than the prices which would maximize its short-term revenues, or what it conceives to be its long-term profits? Should it regard its residual profits, not as "belonging to" its stockholders in some ultimate sense, but as a pool of funds to be devoted in considerable part to the public interest, as the directors conceive it—to hospitals, parks, and charities in the neighborhood of its plants; to the local symphony or the art museum; to scholarships for the children of employees, or to other forms of support for the educational system of the nation at large? If what is good for the country is good for General Motors, as is indeed the case, does this view of managerial responsibility set any limit upon the directors' discretion in spending corporate funds for what they decide is the public good?

If the rhetoric of managerialism is properly interpreted in this way, two general classes of difficulties are immediately apparent: one economic, the other legal and political. The new corporate morality may result in prices and wages which sabotage the market mechanism and systematically distort the allocation of resources. Such pricing practices would make the task of monetary and fiscal authority in controlling general fluctuations of trade more expensive and more difficult, and could well make it impossible to sustain high levels of employment save at the cost of considerable price inflation. Secondly, the new theory of corporate responsibility may produce patterns of corporate expenditure which could disturb the present equilibrium of opinion about corporations, and invite public restrictions on the present freedom of corporate management.

If, as is widely thought, the essence of corporate statesmanship is to seek less than maximum profits, postwar experience is eloquent evidence that such statesmanship leads to serious malfunctioning of the economy as a whole. In recent years, many industries having some degree of power over the prices they charge have tended for a variety of reasons to charge less, in all probability, than the market would bear in the short run. Prudence and a bias in favor of long-run price stability; the twin mottoes of "wait-and-see" and "live-and-let-live"; a concern for the firm's relations with government, labor, and the public; a fear of new entrants and of "excess" capacity—all these combine to persuade the firm and the industry that the upward movement is temporary, that demand is weaker than it is, that it would be better, on the whole, to pursue a cautious line than to risk being wrong about the new shape of the schedule of demand.[38]

Many economists and public officials have praised the great companies in markets of the few for their statesmanship in keeping prices low, or raising them relatively slowly, during periods of recovery. Indeed, President Eisenhower has preached this doctrine to both business and labor as their highest social duty.[39]

Viewed against the background of the flow of national income as a whole, a policy of profit abstinence seems neither tenable for extended periods, nor sound, especially during a recovery period of rising total spending.

The first consequence of such moderation in pricing is that demand is unusually high for the product of such industries, but prices rise less than in others. Relatively low profits are earned. The pressure of rising demand is diverted to other sectors of the economy, where prices and profits rise more rapidly. Thus capital is attracted to areas which would have claimed less if the market mechanism had

---

38. J. K. Galbraith, *Market Structure and Stabilization Policy,* 39 REV. ECON. & STATISTICS 124, 127 (1957); Eugene V. Rostow, *Market Organization and Stabilization Policy,* in MAX F. MILLIKAN, ed., INCOME STABILIZATION FOR A DEVELOPING DEMOCRACY 439, 460–69 (1953).

39. Economic Report of the President, January 1959, at v.

been more accurate in measuring the comparative intensity of consumers' desires for different products. On the other hand, since demand for the product is high, public policy may intervene, as it has through accelerated depreciation and other policies, to subsidize expansions of capacity within existing firms despite their relatively low profits. Big firms, having great advantages in any event in their access both to long- and short-term capital, may be able to finance expansion without subsidy, despite their relatively low profits during such periods. The result may be the paradox of low profits and capacity which is genuinely, if temporarily, excessive in the real sense —that is, excessive at competitive prices, even at full employment levels of demand.

This kind of policy, in either of its aspects, records a failure of the market as the chief instrument for guiding the allocation of capital and labor. If long continued, policies of self-restraint may result in a serious distortion in the pattern of resource use. The classic example of French rent control represents an extreme case of this phenomenon. Rents in France have until very recently been frozen at their World War I levels. The result is that tenants pay less rent for their Paris apartments than they do for cigarettes. Leases, of course, are sold, at high prices. But landlords have no incentive to build new apartment houses, and the housing situation, after forty years, is almost insoluble, save through public action.

I do not suggest that we have yet reached this point in the great oligopoly industries which have been so widely applauded for price moderation during the postwar inflationary boom. But the phenomenon has been visible, in varying degrees, signaled by the appearance of occasional "gray" markets for certain key products. And it has been a major barrier to the possibility of entry by new firms, since the earnings of existing capital resources have often been lower than the return to be anticipated, at prevailing prices, on investment in totally new capacity.

One of the consequences of so-called moderate price policies has been to delay and prolong the process of adjustment to episodes of inflation—that is, to periods when demand is excessive in relation to full employment supply. During such periods, competition for scarce resources bids up prices, as businessmen persist in optimistic views about the future of demand, price, and profit in their bailiwicks. Prices of raw material rise; inventories are accumulated; and wages of junior executives, foremen, and good machinists are pushed up by the offers of unusually efficient, productive, well-located, or optimistic firms. The entire economy must adapt its system of notations to the impact of such changes on the marginal product of work, the norm around which the general wage structure is crystallized. Price moderation, like other lags in the process of market adjustment, prolongs the agony. Long, slow-rolling movements of prices and wages have characterized the response of the economy to the pressure of such inflation-induced changes in the general wage level. The length of time required for these adjustments explains the apparent anomaly of costs and prices rising slowly during the early part of a recession, as they did in 1957 and 1958, and again in the prolonged stagflation after 1973.

Of course, even the latter-day policies favoring price stability in markets of the few cannot indefinitely postpone action to keep even short-run profit at a maximum. Pessimistic views about the nature of demand schedules do not usually survive for long. It is difficult for a firm, or even for an industry, to buck the tide. The result is that companies in this position take every opportune excuse, such as a labor negotiation, to raise their prices, and catch themselves up to a position which gives them as much as they could earn in their market. Guided by experts in public relations, the companies make matters worse by trying to blame others for their mistakes of price policy.

The standards of corporate statesmanship so far announced do not, however, supply a price theory which could supplant the traditional lore of economics. I certainly do not object to corporate management which takes a civilized and democratic interest in the morale of its employees, treats them with dignity and respect, and deals with them as equals, through collective bargaining procedures and otherwise. Nor do I oppose trade-union leadership which is willing to acknowledge the common humanity of management. But the basic service for which society looks to business and labor is the production of goods and services at the lowest possible cost, and at prices which measure the comparative pressure of consumers' choices. This is a hard and demanding task. The literature of "managerialism," from Commons and Veblen to Drucker, Burnham, Galbraith, and Berle, suggests no criteria to replace the standards for judging the propriety of wages and prices which the economists have painfully developed during the last century or so.

We have tended to misconstrue the fascinating sociology of the modern endocratic corporation, with its divorce of ownership and management, and its hierarchical features. There is a rich literature which describes corporations and trade unions as institutional entities. These studies have much to contribute to our understanding of the dynamics of economic life. But studies of social and human relations, however valid, do not provide a substitute for the competitive norm in defining an acceptable social goal for the process of price making. Indeed, the literature of managerialism has not so far squarely faced the issue. I doubt very much whether it can produce a standard for "fair pricing" which expresses the idea of efficiency in the use of resources otherwise than in the familiar guise of the concept of competitive equilibrium. It is an ironic comment on the problem that many of the younger socialist economists, especially in England, propose procedures for pricing under socialism which would in fact achieve the classic purposes of competition, both in distributing goods and in determining which branches of the economy should expand or contract. Their effort comes perilously close to the thought that the first task of a socialist society should be to restore competitive markets—the traditional hallmark of capitalism, and its most characteristic institutional ideal.

The political and legal aspects of corporate statesmanship present vistas which are quite as disturbing as its economics. The endocratic corporations are accepted as powerful and effective instruments for carrying on the business of society. If their directors begin to act as if they really were general trustees for the public at large, they may well imperil their present freedom. Corporations are not accepted in public opinion as institutions through which society makes its educational policy, its foreign policy, or its political policy. Programs which would give reality to the idea of spending corporate funds to advance the general welfare, as the directors visualize it, will sooner or later invite the critical attention of legislators, governors, and Presidents, who consider that they have been elected by the people to advance the general welfare, and know more about it than the directors of endocratic corporations. As Professor Ben W. Lewis has recently said, commenting on the thesis that "the corporation, almost against its will, has been compelled to assume in appreciable part the role of conscience-carrier of twentieth century American society":

> It is not going to happen; if it did happen it would not work; and
> if it did work it would still be intolerable to free men. I am willing
> to dream, perhaps selfishly, of a society of selfless men. Cer-

tainly, if those who direct our corporate concentrates are to be free from regulation either by competition or government, I can only hope that they will be conscientious, responsible, and kindly men; and I am prepared to be grateful if this proves to be the case. But I shall still be uneasy and a little ashamed, with others who are ashamed, to be living my economic life within the limits set by the gracious bounty of the precious few. If we are to have rulers, let them be men of good will; but above all, let us join in choosing our rulers—in ruling them.[40]

The responsibility of corporate directors requires redefinition. It may give us a warm and comfortable feeling to say that the director is a trustee for the community rather than for his stockholders; that he is a semi-public official, or a quasi-public official, or some other kind of hyphenated public officer. It would be more constructive, however, to seek redefinition in another sense: to restate the law of corporate trusteeship in terms which take full account of the social advances of this century, but which direct the directors more sharply to concentrate their efforts on discharging their historic economic duties to their stockholders. The economic job of directors and management is quite difficult enough to absorb the full time of first-rate minds, in an economy of changing technology, significant general instability, and considerable competition, both from rival firms in the same industry and from those which steadily offer rival products.

Similarly, watching the investment of trade-union funds in a variety of banks and other business enterprises, one wonders whether the public interest is really served by the present freedom of trade unions. Is it sound public policy to allow unions to accumulate funds not required by their primary needs, and to invest those funds at will, in ways which often lead to grave conflicts of interest?

VI

Would such a redefinition of goals for large endocratic business units and trade unions serve any useful purpose? How could such rules be enforced? Could they have any impact on the flow of events? Is "the long-run economic interest of stockholders" any more mean-

---

40. *Economics by Admonition,* 49 AM. ECON. REV. (Supp. 2) 384, 395 (1959).

ingful, as a standard to guide the deliberation of directors or the decisions of courts or other public bodies reviewing what the directors have done, than "the interests of the enterprise as a whole," or "the interests of the community"? Such a "rule" would comfort the few remaining adherents of the older orthodoxy. What else would it accomplish?

The Dodd-Berle exchange and its sequels are strongly colored by economic and social views popular during the NRA era, when the trend toward "planning" was viewed as necessarily involving something close to the direct control of business enterprises by the state. The climate of opinion has been greatly altered by thought and experience since that time. Another view of the relation of the government to the economy has become ascendant. This theory of "planning" contemplates government control of the level of employment, through fiscal and monetary policy, which could provide a favoring environment for the effective functioning of comparatively free and competitive markets for goods and of comparatively free markets for labor.[41] The controversy over managerial responsibility should be viewed in this context, which significantly alters perspective.

In this setting, does the debate over competing "rules," exemplified in the Berle-Dodd exchange and the subsequent literature, have any substance? Save in the area of managerial salaries, options, and pension plans, and perhaps that of charitable contributions, is endocratic big business really doing anything which the directors could not justly claim was in the best long-term interests of stockholders? The conduct of pricing policies is more a matter of antitrust enforcement than of alternative doctrines of managerial discretion. So long as enterprises are not subjected to the pressure of effective market competition, they will have considerable discretion as to the prices they charge, and will be tempted, in perfect good faith, to make plausible "mistakes" in resource allocation. If they do function in the matrix of effective competition, their opportunity to pursue price policies of "philanthropy" or "public welfare" rather than of "profit seeking" will be correspondingly reduced. The conduct of labor relations, again, is more directly a function of the law and economics of the labor market than of rival philosophies of corporate management.

41. I have attempted to develop this thesis in PLANNING FOR FREEDOM: THE PUBLIC LAW OF AMERICAN CAPITALISM (1959).

The function of rules of law is both descriptive and normative. Such rules reflect the pattern of accepted behavior and the standards which the community seeks to have upheld in the daily conduct of business affairs. They are at best hypotheses, articulated to guide and explain the wayward course of events. As an abstract statement of the social duty of business enterprise in the middle of the twentieth century, I believe the "rule" I have suggested—that of long-term profit maximization—conforms more concretely than any alternative both to the image of preferred reality for business behavior in public opinion, at this state in the evolution of our legal and economic order, and to the ends business enterprise is expected to fulfill as part of the nation's system of law for governing the economy.

But how can such policies be enforced? Are the votes of stockholders, or of some agent for stockholders in endocratic corporations, such as the optional voting trustee suggested earlier, a better guide to the long-term economic interests of stockholders than the business judgment of directors? Are minority stockholders' suits, even if brought by a public officer in the name of the inherent visitorial powers of the state, a suitable or sufficient remedy? Such devices, backed by strong policies of required disclosure, may help curb overreaching, the wrongful taking of corporate opportunity, excessive managerial compensation, trading on inside information, and other abuses. Professor Manning's "second chamber" is a provocative thought which deserves extended consideration in this connection. It can hardly be assumed, however, that any of these procedures, or all of them in combination, would provide a better basis than the directors' judgment for determining the long-term economic interest of the stockholders.

The voting of active stockholders, or, in the case of endocratic corporations, voting by an independent trustee for stockholders, would have one advantage over the present rule of untrammeled managerial discretion: it would provide a less dubious base for the authority of directors and officers of great enterprises, now almost cut off from their source of power.

On the other hand, a clear acceptance of profit maximization as a legal principle might well do something, perhaps a good deal, to order the pattern of corporate policy. Legal rules are not always fully self-enforcing, of course. But they do exert an influence, even though procedures of enforcement are not comprehensive. Adequate means for surveillance and accounting can and should be developed to minimize abuses of corporate power. The more important problem, how-ever, is the orientation of legitimate business policy: should it be essentially economic in purpose, or should it become an ambiguous amalgam of economic and noneconomic themes? I, for one, con-clude that a clear-cut economic directive should help directors to discriminate more effectively among competing claims upon them, in carrying out their public trusteeship for the economic system as a whole.

Part Four

Force and Morals in International Relations

As a presentation of my views on the relations between law and morality, this book would have been incomplete without a sample of my work on international problems.

I have been interested in foreign policy since my student days in the thirties, when my friends and I began to face the probability of war. Since 1969, when I left the State Department, this interest has absorbed nearly half my working time. I have published two books and many articles on foreign affairs and international law in recent years; lectured; testified before congressional committees; and participated in a number of commissions, colloquia, and political groups concerned with these matters.

The paper which constitutes chapter 9 was written in 1977; it distills and summarizes my views on American foreign policy in the perspective of international law. Building on the analysis offered in chapter 9 of *Peace in the Balance* (1972), it attempts to identify the changing role of international law in world politics since 1945. It considers the implications for world society of the marked decline in the restraining influence of law on the international behavior of states since 1972.

Nine

Is the United Nations Charter Going the Way of the League of Nations Covenant?

I

The events of the early 1970s are forcing a reconsideration of the ideas which have been accepted for a quarter of a century as the axioms of modern American foreign policy—the self-evident truths on which it had been built.

Until now, the continuities of our foreign policy have been striking. Since 1945 each President and each Congress has faced a different combination of pressures and opportunities in what the Supreme Court once called the "vast external realm." Each challenge has been stronger and more threatening than the one before, rising in quite a steady curve from the feints of Azerbaijan and Berlin to the massive wars in Korea, Indochina, and the Middle East. The opportunities have been less patterned, although some—the rapprochement with China, particularly—have been important. The seven postwar Presidents have differed widely in temperament, character, experience, style, ability, and luck. But until the numbing catastrophes of 1973 and 1974, at least, the United States perceived its national interests in much the same way. And those perceptions were translated into programs which, for all their shortcomings and mistakes, constituted a coherent foreign policy.

The principal features of that policy have remained constant through this period.

First, the Marshall Plan and its progeny led to the reconstruction of the industrialized democracies and the formation of Europe. The industrialized democracies became an integrated and progressive capitalist world economy, built on liberal principles of trade and investment. Despite weaknesses and mistakes, notably in the monetary field, the capitalist world economy has been a success, thus far—

a remarkable success, if one recalls the damage of the war years, and the stagnation of the thirties. Its dynamism and stability have become quite as important to the well-being of the developing nations and the communist states as they are to the industrialized democracies themselves.

Secondly, President Truman put the political influence of the United States strongly on the side of decolonization. And he initiated the Point Four program, the first of many far-reaching and often useful efforts to help the developing nations achieve modernization.

And finally, the United States proposed the Baruch Plan, thus far a failure, but the first step in a continuing effort to minimize the danger of nuclear war and to bring nuclear energy under international control as a resource for peaceful development. No other American initiative in the field of postwar international relations was of comparable significance. The growing risks of nuclear proliferation and nuclear coercion confirm the wisdom of Dean Acheson and David Lilienthal, who developed the Baruch Plan, and underscore the tragic consequences of its rejection by the Soviet Union.

A state of general peace was the hypothesis on which this array of ongoing enterprises depended. And peace is a necessary condition of their success, and the success as well of related efforts to promote human and political rights, and social improvement.

The statesmen of the early postwar period assumed that the nations would profit from the mistakes they had made in the thirties, and enforce the Charter of the United Nations as a system of peace. For the men and women who lived through the collapse of the League of Nations in the thirties and the Second World War which followed, for the delegates who drafted and ratified the Charter in 1945 and the North Atlantic Treaty in 1949, and for those who authorized and fought the war in Korea between 1950 and 1954, it was obvious that "peace is indivisible," in the phrase often used by Foreign Minister Litvinov some forty years ago, and that man's best hope for progress of every kind lay in enforcing the rules of the Charter against aggression.

The men and women of that generation were convinced that the Second World War would never have taken place if the democratic nations and the Soviet Union had upheld the Covenant of the League, and stood firm against aggression during the thirties in Manchuria, Ethiopia, and Spain, and particularly in the Rhineland and Czechoslovakia. Their minds were dominated by the searing memory of the Emperor of Ethiopia, who asked the League for protection against

Italian aggression in 1935, and was heard in silence. The presence of Ethiopian troops in Korea was the ultimate symbol of what collective security meant to them.

The American policy of collective security began to take shape immediately after World War II in response to the Soviet takeover of Eastern Europe, and a series of Soviet probes in Iran, Turkey, and Greece. It was announced in 1947 as the Truman Doctrine, and followed by the Vandenberg Resolution, the NATO Treaty, and many other unilateral and multilateral statements and actions. The essence of the policy was that the United States and its allies would insist on the enforcement of the Charter through the Security Council or, failing that remedy, through arrangements of collective self-defense, at least in cases of aggression directed against free nations, and conducted or sponsored by the Soviet Union or its proxies. The application of these principles led to the checking of Soviet expansion in Iran, Turkey, Greece, Berlin, Yugoslavia, and South Korea, and the development of a network of alliances and coalitions, designed to deter aggression directed against our interests, and to maintain a strong and stable balance of power.

On that footing, the United States and its allies, year after year, sought not only to fulfill their programs of economic and social development, and of nuclear control, but also to reach political understandings with the Soviet Union and with China, and to induce them to join in a process of genuine détente. The United States made overtures to China regularly, starting in 1949, shortly after the communists came to power. And it offered participation in the Marshall Plan to the Soviet Union and the nations of Eastern Europe, as well as the Baruch Plan and other proposals for reducing tensions.

The word "détente" has been much abused in the political battles of recent years, and has become almost magically ambiguous. But the concept identifies one of the most important on-going objectives and aspirations of American and, indeed, of all Western foreign policy—the achievement of political understandings with the Soviet Union, and the relaxation of tensions. In Western eyes, the only tenable definition for the word "détente" must be the practice of reciprocal respect for the rules of the Charter against the international use of force. "Détente" in that sense has not been achieved. The West can hardly accept the notion of "détente" as a Soviet commitment to refrain from aggression in Europe and as a license to pursue expansionist aims elsewhere in the world.

The power of the idea of the Charter in American thought about the nature of its foreign policy is dramatized by our behavior during the Suez Crisis of 1956 and 1957. There, as the result of American diplomatic ineptitude on a scale difficult to believe, and the breakdown of allied solidarity to which that ineptitude led, the United States felt itself obliged to uphold the Charter against two of its most important allies and a small and friendly nation it was under obligation to protect.

In the aftermath of Korea and Vietnam, this view of world politics has been weakened. A change in consciousness, confidence, and perception has occurred. Whether it is a transitory reaction to the Vietnam experience, or a deep mutation in outlook, remains to be seen. For the moment, at least, Western public opinion is not convinced that peace is indivisible, and that the collective enforcement of the Charter—that is, collective security against aggression—is the best way to protect our interests in world politics. If the Emperor of Ethiopia asked for help today, as he did in 1935, would the Western nations rally against aggression, or would they point out that Ethiopia is hardly a democratic country, and pass by on the other side? Many have come to the view that there must be a better way to keep the peace than by fighting small wars to prevent big ones, when the small wars become as unpleasant, and as costly, as the "peace-keeping" actions in Korea and in Vietnam. "No more Vietnams" is just as popular a slogan today as "no more Koreas" was during the Eisenhower administration.

The difficulty is that while many inveigh against the policy of collective security, no one has proposed a coherent alternative. Apart from true isolationists and those who in fact favor the spread of Soviet power and influence, the main opponents of American military action in Korea and Vietnam register their protest, and then put forward programs which differ in tone but not in substance from the official programs. Many approach these problems, as Ambassador Andrew Young remarked in April 1977, "as children of Korea and Vietnam." For them, an attitude is itself a policy. The struggle to develop a post-Vietnam American foreign policy, based on a perception of the national interest in the context of reality, is only starting.

American writers and politicians have thrown out vague hints about alternative policies, but none has so far impressed either professional or general opinion as realistic. Some favor a return to "massive nuclear retaliation"—an idea which was unworkable even when we had a nuclear monopoly, and is unthinkable now. Others would have the nation use force only if an enemy should land on Long Island. They underestimate the coercive pressures which could be exercised against us through the hostile control of raw materials or the threat of overwhelmingly superior military power. And those who favor drawing a perimeter around the industrialized democracies, and ignoring the rest of the world, ignore also the fact that the industrialized nations can be outflanked, invested, and reduced to impotence through the Third World. A Maginot Line defense would be quite as foolish for the industrialized democracies today as it proved to be for France in 1940. For example, the defense of South Korea is vital to the defense of Japan from the west and south, and the defense of Israel and other American interests in the Middle East is essential to prevent Soviet hegemony in the area. With such hegemony, the Soviet Union could take over the control of Europe, and of much else besides. Examples could easily be multiplied. The conclusion they support, I should suggest, is that the significance of many parts of the Third World to the security of the United States depends on time and context. None can be excluded *a priori* from the horizon of national concern.

The question remains, therefore, as the central issue of American foreign policy after Vietnam: "Is there any feasible way to protect the security of the nation short of general, if not universal, enforcement of the Charter?" Until the American people can agree on an answer to this question, the United States and its allies continue in the older pattern of collective security, but without conviction, flexibility, energy, or imagination. As the Chinese remark with increasing concern, Western foreign policy in recent years has been marked by "strategic passivity."

Against the background of recent history, and with war in open violation of the Charter now raging or proclaimed in many parts of Africa, Asia, and the Middle East, the future of collective security will be the principal preoccupation of United States foreign policy during the late seventies.

The scale and pace of aggression have increased markedly since the early seventies, and resistance to aggression has declined. The restraining influence of international law in international politics has correspondingly diminished, as it did in the period before World War II. The practice of aggression is contagious. As fear spreads, violent conflict becomes more frequent, and more difficult to control.

Unless general respect for the Charter is restored soon, no state will regard itself as bound by the Charter rules. The Charter will vanish completely as a curb on the aggressive appetite, and we shall once more confront the problem of living in a world without the pervasive influence of a basic law.

The fact challenges the possibility of the political system posited by the United Nations Charter: a system of world politics ordered by law; a system more just than the imperial system of the past, and more progressive; a system which aspires to develop peaceful procedures for vindicating human rights and the self-determination of peoples; but, above all, a system of international peace.

II

In his Inaugural Address, President Carter declared that the goal of American foreign policy is "to help shape a just and peaceful world that is truly humane."

The only possible predicate for President Carter's concept of world order is the Charter of the United Nations. As a constitution for the world community, that document restates the political, social, and moral aspirations of modern humanism, and establishes procedures of international cooperation for making progress towards their realization. The relationship among the purposes and goals of the Charter will be discussed more fully at a later point. Suffice it to note here that the Charter goes far beyond the Covenant of the League in seeking to encourage and promote the protection of human liberty and dignity. But the Charter contemplates that the political, economic, and social goals of the instrument be sought by persuasion, diplomacy, and other means of peaceful international cooperation, and not through the use of force. The central core of the Charter—the idea from which all the rest flows—is the ban of Article 2 (4) against the international use of force, except for individual and collective self-defense and enforcement actions under the direction of the Security Council.[1] The Charter was born from a terrible, worldwide war. Its first concern is to end the scourge of war.

---

1. Article 2(4) provides that "All Members shall refrain in their international relations from the threat or use of force against the territorial integrity or political independence of any state, or in any other manner inconsistent with the Purposes of the United Nations."

It is commonplace both in journalism and in politics, and sometimes even in academia, to contrast a foreign policy of "world order"
with one based on "the balance of power." Other pairs of words and
phrases are used to the same end: "idealism" versus "realism";
"morality" versus "security"; "international law" versus "naked
power"; reliance on the United Nations versus reliance on national
military strength. This way of looking at foreign policy has strong
roots in American history. Echoing Wilson, President Franklin D.
Roosevelt once said that the United Nations would provide an al-
internative to "the system of unilateral action, the exclusive alliances,
the balance of power, and all the other expedients that have been
tried for centuries—and have always failed."

But the supposed antinomy between a foreign policy of "morality"
and "world order" and one of "power politics" is a false one. The two
ideas are not necessarily in opposition. In 1945, when the Charter
was drafted, it was widely hoped that the great powers would understand their common interest in the enforcement and fulfillment of
the Charter. Today, no such hope can be entertained. Since the great
powers do not share a common and concerted view of the requirements of the Charter, world order in accordance with the Charter is
inconceivable without a firm balance of power to sustain it. As President Carter remarked in his Inaugural Address, "it is clear that a
world which others can dominate with impunity would be inhos-
pitable to decency and a threat to the well being of all people."

Responding to the events of his time, Jefferson defined the American national interest much as President Carter did. Immediately
after 1789, Jefferson was a passionate enthusiast for the French
Revolution and the cause of the French Republic. But he became
more and more concerned as Napoleon conquered Europe, invaded
Russia, and threatened to bring all Europe, including Britain, under
French dominion. "Put all Europe into his [Napoleon's] hands," Jefferson wrote, "and he might spare such a force . . . as I would leave
not have to encounter. It cannot be to our interest that all Europe
should be reduced to a single monarchy"—even a monarchy devoted
to the Rights of Man.

The Charter of the United Nations cannot enforce itself. It can be
the effective organizing principle of a peaceful world society only
when there are strong coalitions and alliances ready and able to
insist upon general compliance with its rules purporting to govern the
international use of force. The Charter itself anticipated the problem.
Legally, the paralysis of the Security Council does not suspend the

binding force of the Charter. When the Security Council is unable to function, the vindication of the Charter is left to the recommendatory powers of the General Assembly, and the efficacy of individual or collective self-defense: that is, to trial by defensive battle, supplemented by the persuasive and mediating influence of diplomacy and public opinion.

In this perspective, foreign policies based on morality, idealism, and international law are not alternatives to foreign policies based on the balance of power. They complement each other, as ends and means. "World order" and "the balance of power" are not antonyms. They are two sides of the same coin. Their true antonym is a society of uncontrolled aggression—that is, the state of anarchy. All societies ordered by law, and especially the democracies among them, are necessarily pluralist: only a wide dispersal of influence and authority among the classes and institutions of such societies can protect them from the risks of abuse of power, and of lawless power. Even the most peaceful and homogeneous societies require a mild police power as an indispensable component of the legal process. There is a profound difference between power in the service of law, and power as its enemy.

To talk of the influence of international law in international relations is not an indulgence in pedantic illusion. Law is not a remote and technical abstraction, but an integral part of the social process—profoundly influenced by it, and at the same time a profound influence on its course. The rules of the Charter regarding the international use of force are not sentimental dreams, or the idle chatter of monks. They are the norms of a system of law fulfilling for international society the essential roles of law in the on-going life of every other kind of society.

I use the word "law" here in its simplest and most realistic sense."[2] The society of nations today is not as homogeneous as it was when it was controlled by a loose cartel of the European empires. But it is nonetheless a society, bound by the necessities of shared self-interest to agree on a few minimal rules of public order which embody their aspirations and their common expectations. These rules, and the principles they apply, constitute a body of law.

A society governed by law does not invariably live in accordance with its own rules of right behavior, nor does it always follow its

2. See p. 1, *supra,* for an attempt at definition.

established procedures for resolving conflicts. A model for behavior can remain a legal norm if it is not universally respected. But it ceases to be a norm, and becomes a dream, when it no longer corresponds to the generality of usage, and society abandons any attempt to vindicate or protect it.

Lawyers of a positivist outlook, and political scientists influenced by them, often say that international law "does not exist," since there is no sovereign to command obedience to its norms. This is a shallow view. Law draws its strength and sanction more from custom than from fiat. Its most fundamental sanction, as Grotius pointed out, is the reciprocal perception of a common interest. And no ruler, however "sovereign," can make law which runs counter to the customs of his people, and to the deeply held common values which make them a culture, a community, and a society.

Alternatively, writers of the positivist persuasion agree that the sensitive body of international law dealing with the use of force by or from states "does not exist," since the international use of force touches the ultimate interests of states—the nerve roots of their sovereignty and existence. Dean Acheson often spoke and wrote in this vein, with his usual force, color, and clarity.

But when Acheson was Secretary of State in 1950, he confronted the barefaced invasion of South Korea by North Korea, backed by the Soviet Union—the most important of the many important problems with which he had to deal during his tour of duty. Acheson advised President Truman that it was in the national interest of the United States to lead a worldwide crusade of collective security in behalf of South Korea, and of the Charter.

The Korean War was long viewed as the heroic model of what collective security was for—an action intended to remind predators that aggression had been outlawed, and that the ban would be maintained. Since the Korean War was supported by nations which at the time were willing and able to insist on their view, the aggression was defeated.

III

The rules of the Charter on the international use of force grow naturally from our culture, and its experience of war. Like so many other moral achievements and aspirations of nineteenth- and twentieth-century Western society, from the abolition of slavery to the recognition of the equality of men and women, these rules measure the influence of the eighteenth-century Enlightenment, which has so profoundly transformed our minds and our lives.

The provisions of the Charter regarding the international use of force particularly represent the influence of the American school of eighteenth- and nineteenth-century Enlightenment, with its emphasis on the importance of law among the instrumentalities of social policy. The American Constitution was not the only manifestation of this singular outlook. From the day that American Presidents and Secretaries of State emerged as actors in world politics, they became important spokesmen for international law, and contributed disproportionately to its development. During much of the nineteenth century, Americans pressed international arbitration and international tribunals as means to achieve the peaceful resolution of international conflict. And Americans played a critical part in the drafting and adoption both of the League Covenant and of the United Nations Charter.

The effort to impose generally accepted rules of restraint with regard to the international use of force in world politics goes back to the Congress of Vienna and the volcanic and devastating war which preceded it.

Before 1815, no rule or principle claiming to be a norm of law in this sense effectively challenged the right of states to go to war at will. Philosophers and theologians had contended for centuries that international law should prohibit war, or at least that it should prohibit unjust war. Before 1815, opinions of this kind belonged to the realm of visionaries, not of practical men. They had little or no visible effect on behavior.

After the terrible cycle of nearly universal war which began in 1789, however, the European statesmen assembled at Vienna started on a course which continues to preoccupy our minds. Seeking to apply the maxims of the philosophers, they undertook to achieve new norms for international law—norms which would effectively limit the right of states to use force against each other.

"A Europe in which the rights of everyone resulted from duties from all," wrote the historian Albert Sorel, "was something so strange to the statesmen of the old regime that the Revolutionary and Napoleonic wars, lasting a quarter of a century and the most formidable yet seen, were required to impose the idea upon them and demonstrate its necessity. The attempt to give Europe an elementary organization at the Congress of Vienna and the Congresses which followed was a step forward, not a return to the past." This step, Sorel said, was not an "august abstraction," a beautiful chimera "with which Utopians rocked themselves to sleep." It was, rather, part of the "biological" process through which the real law of nations —the living law—is precipitated from history. Following Montesquieu, Sorel wrote that law develops from the customs and aspirations of cultures, reflecting what he called "relationships based on the very nature of things." For the society of nations and the substance of international law, the critical factors were the nature of states, and the conditions essential to their living together.

The ideas behind the new norms for international law have been asserted with more and more insistence now for nearly two centuries. Sometimes—and sometimes for extended periods—they have been respected in practice about as much as the norms of municipal law. And throughout this period, their influence on the minds of men has increased—at least in societies faithful to the liberal Western tradition. One need only recall the remark Undersecretary of State George Ball made at the time of the Cuban missile crisis to realize the importance of this fact. Arguing against the proposal to bomb Cuba, he said, "We should wake up a different people." Manifestly, the record is spotty and uneven. But the line of development is clear.

Between 1815 and 1914, the principal thrust of the effort was not to abolish war, but to confine it. Conscious of their equal interest in avoiding the catastrophe of universal war, the statesmen of the period found compromises which restricted their rivalry. It became the understood rule that states should seek to settle their disputes by peaceful means, and go to war only as a last resort. The Great Powers recognized a special responsibility which they possessed because of their size—a responsibility to constrain their ambitions, and concert their influence, in the interests of peace. The Concert of Europe, and its occasional diplomatic congresses, were the ancestors of the Security Council of the United Nations, and of its veto provisions. They functioned often, and sometimes well, to find diplomatic solutions for many conflicts which might otherwise have led to war. And, when wars came, they were confined, and their goals limited. During the century before 1914, war was a phenomenon of the political order, and within it, not a means for destroying it. The wars of the nineteenth century tended to be limited, both in space and in purpose. They never involved the destruction of states or societies. In the end, they were smothered in diplomacy. The Crimean War, the Franco-Prussia War, and the War over Schleswig Holstein were not fought to the point of unconditional surrender.

The regime of the nineteenth century collapsed in the tragedy of the First World War. For at least two decades before 1914, Wilhelmine Germany had broken its rules. All its restraints were finally swept away. In revulsion, the nations adopted the Covenant of the League of Nations, seeking again, as they had done at Vienna a century before, to commit themselves to rules which could exorcise the demon of general war: rules of balance and restraint, of conciliation and compromise; rules which might help them to maintain peace at least as well as it had been maintained by the Concert of Europe in the nineteenth century.

Once again the effort failed, this time after only twenty years. Once again men reacted in revulsion by trying for a third time, and this time more categorically than ever, to codify as norms of law the system of ideas about the international use of force which had been evolving since the Congress of Vienna.

The Charter of the United Nations was the result of that effort. It was achieved at a rare and brief moment—a moment of relative harmony among the victorious allies who came together in San Francisco as a constituent assembly at the end of a desperate war they had barely won. Their principal purpose was to establish a world organization, an organization not of peoples but of states—states of different cultures and social systems, all claiming to be "sovereign." The Charter was thus a constitutive act, an attempt to state fundamental principles for conducing the diplomacy of a diverse society of "sovereign" states.

The hopes and dreams men entertained for the United Nations went beyond diplomacy, and beyond peace. The Charter expressed other ambitions: the promotion of fundamental human rights and the advance of economic and social welfare. But the modern world consists of many cultures, and of states dominated by different ideologies. Many do not accept, or do not fully accept, either the political and human aspirations of the Charter or its rules about the international use of force. The implementation of the Charter rules of minimal public order would therefore have been a difficult and uneven process under ideal circumstances. But circumstances have hardly been hospitable to the notion of peace since 1945.

The Charter is not the whole of international law, any more than a written constitution or statute is the whole of the law on the subjects with which it deals. Like any document of positive law, the Charter must be read against a tenacious background of customs, practice, history, expectation, and hope. And, like any other document of positive law, its meaning evolves continuously in response to social and moral change, and to changes in its own code of aspiration as well. The Charter is thus an effort to reorient and in some areas to restate the preexisting international law. It should be read in its matrix of purpose, with primary emphasis, always, not on the words alone but on the underlying theory of governance the words seek imperfectly to express and to fulfill.

IV

What is that theory of governance, with regard to the responsibility of states for the international use of force?

The Charter articulates a number of axioms, postulates, and aspirations for the society of nations: to defend and advance fundamental human rights and the equality of men and women, and of nations large and small; economic welfare and social justice; respect for the integrity of treaties and other sources of international law; friendly relations among nations based on the principle of equal rights and self-determination of peoples; and, above all, international peace and security. These goals of the Charter system are to be sought through peaceful means, and never by the use of force—through political cooperation, compromise, mediation, arbitration, adjudication, and the good offices of friendly powers, and of the organs of the United Nations.

If there is any one proposition about the Charter which history makes manifest, it is that its primary and overriding purpose is to minimize the use of force in international relations. All scholars on the subject do not agree about the extent of that restriction. But if the Charter does not revise international law in this regard, by making peace the first among its goals, it is hard to imagine what it can be supposed to intend.

The regime posited by the Charter with respect to the international use of force is reflected in two key passages of the document, Article 2(4) and Article 51. The modern law concerning the international use of force is a counterpoint of themes drawn from these two provisions.

Article 2(4) specifies that "all Members shall refrain in their international relations from the threat or use of force against the territorial integrity or political independence of any state," while Article 51 notes that nothing in the Charter "shall impair the inherent right of individual or collective self-defense if an armed attack occurs against a member of the United Nations, until the Security Council has taken measures necessary to maintain international peace and security."

The background of Article 51 in customary international law is well developed. States have always been conceded the legal right to ask others for help in dealing with external and internal threats to their security, and, indeed, to cooperate freely with other states in the military area. They have also been conceded the right to use limited and proportional force in peacetime to defend themselves against armed attacks and other threatening and coercive breaches of international law for which there was no practicable diplomatic or judicial remedy. The classic paradigm of permissible self-help against the fact or the threat of external attack in peacetime is the situation of the famous *Caroline* episode in 1837, in which the British sent armed forces into New York to disperse a military group that had assembled along the Niagara River to assist an insurrection in Canada. The United States had failed to break up and arrest the armed band.

The principle of self-help recognized in the correspondence over the *Caroline* episode was applied widely and generally accepted as right in situations involving international raids, arms smuggling, threats to the safety of citizens abroad, breaches of neutrality, or other failures to carry out legal obligations owed to individual states or the international community at large. Where a state was subjected to armed attack or other forms of coercion by or from another state, and there was no practical peaceful remedy available, it had a right to use a proportional amount of force against the state responsible for the breach—enough force under the circumstances to cure the breach.

Such limited uses of international force by way of self-defense were not acts of general war. And they were not deemed to threaten the territorial integrity or political independence of the state. Under the

Charter, a use of force does not violate Article 2(4) if it is justified under Article 51.

Article 2(4) is thus the critical change sought to be accomplished by the Charter in customary international law. Building on the Kellogg-Briand Pact, and the jurisprudence of Nuremberg, it would deny states one of their historic "inherent rights" as sovereign states —that of making war on their neighbors for any reason, or for none.

The inherent right of states to use force internationally in ways which do not violate Article 2(4) is left unimpaired by the Charter. The expectation was, of course, that the permanent members of the Security Council would agree on the peacekeeping policies to be applied by the council in carrying out its responsibilities under the Charter. When it became clear that no such agreement was possible, the enforcement of the Charter rules was remitted automatically to the inherent right of states to undertake policies of individual or collective self-defense, in accordance with Article 51.

While states necessarily make provisional determinations that an attack has occurred when they exercise their rights of self-defense under Article 51, the Security Council has the final authority under the Charter to determine when a threat to the peace, a breach of the peace, or an act of aggression has taken place. It may then call upon the parties to settle their dispute by peaceful means, recommend a settlement, provide a mediator or diplomatic midwife, or recommend the submission of the dispute to the International Court of Justice. If these means fail, it may make legally binding decisions and, in extreme cases, use economic or military sanctions to implement them in order to maintain or restore international peace and security. Under the Uniting for Peace Resolution passed during the Korean conflict, the General Assembly can make recommendations but not binding decisions on breaches of the peace and acts of aggression when the Security Council is unable to act.

Thus the first class of international uses of force contemplated as legal by the Charter consists of those undertaken pursuant to recommendations or binding decisions of the Security Council, either by the national forces of member states or by special United Nations forces. Not all such episodes, properly speaking, have been "enforcement actions" of the United Nations rather than procedures of self-defense encouraged, or not opposed, by the Security Council. Their legality under the Charter is the same in either case. In other instances, United Nations forces have been established more for diplomatic than for combat purposes—to keep combatants apart, and to reduce anxiety about possible breaches of cease-fire or armistice agreements, as was the case in the Middle East, Cyprus, and other troubled areas.

Under the political circumstances of recent years, the power of the Security Council to make binding decisions on issues of international peace and security has not been used often. But on great occasions, when the major powers can agree, the Security Council has acted, and acted with considerable effect. One such occasion occurred on October 22, 1973, when the council voted a binding decision requiring the parties to the Middle Eastern conflict to negotiate a just and durable peace in accordance with the principles and provisions of the resolution on peace in the Middle East the council had adopted in November 1967. Security Council resolutions are drafted in a political atmosphere, and avoid explicit language to which some of the nations might be sensitive. They must be interpreted, therefore, like the holdings of common law judges, in the light of the principles and propositions from which they necessarily derive. Read in this way, Resolution 338 of October 22, 1973, authoritatively reaffirms the basic decisions of the League of Nations, and the long line of decisions and other resolutions of the United Nations, which uphold the legitimacy of the Palestine Mandate and the lawful emergence of Israel and Jordan as the successor states to Turkey in the territories of the Mandate, and declare the United Nations' special interest in the future of Jerusalem.

The Security Council has not often authorized the use of force to carry out its occasional decisions. It has relied primarily on the slower processes of political persuasion to achieve compliance. This is the case today with respect to both Namibia and the Middle East. There are instances of prolonged noncompliance in international law, as there are in any other system of law. It remains to be seen whether those instances of noncompliance are going to become the rule rather than the exception in the near future, and destroy the United Nations system as the system of the League of Nations was overwhelmed forty years ago.

The second category of international uses of force contemplated as legal by the Charter are those undertaken by a state in the name of its inherent right of self-defense. While each state is subject to the obligation to exhaust available peaceful alternatives before exercising its right of self-defense under Article 51, the Charter leaves to the state itself the right to decide in the first instance when to respond to what it regards as an armed attack, the imminent threat of armed attack, or a breach of international law which it regards as comparably coercive. A state need not obtain a ruling from the Security Council before using force in self-defense. The Security Council can support a state's decision, as it did when North Korea attacked South Korea in 1950, and as it did repeatedly in the course of the prolonged conflict over Israel's right to exist. The Security Council may disagree with the action of the state claiming a right of self-defense, and rule against the propriety of its decision: i.e., rule that its use of force was a violation of Article 2(4), and therefore a breach of the peace or an act of aggression. This happened in effect during the Suez crisis of 1956, although the Security Council was paralyzed by the British and French vetoes. Nonetheless, it was clear that an overwhelming majority of the world community had concluded that Great Britain and France, at least, had not been attacked, or threatened by attack, and therefore that their use of force against Egypt was not justified under Article 51.

The Cuban missile crisis was the most extreme instance thus far of the exercise by a state of its inherent right of self-defense. The United States made no claim that a nuclear attack on it from Cuba was imminent. On the contrary, our nuclear superiority at the time made it clear that no such threat existed. We did take the position, which subsequent events demonstrated was correct, that the secret emplacement of missiles in Cuba, in violation of diplomatic assurances the Soviet Union had made to us, was a substantial political-military threat, against the background of contemporary pressures in Berlin, in Laos and Cambodia, and elsewhere, though not an armed attack or even an imminent threat of armed attack. We elected to treat that threat as one justifying limited acts of self-help, including some use of military force. Article 51 is the only possible legal basis for that claim, although the United States government of the day relied on another legal argument. Most of the world agreed with our assessment.

In this connection, two related uses of force in international affairs should be noted: assistance by a state to another which is defending itself against armed attack; and a broader form of international military assistance—the emplacement of the forces of one state on the territory of another, with its permission, to assure their common defense interests or, indeed, to assist it in dealing with domestic disorders, including riot, insurrection, or civil war. The first case is generally thought to be referred to by the language of "collective self-defense" in Article 51, despite its clumsy drafting. The second is simply an aspect of customary international law accepted as the order of nature in the states system, and never seriously challenged under the Charter. For example, when civil war raged in Nigeria in the 1960s, it was considered altogether normal and legal for Great Britain, Egypt, and the Soviet Union to provide military assistance to Nigeria, although military assistance to the Biafran rebels would have been considered an armed attack against Nigeria. The Organization of African States and a number of interested nations made strenuous efforts to prevent any international assistance to Biafra. The minute assistance the Biafrans did receive from abroad was covert, and understood to be illicit. The Biafran case was discussed and treated by the international community as comparable to that of Greece in the late 1940s, although there were differences between the two episodes. In Greece, the internal rebellion was helped significantly from neighboring communist states, a fact which was verified publicly by a United Nations Commission. But the pattern of reaction by the international community was the same as in the case of Biafra. International assistance to the Greek rebels was condemned, while the action of Britain and the United States in helping the Greek government was regarded as legal and proper. Similarly, Britain and France have assisted a number of African countries dealing with disorders, or movements of revolution or secession.

Many writers and governments have sought to identify an exception to this doctrine of international law which would authorize international assistance to revolutions they favor. They seek to distinguish international "intervention" in civil wars from open forms of interstate aggression. The uniform pattern of state practice, and the conditioned reflexes of the states system, deny their thesis. On analysis, their distinction vanishes. The rule that other nations may assist a state in putting down a rebellion, but not the rebels themselves, seems to correspond to the imperative necessities of international society viewed as a society of states.

Force is sometimes used internationally under customary international law and Article 51 to protect the citizens of a nation in a situation of distress or to remedy severe breakdowns in public order after earthquakes, riots, or other disasters. In the 1976 raid to rescue

Israeli and other hostages being held at Entebbe in Uganda, for example, the government of Uganda owed a clear duty under international law to protect the plane and its passengers from the hijackers. Since Uganda was not fulfilling that duty, and the risk to the passengers was imminent, the prevailing view—a correct one, in my opinion—was that under Article 51 the governments concerned were entitled under international law to use the amount of force reasonably necessary to deal with the effects of Uganda's breach of international law. Such actions do not violate the principle of Article 2(4), since they do not threaten either the territorial integrity or the political independence of the state where limited military operations occur. In the *Caroline* affair it was obvious that Great Britain was not waging general war against the United States, or planning to annex upper New York state.

Much of the modern law regarding the use of force in international politics concerns the interpretation and enforcement of Article 51. In practice, the law of Article 51 has gone far beyond its text in adapting its principles to the realities of the political process during a period when the Security Council has often been paralyzed by the rivalries of the Cold War, and the passions of world politics. Like every document in the history of law, Article 51 cannot be given a literal interpretation. In terms, it seems to apply only to members of the United Nations. But nonmember states, like South Korea, have been given its protection. And the right to use force under Article 51 against "an armed attack" extends to the threat of armed attack, although Article 51 seems literally to apply only after an armed attack has begun. Such a construction would be absurd, as a practical matter, especially but not exclusively in a nuclear setting. As Elihu Root once wrote, "No state can be expected to wait until it is too late to defend itself effectively." There is no evidence that those who drafted the Charter or have since construed it contemplated so drastic a change in customary international law. On the contrary, long-standing usage in this regard has been relied upon as obviously sensible. It should be recalled that in the celebrated *Caroline* episode the United States conceded that self-help might sometimes be justified to deal with the imminent threat of armed attack. And in the *Corfu Channel* case, for example, the International Court of Justice held that Albania had committed a serious breach of its international legal obligations, justifying a limited use of force by Great Britain in response, in failing to issue public warnings as to the presence of mines in the Corfu Channel. The court inferred that Albania must have known of the presence of those mines, which caused serious damage to British ships found to be legally passing through the channel. Heavy damages were awarded against Albania for its failure to act—hardly an "armed attack." In a demonstration of political balance, the court also ruled that Britain had used excessive force in responding to Albania's illegal act, although it did not award damages against Great Britain. Paradoxically, the principal evidence in the case concerned the mines which the Court ultimately ruled had been wrongfully swept by the Royal Navy.

The rules of the Charter with regard to the international use of force have been interpreted and restated with surprising consistency over the years since 1945 not only by scholars, diplomats, judges and ministers, but by a number of United Nations committees, commissions, and special bodies charged with codifying and expounding this branch of international law. Despite the intense political interest of many states in establishing exceptions which might legitimize categories of war they happen to favor—most notably, wars of national liberation, wars of communist revolution, and wars against the surviving white regimes of Africa—it has proved intellectually and politically impossible to do so. The needs, interests, and anxieties of all states in this regard are the same. In the end, no state can vote in favor of a doctrine which might be read to authorize guerrillas, mercenaries, or armed bands to operate against it from foreign bases, nor can it bring itself to abandon its inherent right under international law to obtain foreign help either against insurrection or invasion.

In 1950, the General Assembly, "condemning the intervention of a state in the internal affairs of another state for the purpose of changing its legally established government by the threat or use of force," solemnly reaffirmed "that, whatever the weapons used, any aggression, whether committed openly, or by fomenting civil strife in the interest of a foreign power, or otherwise, is the gravest of all crimes against peace and security throughout the world." And, in 1954, the International Law Commission defined as offenses against the peace and security of mankind the tolerance by a state of the use of its territory by armed bands or terrorists planning to make incursions into another state, or by groups intending to foment civil strife in another state.

A quite different General Assembly adopted the same sentiments in 1970, and again in 1974. The General Assembly's 1970 Declaration on Principles of International Law Concerning Friendly Relations and Cooperation among States provides that "every state has the duty to refrain from organizing or encouraging the organization of irregular forces or armed bands, including mercenaries, for incursion into the territory of another state." And the 1974 Definition of Aggression adopted by the assembly defined as aggression "the sending by or on behalf of a state of armed bands, groups, irregulars or mercenaries, which carry out acts of armed force against another state . . . , or its substantial involvement therein."

It is sometimes urged that these rules enshrine the status quo, and that an exception should be recognized in behalf of international assistance to revolutions which a majority of those voting in the United Nations might consider to be just, especially for so-called "wars of national liberation." International law does not condemn revolutions which occur within states. It is opposed to international war, not to social or political movements seeking social change within the states which have been formed by history. There are almost no states which do not contain groups which could be described as "peoples" claiming the right of self-determination. Spain, one of the oldest states of the international community, contains Catalonians and Basques who assert rights of self-determination. There are problems of this order in Belgium, in Canada, in the Soviet Union, in most of the states of Africa, and in many, many others. Each time an effort is made to formulate a rule which would allow force to be used internationally in behalf of "the self-determination of peoples" or other popular causes, the obstacles prove to be insuperable. No state is willing to concede to others a right it would resist if it were applied to itself. For international law and practice to acknowledge a right to use force internationally in behalf of such claims would be to authorize lynching, and to repudiate the principles on which the Charter is based: the principle of the equality of states, and their right to order their domestic affairs in accordance with their own ideas of social justice.

This is not to say that a state's internal affairs may never be a matter of international concern. The Charter does contemplate the use of peaceful means to promote the universal acceptance of human rights. And the precedent of international military interventions where minimal standards of decency are being violated has by no means vanished from our consciousness. Such humanitarian interventions—a limited and controversial category at best—are not

considered to violate Article 2(4), because they do not threaten
the territorial integrity or political independence of the state. But
the pattern of state practice, and the repeated formulations of international law by groups purporting to be authoritative, uniformly
deny the claim of a legal right to use force in behalf of rebellions,
secessions, or revolutions, whether labeled those of self-determination, national liberation, or one or another sect of communism.

Formally, therefore, international law prohibits the Brezhnev
doctrine as categorically as it forbids all other forms of aggression;
it cannot be stretched to authorize uses of force like the Soviet invasion of Hungary in 1956 and of Czechoslovakia in 1968, when the
Soviet Union used force to depose a government which in its view
had deviated from the true faith. The principles of international law
which made Great Britain responsible to the United States for failing
to prevent the Confederate cruiser *Alabama* from putting to sea
retain their nominal vitality.

V

The effective validity of these rules as law is an illusion, however,
despite the unanimity with which they are pronounced. Under the
impact of a series of large-scale and successful recent aggressions,
they are rapidly ceasing to correspond to the practice of states.

Even in the heyday of the Truman doctrine, exceptions to the
apparent universality of the Charter were tacitly recognized.

The United States and its European allies made no attempt to invoke the Charter against Soviet aggression in East Germany, Hungary, Poland, Czechoslovakia, and other countries of Eastern Europe.
In fact, if not in form, the area was treated as a Soviet sphere of
influence, and the promise of free elections given at Yalta and Potsdam was ignored. The allies reacted effectively only when the Soviet
Union attacked or threatened areas outside the Soviet protectorate—
Greece in the late forties, and Yugoslavia in the early fifties and again
in 1968.

Secondly, the rules of the Charter have never been seriously invoked in connection with the process of African decolonization. In
the first stages of that process, groups seeking independence from
France, Great Britain, and Belgium were rarely helped by forces
from beyond the frontiers of their own colonies, and then only on a

small scale. The spread of the practice of using force internationally in wars against white authority in Africa, and the increase in the scale of such interventions, is only some fifteen years old. It began with attacks from neighboring states against the Portuguese and then the Spanish provinces in Africa: attacks which no effective group in the world community was prepared to resist. Now the practice has become epidemic, and virulent. While the African states have often invoked the Charter in order to protect themselves—as in the Biafran case, the Katangese secession in the Congo, and a large number of other episodes involving the international use of force in Africa—neither the African states nor other members of the United Nations so much as comment on the illegality of the warfare now raging in Africa.

The Charter is based on the principle of the sovereign equality of states. While consistency is not in itself the ultimate goal of law, the political and social policies embodied in the principle of "sovereign equality" have formidable support. They embody realities about the nature of the state system which are difficult for the legal process to deny. The state has proved to be a tenacious institution in the modern world, despite the frequent predictions of its demise. The principle of sovereign equality cannot therefore be interpreted to authorize aggression against a state, however offensive other members of the world community may find its internal policies. State after state now faces frontiers festooned with armed camps—the camps of troops actively engaged in aggression against neighboring states. The troops may be exiled natives or mercenaries fighting for money or for ideology. They may represent the cause of conquest, of adventure, of racial warfare, or of one or another brand of revolution. Whatever their cause, the effect of what they do is the same.

The intensification of international conflict since the early seventies rests on a basic challenge to the political and legal doctrines of the Charter. What is happening in Africa is no more than an extension of trends long manifest in the Middle East and the Far East. That challenge is encompassed in the theory of wars of national or indeed of ideological liberation. In legal terms, the argument is that international law must acknowledge as sacred the right of self-determination of peoples who happen to live within the states which constitute the atoms of the system of international politics. By treating "states" as fictions, and "peoples" as realities, the advocates of this theory claim that international law should recognize the right of states to use force internationally in order to assist movements of secession, and other revolutionary movements against the authority of states. Furthermore, they claim that when revolutionary movements of this character gain sufficient momentum, no state should be allowed to provide assistance to the governments being attacked.

These theories would revive two unhappy precedents, and make them operational principles of international law and politics.

The first of these precedents would legitimize international assistance to peoples in revolt. Before the First World War, the Russian government provided assistance to the Slavs of Eastern Europe—a process which contributed to the turmoil of the Balkans, and helped to bring on the war. The argument is made in behalf of the Palestinian Arabs today. It was the theory Hitler invoked to justify his seizure of the Sudeten province of Czechoslovakia in 1938.

The second theory much in vogue today is that of the nonintervention policy adopted by Britain, France, and the United States during the Spanish Civil War of the 1930s. That theory asserts that it is the duty of states to refrain from assisting either side in a civil war, at least when the conflict reaches the level of belligerency.

I should argue that international law does not and cannot accept either the Sudetenland precedent, or that of the nonintervention policy of the 1930s toward the Spanish Civil War. The Charter of the United Nations repudiates them. They do not correspond to what has until recently been the almost instinctive pattern of practice. And they are contrary to the necessities of peace in a political system which is and will remain a system of states.

The true norm of international law for situations of this kind is illustrated by the way in which the international community reacted to the Biafran case in the mid-1960s; to those of Tanzania, Chad, and Ceylon; and to that of Greece in the late 1940s. In all these instances, the international community regarded it as clear that governments could legally obtain international assistance in putting down insurrections, while open or covert assistance to the rebels under such circumstances was treated as categorically illegal. Both in the Hungarian case of 1956, and the Czech case of 1968, the argument before the United Nations and elsewhere was not that the Soviet Union could not legally assist a widely recognized government which asked for help in suppressing a rebellion, but that there was no such government, and therefore no such request for assistance. In both those instances, the Soviet Union invaded not to support but to destroy a government. The United Nations intervention in the Congo which ended the secession of Katanga rested on exactly the same principle—that nations could assist the government of the Congo, at its request, but not the secessionists. And in the Bangladesh war, the preponderant view of the international community, at least as expressed in votes in the Security Council and in the General Assembly, was that the Indian intervention in behalf of the secession of Bangladesh from Pakistan was contrary to international law. India did not claim its action was justified on humanitarian grounds. Only the Soviet veto saved India from explicit condemnation.

The principle is particularly familiar to Americans. When France assisted the secessionist cause in America after 1776, everyone understood that French help for the American colonists in their revolution was an act of war against Great Britain. It was treated as such, legally and politically. This is one of the categories of war the Charter now purports to forbid.

The political process mirrored in these legal developments reached a climax in the Indochinese War after 1967 or 1968. That traumatic sequence of events precipitated a profound if thus far inconclusive disturbance of public opinion, particularly in the West, about the nature and extent of the Western commitment to the policy of collective security, and, indeed, about the viability of a policy of world order based upon the enforcement of the Charter rules regarding the international use of force. In Europe and the United States, public support for collective security had been weakening steadily since the war in Korea. In the final stages of the war in Indochina, the decline became precipitate. The emotional and political intensity of the reaction of American and world opinion to the Vietnam experience measures its significance as a protest not only against American participation in the war, but against the nominal state of international law, and the policy of collective security developed to enforce it.

In the perspective of this paper, these aspects of the Indochina drama should be recalled.

The Geneva Conference of 1954 resulted, as Chester Cooper concluded, in another "divided country," like Korea and Germany, "which, sooner or later (probably much later) would somehow be reunified." The conference, he says, gave "international blessing to the independence of Laos and Cambodia, and establish[ed] two political entities in Vietnam."

Later in 1954, eight nations signed and ratified the Treaty of Manila, the South East Asia Collective Defense Treaty, which specifies in Article 4(1) that each party to the treaty "recognizes that aggression by means of armed attack in the treaty area against any of the parties" (or against states or territories designated in the protocol to the treaty, which lists Laos, Cambodia, and South Vietnam, if they choose to be protected) "would endanger its own peace and safety, and agrees that it will in that event act to meet the common danger in accordance with its constitutional processes."

The general expectation of the international community in 1954, expressed both at the Geneva conference and in the SEATO Treaty, was that North and South Vietnam, like North and South Korea, China and Taiwan, and East and West Germany, were states divided by unfortunate political circumstance. They might be united someday by political agreement, but not by force.

Starting in the late 1950s, and in any event well before the first American response in 1961, the North Vietnamese undertook to develop, direct, and conduct what was at first a guerrilla war and at later stages a full-scale conventional war to bring South Vietnam under its control. The United States and other nations responded within the framework of the SEATO Treaty. Starting with President Eisenhower's warning in 1957 that "aggression or subversion against the Republic of Vietnam would be considered as endangering peace and stability" within the meaning of the treaty, Presidents, high administration officials, Senators, and newspaper editorials united in characterizing North Vietnam's assault on South Vietnam as an "armed attack" requiring action on part of each signatory to the treaty under Article 4. President Johnson, in a message to Congress on May 4, 1965, said that South Vietnam has been attacked by North Vietnam, and that our commitment to South Vietnam rested on "solemn treaties, the demands of principle, and the necessities of American security. The South East Asia Collective Defense Treaty 'committed us to act to meet aggression against South Vietnam.'" And Undersecretary of State George Ball, speaking at a SEATO meeting in 1965, said "the evidence establishes beyond the shadow of a doubt that South Viet-Nam is the victim of deliberate aggression. We have provided assistance for the same reason that we aided Greece and Turkey in 1947, that we fought in Korea, that we joined in forming NATO, and ANZUS, and SEATO . . . ."

Beginning in 1961, the United States began to send armed forces to South Vietnam to assist that country in its defense against armed attack. In 1964, Congress, through the Tonkin Gulf Resolution, gave its formal support to what Presidents Eisenhower, Kennedy, and Johnson had done in Vietnam, and declared that "in accordance with its obligations under the Southeast Asia Collective Defense Treaty, the United States is . . . prepared, as the President determines, to take all necessary steps, including the use of armed force, to assist any member or protocol state . . . requesting assistance in the defense of its freedom."

Although a sustained political attack was made against the legality of American and international assistance to the defense of South Vietnam, there is no plausible way in which that charge can be explained, in terms of international law.

Three theories have been advanced to justify the claim that international assistance to South Vietnam was illegal: (1) that the war between North and South Vietnam was a civil war, not an international war, since North and South Vietnam were not separate states at the time but part of a single "state" or "nation"; (2) that the North Vietnamese attack on South Vietnam was justified because no elections were held in 1956 on the possible unification of North and South Vietnam into a single state, as contemplated in the declaration issued at the end of the Geneva Conference in 1954 by Great Britain and the Soviet Union as cochairmen of the conference; and (3) on another legal footing altogether, that the war was a civil war *within* South Vietnam, and that under international law North Vietnam had a right to assist the revolutionary group, but that the United States had no right to assist the widely recognized government of South Vietnam.

Separately and together, these three theories are without foundation in the law of the Charter, as it has developed since 1945, or in the customary international law which is the matrix of the Charter.

According to generally accepted standards of international law, there were two states in Vietnam, not one, certainly after the Geneva Conference of 1954 and, according to Lauterpacht, for a good many years before—two states recognized as states by a considerable part of the world community, and exercising authority after the manner of states. As Professor Wolfgang Friedmann wrote in 1965, "it may be conceded that North and South Vietnam are today *de facto* separate states, even though the Geneva Agreement of 1954 spoke of 'two zones.' " And Professor Telford Taylor concluded that "the two zones [of Vietnam] took on the attributes of separate states."

South Vietnam was therefore entitled to defend itself against attack from North Vietnam, and to receive international assistance in that defense, just as South Korea was held to be entitled to the benefits of individual and collective self-defense under parallel circumstances in 1950.

Secondly, the declaration about elections in the communiqué issued at the end of the Geneva Conference in 1954 had the nominal support of only four of the nine participants in the conference, and both South Vietnam and the United States made it clear at the time through formal statements that they did not accept the proposal, and were not bound by the cochairmen's statement. In any event, even if there had been international agreement on the point, the breach of such an agreement would not justify the use of force by North Vietnam. The Korean people had been promised their unity and independence by the Soviet Union and the Western allies at Cairo and Potsdam. Yet the failure of the great powers to carry out these promises was held not to legitimize the North Korean attack on South Korea in 1950. Similarly, the unification of Germany has been promised by communiqués at the end of many international conferences since 1945. But no one contends that West Germany and its NATO allies would be legally justified in unifying the German nation by force, because those international promises have not been kept. However broadly one reads Article 51, it is difficult to conclude that the breach of such promises is equivalent to an armed attack.

The third ground advanced to support the claim that American aid to South Vietnam was illegal—the argument that North Vietnam had a legal right to assist the Viet Cong within South Vietnam, but that the United States and other nations had no right to assist South Vietnam—is plainly wrong under the Charter, under preexisting international law, and under the prevailing practice of states, for the reasons considered in earlier sections of this chapter.

The ill-fated agreements for peace in Indochina reached in January 1973, and guaranteed by the Act of Paris of March 1973, fully vindicate the legal position of the United States, and reject the three arguments I have sketched. Those agreements treated North and South Vietnam as separate states, and emphasize the right of the

South Vietnamese people to self-determination. They treated the
war in Vietnam as an international war in every sense, not a civil
war. Reaffirming the Laos agreements of 1962, they required North
Vietnam to withdraw from Laos and Cambodia and tacitly at least,
from South Vietnam as well. They also required North Vietnam to
refrain from interfering with the process of self-determination and
political settlement in South Vietnam. American withdrawal from
South Vietnam was the quid pro quo for the North Vietnamese
withdrawals.

Much can and should be said about American participation in the
Indochinese War: that it was badly conducted and badly explained;
that too much effort was devoted to diplomatic probes which turned
out to be deceits, and should have been perceived as such; and, above
all, that the war was not promptly and decisively won. What cannot
be said is that it was illegal.[3]

The breach of the 1973 peace agreements for Indochina by North
Vietnam, with the full support of the Soviet Union, marked a turning point of far-reaching significance in modern world politics—an
event whose full impact on the international political order has not
yet been fully revealed. From the point of view of the Charter, no
more blatant aggression could be imagined—an open conventional-
force invasion of South Vietnam in violation not only of Article 2(4)
but of confirmatory international agreements on which the ink
was hardly dry. From the point of view of world politics, the attack
can be compared only with Hitler's invasion of Czechoslovakia, in
violation of the Munich agreements of 1938.

Yet the final conquest of South Vietnam by North Vietnam was
greeted in the West by silence, or by relief.

Was this episode a minor deviation from the legal norm which will
be corrected in due course? Or did it mark the demise of the Charter
as a significant influence in world politics?

Some of the episodes recalled above in section IV and in the present
section are instances in which the norms of international law were
respected and enforced. In others, of course, those norms were
successfully defied. The three most recent cases—those of Bangla-

---

3. I have examined these problems at greater length in a review of John
Norton Moore's book *Law and the Indo-China War,* 82 YALE L. J. 829 (1973).

desh, Indochina, and the Middle East war of October 1973—
are also the most serious. In Bangladesh and Indochina, irreversible
change has been produced by the illegal use of force.

The Charter was breached—again on a very large scale—when
Egypt and Syria, with full Soviet backing, attacked Israel in October
1973. That major war was a strategic thrust at NATO as well as an
attempt to destroy Israel. The Arab attack of October 1973, was
the clearest case of aggression since the attack on South Korea in
1950, a violation not only of the Charter but of Security Council
Resolutions which authorized Israel to occupy the territories it had
captured in 1967 until the Arab states made peace. The Security
Council had commanded the Arab states to make peace with Israel
as early as 1948, and it reiterated that policy once more in 1967. In
legal terms, the Arab attack on Israel of October 1973, can be defended only as a "war of national liberation," on the ground that the
existence of Israel denies the Arab people of Palestine their rights
of self-determination. That ground, as we have seen, is legally untenable; it has been repeatedly rejected by the Security Council.

In the Middle East, the 1973 attack on Israel failed, thus far at
least. And the claim of a right to wage such a war was authoritatively
denied once again by the Security Council, which commanded the
parties to make peace with Israel through direct negotiations, and in
accordance with Resolution 242 of November 22, 1967.[4]

But the attempt was made, and made with impunity. The outcome
was determined not by judgelike deliberations, but by war.

VI

The attempt to look at recent international conflicts in the perspective
of international law suggests many questions. Can the formal rules
of public order embodied in the Charter, and reiterated with surprising consistency ever since, be expected to become true norms of the
living law for a state system in which the cultures and ideologies of
many states take different views of war? Is the foreign policy of the
Soviet Union compatible with the Charter, or is it now bursting visibly out of the Charter's silken cords? Does the security of the United

---

4. I have considered this point more fully in *The Illegality of the Arab
Attack on Israel of October 6, 1973,* 69 Am. J. Int. L. 272 (1975).

States and its allies require the general enforcement of Article 2(4) of the Charter, or are there alternative courses they could pursue?

For a long time after 1945, the United States and many other nations believed that their national security interests did indeed require a Wilsonian policy of enforcing the Charter. The fervor of that conviction has not survived the tests of Korea and Vietnam. But has the reality itself survived, as a sober if no longer evangelical judgment that nothing short of fidelity to the Charter can arrest the sweep toward anarchy and general war before it is too late? Or are there more limited policies through which the industrialized democracies could protect their own security by maintaining a balance of power as the basis for precarious truce, and ignoring aggressions which in their view do not threaten that balance of power?

There can be no doubt that the Western nations, and everybody else, would be better off if a magic wand were available to make the Charter effective as the prevailing norm of international politics, so that the peoples of the world and their governments could reduce their expenditures on armaments, and concentrate instead on social, economic, and political progress. Can such a miracle be achieved, or expected? And what can be done if the Charter continues to fade as an influence on the bahavior of states, until it finally disappears?

For the Charter will disappear, and disappear in the very near future, if present trends continue. The industrialized democracies cannot continue to tolerate a situation in which they live by the rules of the Charter concerning the international use of force, while the Soviet Union and its proxies, satellites, and allies violate those rules on a scale which becomes larger, more pervasive, and more dangerous with every passing year. The tacit exceptions to the Charter which were acknowledged in state practice in the past—the failure to apply the principles of the Charter in Eastern Europe, or in the process of decolonization in Africa—now threaten to swallow the rules, and destroy them. If the habit of aggressive war continues to spread virtually unchecked and unpunished, as has been the case in recent years, the democracies will be forced to announce that they must treat the Charter as abrogated. Feeling threatened and beset, they will then claim their freedom under pre-Charter international law to use force at will, in defense of their vital interests in what Hedley Bull has called "the Anarchical Society" of world politics.

This would be a tragic development in world affairs, and a most unwelcome one. But it will surely happen unless the slide toward anarchy is arrested, and reversed, before it overwhelms the possibility of general peace.

The ultimate irony of the present situation is that there is no objective reason for it. The United States, its allies, and China, whose security interests parallel those of the United States and its allies, have more than enough military, economic, moral, and political strength to restore the vitality of the Charter, if they wish to do so. The defeats suffered by American and allied policy over the last decade are not the inevitable consequence of changing power relationships in the world. On the contrary, they flow from the intellectual and moral climate of Western civilization, and raise an ultimate question about its instinct for self-preservation.

For the men and women of contemporary and secular Western culture, dominated by the rationalism of the Enlightenment, it is nearly impossible to imagine or to believe that evil exists. We explain aggressive behavior, and even the pathological cruelty of modern totalitarianism, as passing excess caused by fear, poverty, cultural shock, or other factors, which can and will be cured by prosperity and education. Ignoring history, and the world around us, we insist on believing that whatever goes wrong is somehow our fault, and can be put right by a little more aid, higher prices for raw materials, or a few territorial concessions.

Freud knew better. The discontents of civilization, he warned, were caused by the restraints upon the aggressive instinct which the achievement of civilization requires. The aggressive instinct is universal, he believed. It can be curbed and channeled into constructive outlets only by the equally universal human instinct he called love, eros, the power in life which leads human beings to develop religion, law, order, and beauty in their lives. All history, Freud wrote, is a chronicle of the contention between these two immense forces.

The Charter of the United Nations expresses the yearnings of mankind for a peaceful and progressive international society. In Freud's metaphor, it is the voice of Isaiah and Saint Paul. If world politics is not soon brought back to the norms of the Charter, the restraints of civilization about which Freud wrote will be overwhelmed, for a time at least, both in national and in international life.

Only the industrialized democracies and China, acting together, can successfully challenge the rising tide of aggression. If they do not do so, the industrialized democracies will have no choice but to arm, and to act, in a program of naked and ruthless power politics, designed to achieve minimal fortress security in a world dominated by Hobbes's vision of the war of all against all. In such an effort, policies of "power politics" would indeed be in opposition to the precepts of the Charter of the United Nations.

When men are sufficiently exhausted and disgusted by that experience, it is safe to predict that the survivors, if there are any, will come together once again, as they did in Vienna, Versailles, and San Francisco, to pledge allegiance to a better course.

Index